SMALL ISN'T BEAUTIFUL

SMALL ISN'T BEAUTIFUL

The Case Against Localism

TREVOR LATIMER

BROOKINGS INSTITUTION PRESS
Washington, D.C.

Published by Brookings Institution Press
1775 Massachusetts Avenue, NW
Washington, DC 20036
www.brookings.edu/bipress

Co-published by Rowman & Littlefield
An imprint of The Rowman & Littlefield Publishing Group, Inc.
4501 Forbes Boulevard, Suite 200, Lanham, Maryland 20706
www.rowman.com

86-90 Paul Street, London EC2A 4NE

The Brookings Institution is a nonprofit organization devoted to research, education, and publication on important issues of domestic and
foreign policy. Its principal purpose is to bring the highest quality independent research and analysis to bear on current and emerging policy problems.

British Library Cataloguing in Publication Information Available

Library of Congress Cataloging-in-Publication Data
Library of Congress Control Number: 2022949969
ISBN: 978-0-8157-3971-5 (cloth)
ISBN: 978-0-8157-4048-3 (paperback)
ISBN: 978-0-8157-3972-2 (electronic)

The paper used in this publication meets the minimum requirements of
American National Standard for Information Sciences—Permanence of
Paper for Printed Library Materials, ANSI/NISO Z39.48-1992

"Fellow citizens, of everywhere in particular, and nowhere in general . . ."

—from the play *A Glance at New York in 1848*

"If there were a prevailing idolatry of smallness, irrespective of subject or purpose, one would have to try and exercise influence in the opposite direction."

—E. F. Schumacher, *Small Is Beautiful*

"Away ye spirits of discord! ye narrow views! ye local policies! ye selfish patriots, who would damn your country for a sixpenny duty! In the present state of America, local views are general ruin!"

—*Pennsylvania and the Federal Constitution, 1787–1788*, edited by John Bach McMaster and Frederick D. Stone (Harvard University, 1888)

Contents

PART IV
Against Localism and Beyond

Preface

In 2014, Bloomberg News released a list of the "Dumbest Local Ordinances," which included a fine for saggy pants (Ocala, Florida) and a ban against clutter (Oil City, Pennsylvania).[1] In 1969, Skamania County, Washington, banned killing Bigfoot. In Yamhill, Oregon, it is illegal to tell fortunes. And a law in Billings, Montana, prohibits intermissions during live performances.[2]

This book is not concerned with laws like these—as amusing as they are. This book is concerned, in the broadest sense, with their pernicious, terrible, and tragic counterparts: exercises of local power (a form of what I call localism) that hurt people and deny their rights—all for supposedly good reasons.

That last point bears repeating: no one favors localism, the subject of this book, because it hurts people or undermines their rights. That would be ridiculous. People want localism and local control because they think it is the right thing to do or does good things, such as giving ordinary citizens greater control over their lives, encouraging efficient government, protecting group rights, and so on.

In this book, I do not deny that localism and local control sometimes do such things. My argument is that they do these things rarely, and under very special conditions. More often, good intentions for localism and local power undermine rights or the public good. I'll provide a few examples in a moment.

Put similarly, but differently, there really are—in some cases—good reasons for localism and local control. Yet in other cases (many or most cases, I believe), what appear to be good reasons aren't actually good reasons, and when there are good reasons, they are outweighed by other, stronger, good reasons on the other side.

A familiar example of local control comes from American education policy. As Chief Justice Warren Burger put it in one of the most important Supreme Court decisions in desegregation jurisprudence, "no single tradition in public education is more deeply rooted than local control over the operation of schools; local autonomy has long been thought essential both to the maintenance of community concern and support for public schools and to quality of the educational process."[3]

It turns out, however, that localism in education policy exacerbates segregation and inequitable funding (the scholarly literature demonstrating this is large and compelling).[4] In 2012, residents of Gardendale, Alabama, argued that "schools do better when they're part of smaller, city-based districts where they can make hyperlocal decisions." What did they do to apply their argument? They "decided it was time to secede from the Jefferson County School District—because of the changing 'dynamics.'"[5]

The new Gardendale School District had a poverty rate of 7 percent and a nonwhite student body of 22 percent. The school district it left behind (fragments of Jefferson County) had a poverty rate of 22 percent and a nonwhite student body of 55 percent. Whatever its supporters' intentions (good, benign, otherwise), Gardendale's succession left Jefferson County poorer and more racially segregated.

Gardendale was not the first to secede. Eight communities seceded from Jefferson County before Gardendale. As Vox's Alvin Chang argues, the eight communities "didn't want to be subject to racial integration orders that involved busing, and they didn't want to share tax dollars with people who were less fortunate."[6]

Secession in Gardendale and Jefferson County was not an isolated incident. From 2000 to 2017, seventy-one communities in the United States attempted secession, of which forty-seven were successful (with only nine attempts defeated).

A second example comes from the United Kingdom, although there are well-known parallels in the United States. In 2011, the UK Parliament passed the Localism Act. According to the government's plain English guide, the Localism Act "sets out a series of measures with the potential to achieve a substantial and lasting shift in power away from central government and towards local people."[7]

The bill has given local councillors (officials who answer to their constituents) greater control over housing policy in their communities.[8] They have been "quick to remove, reduce, or quietly ignore the planning targets" for new development set by the central government in London.

What has that meant in practice? Fewer new homes in a country (like many countries) facing a severe housing shortage. As Paul Smith puts it: "there is one group of people largely overlooked by the new bill, those desperate to get their first foot on the property ladder or hoping to rent from a social landlord. Localism cannot wish away the need for more homes in this country."[9]

My last example does not have an obvious moral. In the United States, at one point or another during the coronavirus pandemic, Washington D.C., New York City, Philadelphia, Boston, San Francisco, Chicago, Los Angeles, Seattle, and New Orleans issued indoor vaccine mandates.[10] New Orleans ended its indoor vaccine mandate in March 2022, but the Louisiana House of Representatives went ahead and passed a bill to *ban* vaccine mandates in April 2022.[11] On the other hand, North Carolina issued a statewide mask requirement in 2020, but sheriffs in Halifax County, Craven County, and Sampson County refused to enforce it.[12]

Each of these cities and counties thought (if I may personify them) they were doing the right thing and that their state governments were trying to force them to do the wrong thing. The cities believed their states were not doing enough to protect the public against the coronavirus. The counties in North Carolina believed that their state was violating their residents' freedom of choice.

Although there may be a right answer here (that considerations in favor of public health outweigh considerations in favor of personal freedom), that's not the point. Each city or county believed and still believes that there are good reasons for lower-level governments to decide as opposed to letting the higher-level government decide.

This book is about those supposedly good reasons—whether they are good and when, if they are good, whether other good reasons outweigh them.

Acknowledgments

This book did not come into being in the usual way. I started writing it as a scholarly monograph in political theory, but quickly pivoted toward a book that is something else—still scholarly (hopefully), but hopefully fun and interesting to a broader audience. Initial responses to the manuscript were less than enthusiastic, so I thank Steve Macedo and Bill Finan for recognizing its merit and pushing for its publication. I thank Gwynne Latimer for patiently reading every page

Many other people and institutions helped make this book possible. First and foremost, my parents, Dave and Patty Latimer. In close second, the following and others I've missed: Larry Bartels, Elliott Beard, Chuck Beitz, Kelsey Brady, Brookes Brown, Emilee Booth Chapman, Hank Clark, Teresa Davis, Joshua Dienstag, Keith Dougherty, Elisabeth Ellis, Ted Engelhardt, Paul Frymer, P. J. Gardner, Art Goldhammer, David Golemboski, Alex Guerrero, Emily Hallock, Cecelia Hernandez, Amy Hondo, Jennie Ikuta, Jeff Jackson, Desmond Jagmohan, Peter Johannessen, A. J. Julius, Melissa Lane, Sean Latimer, Ted Lechterman, Dean Machin, Russ Muirhead, Herschel Nachlis, Melody Negron, Paulina Ochoa Espejo, Carole Pateman, Brian Phillips, the Princeton

University Center for Human Values, Julia Rabig, Lucia Rafanelli, Daniel Rodgers, Julie Rose, Timothy Rosenkoetter, Alan Ryan, Melissa Schwartzberg, Jason Sorens, Desmond Stevens, Liza Taylor, University of Georgia American Founding Group, Keith Whittington, Sean Wiltentz, and Victor Wolfenstein.

A draft of the manuscript was the subject of a workshop hosted by Dartmouth College's Ethics Institute. I presented a version of the chapter on tyranny (then called "Localism, Centralization, and Tyranny") at the November 2018 meeting of the Northeastern Political Science Association in Montreal.

PART I

Identifying Localism

ONE

Localism and Why It Matters

Localism is the belief or the claim that we should prioritize the local by making decisions, exercising authority, or implementing policy locally or more locally. The demand for local control is a kind of localism. The desire for local autonomy is a kind of localism. Localism is as popular now as it has ever been, as we'll see in a moment.[1] I've written this book because localism can be dangerous and it will continue to inflict harm under the guise of virtue if we let it.

It's not that localism is always an instrument of harm. In some cases, making decisions, exercising authority, or implementing policy locally or more locally has good results. The problem arises, as we'll discover, when localism operates ideologically—when the reasons we think we have to make decisions, exercise authority, or implement policy locally or more locally in some cases, under certain conditions, are taken to justify making decisions, exercising authority, or implementing policy locally or more locally in most cases. When our commitment to doing things locally becomes an article of faith.

The real trouble surfaces when our intuitions about particular cases are used to conjure what masquerade as broadly applicable principles.

3

Or when our good reasons for doing things locally in some cases take root where they do not belong—like invasive species—and wreak havoc. Localism is like kudzu (genus *Pueraria*), a vine that chokes trees to death: "when you introduce one of these species into a new place, it often escapes its natural enemies, its natural parasites and diseases and competitors, and it can just sort of go nuts."[2]

In this book, we'll come to see that our enthusiasm for localism is unwarranted, or at least far less warranted than its proponents contend. The contention that we should, generally speaking, make decisions, exercise authority, or implement policy locally or more locally does not pass muster. The good reasons we have to make decisions, exercise authority, or implement policy locally or more locally in some cases do not magically extend to all cases, or even most cases. That's because the arguments for localism—the reasons people give to justify making decisions, exercising authority, or implementing policy locally or more locally—aren't nearly as good as we have been led to believe. That's my argument. We should reject localism because the case for localism is weak at best, mistaken at worst.

Localism has existed for as long as it has had a foil: power or authority exercised somewhere else—somewhere beyond the local. In that sense, localism is the product of civilization itself. The moment someone decided to extend the scope of political authority beyond the primeval village, localism was born. Once power leaves, someone will want it back.

This is anachronistic, I readily admit. *Localism*, as a term used to describe the desire to make decisions, exercise authority, or implement policy locally or more locally, is undoubtedly newer than that. So is the more or less coherent doctrine I am concerned with in this book.

Although something that looks a lot like localism has existed for a very long time—think of corporate towns in the Middle Ages—localism proper probably began with the rise of the modern nation-state.[3] Once there was a thing, the state, that amalgamated hitherto dispersed communities into novel, and what would surely have felt artificial, national communities, there were reasons to assert the identity, rights, and privileges of what had been, until then, all there was: local communities.

Localism evolved considerably in the late twentieth and early twenty-first century. Earlier forms of localism were reactionary, though not necessarily in the pejorative sense. People wanted to make decisions more locally because that was where they had been made until the king and his henchmen took them away. Throughout its history, many instances of localism have been about restoring the status quo ante.

I should emphasize that the history I am now telling is stylized and conjectural, à la Jean-Jacques Rousseau's *Discours sur l'origine et les fondements de l'inégalité parmi les hommes*. All that matters for this book is that there came a time when people started celebrating the local for its alleged virtues. Instead of saying that we should make decisions locally or more locally in order to protect local interests, restore the cosmic balance, or resist a newfangled state, people began to argue that we should make decisions more locally because doing so was good in its own right. Making decisions more locally could generate previously overlooked benefits: democratic participation, efficiency, local know-how, and so on. It didn't take much to gather these intuitions into the loose doctrine I am calling localism.

Although I believe it is impossible to say so definitively, we can mark the emergence of contemporary localism using E. F. Schumacher's *Small Is Beautiful*, published in 1973.[4] Until that point, the local had been kept at arm's length, and for historically good reasons. In *Federalist* No. 22, Alexander Hamilton told his fellow countrymen that if the system then in place, the Articles of Confederation, were to continue, "there will be much to fear from the bias of local views and prejudices, and from the interference of local regulations."[5] At the height of the Great Depression in the United States, Franklin Roosevelt, the future president, insisted that "in many instances the victory of the central Government, the creation of a strong central Government, was a haven of refuge to the individual. The people preferred the master far away to the exploitation and cruelty of the smaller master near at hand."[6]

The local was backward, parochial, small-minded—choose your favorite synonym. For much of human history, the local had been an obstacle to peace and progress. However, as with most good ideas, centralization was taken too far, with some notoriously ridiculous—and

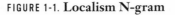

FIGURE 1-1. **Localism N-gram**

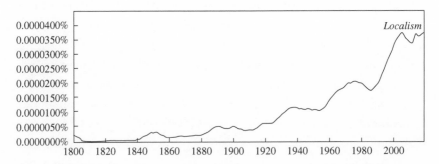

Notes: Localism as a percentage of all unigrams published in English, 1800–2019. Three-year moving average.
Source: Google Books NGram Viewer, https://books.google.com/ngrams/graph?content=localism&year_start
=1800&year_end=2019&corpus=26&smoothing=3.

sometimes tragic—results. I don't think it would distort history too much to say that the period from the turn of the twentieth century to the 1960s were the golden, though not entirely salutary, age of centralization, so-called rational administration, and planning.

Localism could be seen as a simple reaction to the age of centralization in the developed world. But that would be a mistake, as Schumacher shows. His book was not called *Big Is Ugly*. He had plenty of nasty things to say about bigness and centralization, but he cared far more about introducing a notion that seems perfectly natural now but probably felt blasphemous then: that the small and the local are aesthetically, practically, and morally praiseworthy. The small and the local are not violent or parochial, as Hamilton and Roosevelt thought; the small and the local had been unfairly maligned, Schumacher argued.

In a moment, I'll explain how this book is put together. Before that I want to introduce localism in all its dizzying variety. Local control of education and local housing regulations are localism, as we saw in the preface, but there's so much more. Localism appears in so many places, periods, and guises that I'm certain I'll miss your favorite example.

Readers of this book are surely aware that we're supposed to be eating the delicious locally grown food available at the farmers' market down the road.[7] We've learned from popular books like *Plenty: Eating Locally On the 100-Mile Diet* and the work of Michael Pollan that local food tastes better, is better for the environment, and supports the livelihood of local farmers.[8]

Local food has become so popular that traditional national brands are now cashing in on the craze. As Fiona Simpson of *Forbes* puts it, "a significant and highly valuable proportion of consumers are looking to spend their hard earned cash with small businesses in their own neighborhood and support their local economy."[9] Starbucks has "even taken steps to 'unbrand' some of their stores, making them appear more like locally run cafes and using them to carry out market research on customer trends and desires."[10] It seems, then, that the market for local food is following the trajectory of its predecessor: organic food.

When I was a kid, I remember being told to "Buy American." In my car crazed California suburb, there were always a few conspicuous driveways replete with Ford, Chevy, and General Motors automobiles; their owners wouldn't be caught dead with a Honda or a Toyota. These days, more often we're told to "buy local" than to buy American (perhaps, at least in the automobile industry, that's because the latter is pretty much impossible). Buy local simply spreads the logic of the local food movement to a wider range of goods. The coronavirus pandemic only accentuated this trend.[11] Breweries, in particular, like to point out that their beer has been brewed locally and to remind their patrons to "drink local."

Some of this is thinly veiled elitism, to be sure. Upper-middle-class and affluent liberals are horrified by chain restaurants, big box stores, and cheap, mass-produced goods (except when they come from Amazon). Buying local is a way to fight the homogenizing and corrupting influence of globalization, one purchase at a time. I'm being a little glib, of course. But it would be a mistake to discount the extent to which globalization, both economic and political, has produced localism in many of its current forms. Hans Beck has argued that localism is "a potent response to the seismic shifts of globalization" and that "prioritization of local governance, culture, and production [has] inspired a towering wave of localism."[12]

Or as Donald Trump put it in 2016, "people talk about how we're living in a globalized world, but the relationships people value most are local—family, city, state, and country. Local, folks, local."[13] The former president certainly struck a chord. Some Democratic communities that supported Donald Trump in the 2016 election have adopted their own local versions of "America First," which Stephanie Muravchik and Jon Shields describe as "locally grown political ethoses that are concerned primarily with the welfare and preservation of small communities."[14]

You may be surprised to hear that Brexit, the United Kingdom's decision to leave the European Union, is a kind of localism. Some people think localism is all about neighborhoods and towns, but it's not. As we'll see in the next chapter, localism is about doing things someplace smaller, geographically, or lower, in what I call a "multilayered jurisdictional hierarchy" for lack of better terminology. Brexit is localism because the citizens of the United Kingdom believe they should make decisions about trade, regulation, and immigration on their own in London (or Cardiff, Belfast, or Edinburgh), rather than with the rest of Europe in Brussels and Strasbourg.[15] If you don't listen too closely (try ignoring the proper nouns), arguments for Brexit are virtually indistinguishable from those of Chief Justice Burger on behalf of local school districts (quoted in the preface). The "Vote Leave" campaign claimed that "it's safer to control our own borders and decide for ourselves who can come into this country, not be overruled by EU judges."[16]

Because of its affinities with states' rights in the United States, localism has been associated with John C. Calhoun and nullification as well as the conservatism of Barry Goldwater and Ronald Reagan. If it ever was, localism is no longer exclusively conservative, however. During the Trump presidency, self-described liberals took up the mantle of localism, most notably Bruce Katz of the Brookings Institution and his late colleague Jeremy Nowak. In their book, *The New Localism*, published in late 2017, and in outlets such as CityLab, liberals herald localism as a way to "get things done" in the face of a sclerotic national government controlled by their political opponents.[17]

As Katz and Nowak's website puts it, "Power is shifting in the world downward from national governments and states to cities and metropolitan communities, where problem solving is less partisan and more pragmatic. This new locus of power—this New Localism—is emerging by necessity to solve the grand challenges characteristic of modern societies: economic competitiveness, social inclusion and opportunity; a renewed public life; demographic transformation and the imperative of environmental sustainability."[18] Cities are the wave of the future, apparently.

The American Enterprise Institute's *Localism in America* maintains that "solving big problems may work better with smaller units of government" and that "localism involves the integrity of essential units in society such as families, neighborhoods, and other locally proximate communities."[19]

A conservative contributor to the left-leaning Vox insists that "it's time for a new emphasis on localism in American politics."[20] According to the author, Lyman Stone, "a diverse society can sustain itself peacefully when its members are committed to solving problems as locally as possible, involving higher levels of government only when absolutely necessary."[21] Stone should be applauded for at least being consistent in his localism; he claims that conservatives committed to localism have to leave so-called "blue cities" free to experiment with progressive policies like higher minimum wages and sanctuary cities.[22]

But sanctuary cities are not unprecedented, especially not their analogue at the state level. Colorado legalized marijuana in 2012, despite the federal ban. Even further back, in the antebellum era, most Northern states passed liberty laws, which were designed to circumvent the Fugitive Slave Act and the fugitive slave provision in the U.S. Constitution. These laws made it a crime at the state level to turn fugitive slaves over to federal authorities.

In all these cases, there is a conflict between local preferences and national law. The locality—city or state—claims the issue is within their purview, either because it is better handled locally or because handling it locally is what local people want.

This is a good place to state a curious but obvious fact. Localism transcends the ideological spectrum. Some conservatives will tell you that localism is fundamentally conservative because conservatives favor local as opposed to national power. Maybe there are some forms of conservatism for which this is true. But we all know that, in practice, conservatives wield national power just like liberals when it suits their purposes. George W. Bush ushered a new entitlement, Medicare Part D (prescription drugs), into law in 2003. Liberals and progressives are no different, as sanctuary cities, liberty laws, and marijuana legalization demonstrate. It's rare to find a completely consistent localist. That's part of what makes the ideologically neutral, or what appear to be ideologically neutral, arguments for localism so fascinating and troubling.

There is even such a thing as "firearm localism." Writing in the *Yale Law Journal* and for Vox, Joseph Blocher argues that we should "pursue gun regulations tailored to local experiences, preferences, and needs."[23] Since the costs, in terms of gun violence, are concentrated in urban areas, and the benefits, in terms of liberty to hunt and the like, are concentrated in rural areas, Blocher contends that it would be better if localities, rather than the national government, were permitted to pass their own gun regulations.

Localism is becoming increasingly popular in issue areas like education and policing. Archon Fung is a notable advocate of a kind of localism he calls "empowered participation." His core argument in *Empowered Participation* is that "troubled public agencies such as urban police departments and school systems can become more responsive, fair, innovative, and effective by incorporating empowered participation and deliberation into their governance structures."[24]

Fung is just one of the most sophisticated recent proponents of an old idea. Although active participation by citizens goes all the way back to ancient Athens, Fung is really a successor of the 1960s and the New Left, especially Students for a Democratic Society's calls for "participatory democracy." SDS argued that getting people to participate would invigorate democracy and eliminate poverty and injustice in the process. Until the end of the 1960s, SDS adhered to the reform tradition; it reasoned that it should start small and build gradually toward its goal: what Carole Pateman later called a "participatory society."[25] Starting small meant starting local. You couldn't get everyone off their butts at once, but you could try to demonstrate the value of political participation to a few people in a few places—by getting them to participate more actively in local government. If they saw what they could do locally (cleaning up streets, planting trees, taking on shady landlords), they would realize that they were not powerless at the national level. Participatory democracy made its way into Great Society legislation of the 1960s as "maximum feasible participation."[26]

In the United States, the Personal Responsibility and Work Opportunity Act of 1996, more commonly known as welfare reform, devolved authority over welfare programs from the national government to the states primarily by replacing matching grants with block grants. Matching grants give money to the states on the condition that it's used in certain ways. Block grants, by contrast, give states more discretion over the funds they receive from the federal government. The justification for welfare reform was hardly surprising. The thought was that if states had more flexibility, they could experiment with new ideas, ideas that might fight poverty more effectively.

As Juliet F. Gainsborough explains, some states decided to experiment by devolving authority even further, to localities.[27] Joe Soss, Richard C. Fording, and Sanford F. Schram have since shown that "devolution to local authorities has proceeded along racial lines in ways that intersect with racial patterns of welfare paternalism and carceral investment."[28] In short, "welfare localism has consistently facilitated racialized practices of social control."[29]

Most of the examples in this book are drawn from the United States, not because localism is exclusively American but because I'm an American and I know America best. Localism is so deeply entrenched in the American consciousness, in our *mores*, as Alexis de Tocqueville would say, that we hardly ever bother to state our commitments explicitly.[30] For that reason, it is sometimes helpful to turn to Europe, where localism is easier to pin down.

Though my focus here is primarily the United States, I have written elsewhere about the principle of subsidiarity, a form of localism that is tremendously influential in Europe.[31] Subsidiarity, according to the European Union's Treaty of Maastricht, requires that in "areas which do not fall within its exclusive competence, the Community shall take action . . . only if and in so far as the objectives of the proposed action cannot be sufficiently achieved by the Member States and can therefore, by reason of the scale or effects of the proposed action, be better achieved by the Community."[32] Subsidiarity generates a presumption in favor of local action—in favor of making decisions more locally—that is overcome only when lower-level governments can't do the job. The Treaty of Lisbon amended the earlier treaty so as to apply subsidiarity to regional and local governments, in addition to the member states.[33]

According to the European Charter of Local Self-Government, ratified in 1985, "local self-government denotes the right and the ability of local authorities, within the limits of the law, to regulate and manage a substantial share of public affairs under their own responsibility and in the interests of the local population."[34] The charter adds that "public responsibilities shall generally be exercised, in preference, by those authorities which are closest to the citizen."[35] Protecting local government in this way "is an important contribution to the construction of a Europe based on the principles of democracy and the decentralisation of power."[36]

I could keep going but I won't. You get the idea: localism is everywhere, despite looking different in different contexts. We'll see why all the examples count as instances of the same thing—localism—in the next chapter. People still defend the local against outside threats, but more so than ever before, they see the local as a site of possibility. People think they can change the world by changing their little bits of it. "Think globally, act locally," as we learned to say in the 1980s and 1990s. Not only that, many of us now believe that trying to change the world at the national or the global level is futile at best, deleterious at worst. We believe that we can do more good by fixing our sights on what's near, what's familiar, what's local.

I started but didn't finish explaining why I've written this book and why you should read it. Earlier, I said that localism can be dangerous, that localism is like kudzu, and that localism often inflicts harm in the name of virtue. All these things are true, but I wouldn't have written this book if these claims weren't surprising to more and more people every day.

The problem, specifically, is that localism is dangerous *and* highly esteemed. There is a growing consensus among scholars and commentators that localism is a great idea, or at least worth a try. Localism is heralded as the solution to the ills of globalization, the sclerosis of the welfare state, entrenched partisanship, the democratic deficit, the culture wars, anomie, apathy, and, in one extreme variety, the failure of liberalism itself.[37]

For whatever reason (I suggested some possibilities above; I'll explore more in the concluding chapter), enthusiasm for localism is on the rise. Localism is on the march. But I worry that it's enthusiasm in the eighteenth-century sense: "excessive religious emotion or fervour."[38] Few appear to have paused to ask whether localism is really as great as it sounds. That's strange, given our postmodern culture's skepticism toward panaceas.

When I say that "no one" has criticized localism, I don't mean literally no one.[39] There are voices in the wilderness, but no one is listening. I'll refer to these voices on occasion as the book progresses. Many of those who have dared to criticize localism have been forgotten, marginalized, or portrayed as either nefarious centralizers or utopian rubes (I've been accused of the former, to my dismay).

Some critics of localism end up praising it despite the force of their own arguments; that's how powerful localism has become. And no critic of localism, to my knowledge, has attempted a direct, comprehensive critique as I have here. Criticisms of localism appear in passing, in particular policy areas, or with respect to specific historical examples. Occasionally, even a proponent of localism mentions potential "drawbacks," but only to set them aside.

Mark Purcell and J. Christopher Brown, both scholars of development, come closest to my position in this book with their claim that "there is nothing inherent about any scale."[40] They insist that "scales should be seen not as things in themselves with inherent qualities, but rather as *strategies* that are pursued by and benefit social groups with particular social and environmental agendas."[41] I completely agree with their point, but it appears not to have made much impact outside of academic circles.

In this book, I am not arguing that localism has drawbacks, that it has failed to work in particular cases, or that it is inappropriate for certain issues. I am arguing that its drawbacks are endemic, it fails to work in most cases, and it is inappropriate most of the time. Moreover, I believe we can salvage the kernels of truth that localism illuminates while rejecting localism. In this book, we'll see why the reasons people give to justify localism and the arguments they make in its favor are mistaken, weak, or confused.

To be perfectly clear, this is by no means an attack on localism, or a "takedown," in contemporary parlance. I am just trying to show that the arguments people make for localism don't show what they are supposed to show. In fact, if the arguments for localism were right and proper, I'd be a localist too. I follow the reasons. But I think, and I'll say this again, that the burden of proof is on those who urge us to adopt localism as a presumption in favor of the local.

I don't think we should use blunt principles like localism (or centralization) to deal with complicated issues like where authority should be exercised. Too much depends on the circumstances, the policy area, its scope, and so on. The best we can do, I think, is to highlight the most important considerations in favor of doing things more locally, the most important considerations in favor of doing things less locally, and the most important considerations in favor of leaving things as they are. That should be the real goal: making sure all the relevant considerations have their due. Despite being mistaken in general, localism has done some good by reemphasizing a perspective that is sometimes lost when enthusiasm for centralization overflows its banks. We haven't been there for some time though.

Let me repeat what I've just said, simply and directly, before sketching an overview of subsequent chapters. I wrote this book because localism is popular, but for reasons that turn out, upon the kind of reflection you'll find in these pages, not to be good reasons. The case for localism is a tempting mirage. Because localism can do and has done real harm to real people, *j'accuse.*

We'll see precisely why localism misses the mark in chapters 3 through 8. There we'll consider six representative arguments—really six clusters of arguments—for localism: arguments from tyranny, belonging, nature, democracy, knowledge, and efficiency. The arguments say, in essence, that we should prioritize the local by making decisions, exercising authority, or implementing policy locally or more locally because doing so promotes democracy, efficiency, and belonging; captures otherwise neglected forms of knowledge; respects nature and human nature; and protects against tyranny.

We consider the six clusters one at a time because it would be too difficult and too confusing to consider the case for localism all at once. Instead of asking, at least at first, whether localism is a good thing, we ask whether localism does what it says it does: promote, capture, respect, and protect the things we care about. We consider each representative argument while holding the others fixed in place.

I've also divided the arguments into two groups: commitments and consequences. The division is mostly for convenience, but it isn't arbitrary. The first group, commitments, is the subject of part II. These are the arguments from tyranny, belonging, and nature. They are grouped together because they are less concerned with the good consequences localism is supposed to produce than the ways in which localism accords with fundamental moral, metaphysical, or political commitments.

I should pause to mention that my approach in this book is roughly consequentialist and welfarist.[42] This is jargon, but not silly jargon. Consequentialism is the view according to which it is the consequences of our actions that ultimately matter. Consequentialism is not utilitarianism. It is not just people's utility or pleasure that counts. Complex values count too.

Welfarism is the view according to which the consequences that matter are those that affect people and their welfare. Philosophers disagree about what welfare is, exactly. It could be utility or pleasure, in which case consequentialism is just utilitarianism. I think of welfare as what makes people's lives go well. This might sound vague; it is, but for good reasons.

The only thing our consequentialist and welfarist approach really excludes is what T. M. Scanlon has called impersonal reasons or values. Impersonal reasons or values are those "that are not tied to the well-being, claims, or status of individuals in any particular position."[43] Natural beauty, for example. It's not that natural beauty never matters. It's that natural beauty counts only when it implicates "the claims or interests of individuals."[44]

This may seem like an innocuous restriction, but it's not. The mere fact that something pleases God, for instance, does not count in its favor, according to my approach in this book. Undoubtedly, what's good for people pleases God, so what pleases God is good, but because it's good for people, not because it pleases God.

Although I have my own views about what matters for people's welfare, I'm keeping things vague intentionally. We disagree about what makes people's lives go well. We exclude impersonal reasons and values because they do not affect how well people's lives go, by definition. If someone can show that what appear to be impersonal reasons or values matter to people's well-being, they are actually personal reasons and therefore count.

We live in a world in which what some people value is incomprehensible to others. Since we share the world with others, I think we have a duty to our brothers and sisters to proceed according to reasons and values we all find comprehensible. This is John Rawls's great insight in *Political Liberalism*.[45] We exclude impersonal values because reasonable people disagree that they are valuable.

I've discussed impersonal reasons at some length because the arguments in part II—from despotism, nature, and belonging—rely, not exclusively but paradigmatically, on commitments and values that many of us don't share. These three arguments are challenging because it's not obvious, at first glance, that they rest on controversial commitments. It takes some work to see that they do. I say not exclusively because there are sophisticated variants of each argument that at least attempt to connect obscure values to people's welfare—to how well people's lives go.

The argument for localism from *tyranny* says we should prioritize the local by making decisions, exercising authority, or implementing policy locally or more locally because doing so generates a bulwark against despotism and tyranny. Strong local governments, with independent bases of authority, stop despots in their tracks, as Alexis de Tocqueville claimed in *Democracy in America*, his panegyric to local government.

The argument for localism from *belonging* says we should prioritize the local by making decisions, exercising authority, or implementing policy locally or more locally because that is where people's loyalties lie. Local communities are where people feel like they belong—where they find meaning. Authority exercised elsewhere is abstract, mechanical, distant, and foreign; authority exercised locally is familiar, tractable, inspiring, and trustworthy.

The argument for localism from *nature* says we should prioritize the local by making decisions, exercising authority, or implementing policy locally or more locally because the local is the natural and therefore appropriate site of human social organization. Human communities are naturally small, intimate, egalitarian, and informal. Governments and institutions beyond the local are artificial, atomistic, hierarchical, and possibly even grotesque and inhumane.

The arguments in part III, from democracy, knowledge, and efficiency, are grouped together because they are far less likely to appeal to controversial moral, metaphysical, or political commitments. It's easy to see how these values—democracy, knowledge, and efficiency—matter for how well people's lives go.

The argument from *democracy* says we should prioritize the local by making decisions, exercising authority, or implementing policy locally or more locally because local governments are "closer to the people," because making decisions more locally promotes political participation by ordinary citizens, or because local governments are more accountable.

The argument from *knowledge* says we should prioritize the local by making decisions, exercising authority, or implementing policy locally or more locally because some kinds of useful knowledge are accessible, or are far more accessible, only at the local level. Distant officials make mistakes and commit injustice because they don't have all the facts, ride roughshod over local people, or have delusions of omniscience and omnipotence. Making decisions more locally is an effective way to put local knowledge to work.

Last but not least, the argument from *efficiency* says we should prioritize the local by making decisions, exercising authority, or implementing policy locally or more locally because doing so is more efficient than imposing uniformity on diversity. When decisions are made more locally, local governments can adapt their policies to the unique preferences of their constituents. Local governments also have to compete for residents and their tax dollars. The latter keeps local governments accountable and encourages useful experimentation.

Each chapter in part II and part III begins with a thorough, and hopefully charitable, reconstruction of the cluster of arguments in question. My goal is to identify each argument's assumptions, its structure and its key moves. The procedure is like an x-ray or an MRI; we see what really matters and how things work. Skeptics of my conclusions in this book and perhaps even proponents of localism will find something useful here. Localists can use what I've done at the outset of each chapter to hone their case.

I can't say too much here about how I critique the six arguments. My strategy is different in each case, though I will generalize a bit in chapter 9, where I synthesize our conclusions from the chapters 3 through 8. It's there that I rest my case. My contention is that even if some of the arguments I have canvassed are stronger than I've allowed, together the arguments come up short. The case for localism is inconclusive at best, mistaken at worst; and it's dangerous to adopt principles with so little support.

In the last chapter, I speculate a bit more about why localism is so attractive—magnetic even. I suggest that it accords with basic features of human psychology; we have an affinity toward what's near, concrete, and familiar. As human beings, we are wired to prioritize the local.

That does not mean we should, however. We can overcome, or at least question, our bias in favor of the local by cultivating what David Bromwich calls moral imagination, the "power that compels us to grant the highest possible reality and the largest conceivable claim to a thought, action, or person that is not our own, and not close to us in any obvious way."[46] It is through moral imagination that we bring distant strangers into our hearts.

The book concludes on a conciliatory note. Critique can guide action. I know that even by the end I won't have convinced everyone, and since localism isn't going anywhere soon, I believe what we learn here about the weaknesses of localism can help us avoid or mitigate its worst pitfalls. Localism is a mistake, but knowing *why* it's mistaken is, to quote James Madison out of context, "a means of controlling its effects."[47] Localism is a mistake, but like Alexis de Tocqueville, we should "find out what precautions" we can take "to keep it under control."[48]

But before all that, we need to get clear about what localism actually is. We need to identify localism and distinguish it from things that just look like it. That is the task to which we now turn.

TWO

What Is Localism?

What is localism, exactly? Nearly everyone thinks they know; everyone else has no idea. For a topic of such importance, that has attracted so much enthusiasm in recent years, very little has been done, carefully that is, to explain what it is, how it works, or why it's distinctive. To quote Alexis de Tocqueville out of context, localism "is a word that is constantly repeated of late but whose meaning no one seeks to clarify."[1] We seek a remedy for that regrettable deficiency here.

As someone who has been thinking about localism for many years, I'm continually surprised by how little thought, by otherwise thoughtful people, goes into specifying, expounding, and delimiting its underlying ideas and concepts. It's not that no one has attempted to define the term—it's that so few have and that those who have disagree, in many cases without realizing it. Those who write about localism are dispersed throughout the academy and the commentariat in fields that don't ordinarily talk to each another: political science (rarely), development studies, urban studies, political geography, policy studies, and so on. I'm painting with a broad brush, exaggerating a bit, but not too much.

As Paul Hildreth explains in an article the title of which begins, promisingly, "What is localism," "not only is there no universally agreed definition of local economic development, but there is a distinct lack of one for localism."[2] "The lack of a common language to describe it," he adds, "makes it challenging to pin down what is localism and what it is not."[3] I agree. Let's see what we can do about it.

Competing Definitions

Hildreth, an urban policy scholar, goes on to say that "in a general sense, localism implies a process of bringing decision-making closer to citizens to enable them to participate more effectively in shaping the public policy decisions and service outcomes that impact upon their lives."[4]

Along the same lines, in *Locating Localism*, Jane Wills, a geographer, suggests that "broadly speaking, localism comprises a shift in policy making and practice to decentralize political power towards local institutions and local people."[5] In a section titled "What is localism?" Wills adds that "localism is about engaging people in local civic life. . . . Localism can be understood as an effort to reconfigure the geographical division of political powers across the nation by shifting power from the centre towards the localities."[6] It is, furthermore, "a proxy for arguments about the place of the people in democratic life."[7]

David Hess, a sociologist and contributor to *The Localization Reader*, calls localism "the movement of movements in support of government policies and economic practices orientated toward enhancing local democracy and local independent ownership of the economy in a historical context of corporate-led globalization."[8] He includes under localism the "buy local" movement, "farmers markets, community gardens, small farms, and other elements of local food networks; community finance and community media; and various efforts to develop locally owned energy and transportation systems."[9]

According to Richard Schragger, a legal scholar, "localism depends on the creation and maintenance of smaller-than-state associations marked off in geographical space by a definable (and often, defensible) perimeter."[10] Note how Schragger includes the words *smaller, geographical*, and *space*. These are important and we'll come back to them.

In 2013, the academic journal *Policy Studies* released a double special issue dedicated to localism. In their introductory article, "Understanding Localism," Mark Evans, David Marsh, and Gerry Stoker (scholars of governance, policy analysis, and political science) provide an explicit definition. For them, "localism is: 'an umbrella term which refers to the devolution of power and/or functions and/or resources away from central control and towards front-line managers, local democratic structures, local institutions and local communities, within an agreed framework of minimum standards.'"[11]

According to Simin Davoudi, a scholar of environmental policy and planning, and Ali Madanipour, an expert in urban design and planning, their edited volume, *Reconsidering Localism*, "brings together new scholarship from leading academics in Europe and North America to develop a theoretically grounded critique and definition of the new localism."[12] In their introductory essay, they argue that "localism evokes multiple and contested meanings," including "a re-ordering and liberalisation of political spaces, a site of empowerment, a locus of knowledge generation, a framework for social integration and community-building, a localisation of economic activities and a site of resistance and environmental activism."[13]

Richard Briffault, an expert in local government law, defines localism with elegant simplicity: "greater local power."[14] According to Roderick Hills, another legal scholar, localism "is a theory that governments ought to be arranged to protect 'democratic decentralization,'" which, he adds, "is the backbone of self-government, both individual and collective."[15] Self-government, Hills clarifies, requires that "on matters that exclusively concern either an individual or a group, that individual or group should have exclusive or preeminent decision-making power."[16]

According to *Localism in the Mass Age*, a manifesto published by the online publication Front Porch Republic, "localism is an idea with a wide array of adherents from academics to hipsters, from city planners to organic farmers. It is becoming increasingly clear that many people across the political spectrum have come to question the wisdom of centralization in all its many guises."[17] Localism, moreover, "represents a clear challenge to the liberal cosmopolitan agenda—found on both the Left and the Right—that champions internationalism over nationalism, that celebrates an abstract global community over concrete local affiliations, and that rejoices in the inevitability of globalization."[18] A specific kind of localism, humane localism, "is characterized by a love for one's particular place, yet at the same time it is not animated by fear of the other, for by an act of imagination it sees through the inevitable differences and recognizes the common humanity we all share."[19] It is "rooted in respect, not in homogeneity, in a recognition that liberty is sustainable only alongside respect for limits, and in the realization that human flourishing is best realized in the company of friends and neighbors sharing a common place in the world."[20]

For the authors of *Healing American Democracy: Going Local* (Mike Hais, a former political pollster; Doug Ross, a former state senator; and Morley Winograd, formerly a policy adviser to Vice President Al Gore) localism "seeks to acknowledge and reinforce what is already happening in the civic arena: Americans are increasingly looking away from Washington, not just to the states, but to their local communities and regions as more promising venues to solve common problems."[21] They propose a "civic ethos" that "intentionally shifts the greatest possible number of public decisions to the community level."[22]

The American Enterprise Institute's *Localism in America: Why We Should Tackle Our Big Challenges at the Local Level* maintains that "solving big problems may work better with smaller units of government" and that "localism involves the integrity of essential units in society such as families, neighborhoods, and other locally approximate communities."[23]

In *The New Localism*, Katz and Nowak argue, similarly, that "practical solutions to economic growth, economic inclusion, and environmental sustainability are more within the local domain than the national."[24]

According to Neil Brenner, an influential figure in critical geography, and Nik Theodore, a professor of urban studies, "the new localism has become a forceful call to arms through which local (and, in some cases, national) political-economic elites are aggressively attempting to promote economic rejuvenation from below."[25]

While arguing that cities should have constitutional status, Daniel Weinstock, a political philosopher, suggests that localism is "the position according to which any collective subject can in principle make an analogous claim for constitutional status."[26]

Then we have the historians. Jackson Turner Main contrasts localism with cosmopolitanism, arguing that the localist is "the man of narrow horizons—most often rural and sparsely educated—whose experience is limited to his own neighborhood: he is provincial, parochial."[27] According to Forrest McDonald, localism is "loyalty to a town or a village or a valley rather than to the state and the nation."[28] For Barry Alan Shain, localism is "the deeply traditional Anglo-American desire of a people 'to be left alone in their villages.'"[29]

Saul Cornell, an expert in American anti-federalism, depicts localism as "a belief . . . that the government needed to be closer to the people."[30] Describing eighteenth-century Massachusetts, Kenneth Lockridge observes a "submerged localism" that "continued to struggle against all higher authorities in the name of a persistent dream of local simplicity and local autonomy."[31] "The dream of religious piety, community, and autonomy," Lockridge adds, "had always been an integral part of a localism that also had political dimensions."[32]

The definition I like best (other than mine), for reasons I'll explain shortly, belongs to David Brooks, the polarizing *New York Times* opinion columnist: "Localism is the belief that power should be wielded as much as possible at the neighborhood, city and state levels."[33]

Problems

I hope I have shown the extent to which commentators disagree about what localism actually means. The general problem, as I see it, is that scholars take their subject, localism, for granted. They assign a label, localism, to whatever phenomenon interests them, without pausing to explain why it counts as localism.

Doing so is perfectly legitimate in many cases—cases in which *localism* is being used as shorthand for isolated phenomena. Matters are different when we want to say something about localism in general. Then we really need to know what we're talking about and whether we're talking about the same thing.

I think most of us who talk about localism are talking about the same thing, but without knowing why, or precisely what that thing is. Despite considerable efforts, we still don't have a satisfactory definition of localism, or even—on the assumption that localism spurns definition—an analytically rigorous account. But before getting to our definition, one that elegantly captures much of what is meant in the foregoing, I want to say a few words about why previous definitions have gone astray.

Bear with me for a moment for what may seem like philosophical quibbling (it's not). Scholars sometimes say what localism is about, what it depends on, what it implies, or what it comprises rather than what it is. This raises an important question: What kind of thing is localism? Is it a theory? An idea? A doctrine? An ideology? A phenomenon? An activity? A process? These options aren't mutually exclusive. If localism is a doctrine, as one meaning of the suffix -*ism* suggests, it makes sense to explain what it comprises or implies.[34] Sheryll Cashin has called localism "the ideological commitment to local governance."[35] Then again, if localism, as Jane Wills suggests, "comprises a shift in policy making and practice," localism is an activity, not a doctrine.[36]

I think we'd best insist that localism is not the same as "the local," though the two are of course related. It strains our language to call localism "a site of empowerment" or "a locus of knowledge generation," as do Davoudi and Madanipour.[37] The local can be a site or a locus; localism cannot.

I also don't like the phrase "closer to the people," as popular as it may be. In Hildreth's version, it's "bringing decision-making closer to citizens."[38] For the European Union, it's "decisions are taken as closely as possible to the citizen."[39] I don't like "closer to the people" because it's unclear whether *close*, *closer*, and *closely* are meant literally or metaphorically, and I don't like metaphors; they obscure.

If *close, closer,* and *closely,* as terms describing spatial distance, are meant literally, where, exactly, are decisions made? In legislatures, in capitals, in board rooms, in people's heads? Where are the citizens? In many places at once, I would think. To whom should decisions be made more closely: the furthest citizen, the closest citizen, the average citizen? (I suspect it's the average, or the median, or some such.) How do we go about making decisions more closely to the average citizen? By narrowing the territory to which decisions apply? By multiplying loci of decisionmaking?

If closer is meant metaphorically, what's the metaphor? It needs to be fleshed out, for we may find that close and local are metaphorically but not actually connected. In which case, is the local in localism itself a metaphor? I hope not! As I'll argue, localism is distinctive because the local refers to a place in space; localism is, at its core, spatial. If "the local" is just a metaphor, localism is not about space; then I don't know what it is or whether it's distinctive in any way.

Nor do I think we should use localism as a synonym for decentralization, federalism, or devolution. Hills says that localism is a theory according to which governments should be arranged to protect democratic decentralization. I'm not sure what's wrong with calling that theory decentralization.

Some definitions are too specific; others are potpourri. For Front Porch Republic, localism is defined by its opposition to centralization, internationalism, and globalization and by its affection for "concrete local affiliations."[40] How, though, does localism oppose centralization? What, exactly, is to be done with concrete local affiliations?

Healing American Democracy, Localism in America, and *The New Localism* reduce localism to local problem solving, or the observation that some problems are easier to tackle in some places (the local ones) than others. Is that all it is?

Is it rejecting cosmopolitanism, being left alone in one's village, local simplicity, local autonomy, community, local loyalty, or parochialism, as the historians suggest, or all of the above?

Wouldn't it be better to identify what these examples have in common, call that localism, and go from there? Doing so wouldn't preclude specificity; it wouldn't deny that localism looks different in different cases and contexts, just as genotype constrains but does not determine an organism's phenotype. Nor would it prevent additional distinctions or categories: for example, economic localism, political localism, and so on. It would, however, provide the common language called for by Hildreth. We'd then be able to say what localism is and what it isn't.

Our Definition

Localism is prioritizing the local by making decisions, exercising authority, or implementing policy locally or more locally. This is our descriptive definition; it's not the end of the story, as we'll see.

I'll say more about one word, *local*, and one phrase, *more locally*, in a moment. For now, however, localism is doing something locally rather than somewhere else. Extra-locally, one might say, if the prefix *extra-* means what I think it means and what the *Oxford English Dictionary* says it means: "situated outside something."[41] Notice the spatial terminology: somewhere, outside.

Other than the geographers, commentators seem to have missed the fundamental fact, "from which all others derive,"[42] that the local is spatial. Not only that, the local is indefinite; the local is relative. Any place can be local, so long as it is local with respect to something else.

Part of the reason scholars have so much trouble nailing localism down is that each has her own frame of reference. For scholars of urban affairs, who primarily study cities, neighborhoods are local. For those who focus their attention on states or provinces, cities and towns are local. At certain periods in the history of the United States, states were local. In federations, provinces, states, länder, cantons—whatever they are called—can be local. And in international or supranational affairs, nation-states are local. Consider Brexit, for instance.

Genuine nationalism (not white nationalism) is the localism of the nation-state.[43] As Wayne Hemingway puts it, "the word 'nationalism' largely brings negative connotations, but isn't 'localism' an extension of the same idea?"[44] Although one might take that as a mark against localism, Hemingway counts it as a point in favor of nationalism: if localism is good, and localism is an extension of nationalism, maybe nationalism isn't so bad after all, if shorn of its racist overtones?

I prefer to think of localism as the type, nationalism as a token. Localism is prioritizing anything smaller, in terms of size; closer, in terms of distance; or lower, within a "jurisdictional hierarchy." It is making decisions, exercising authority, or implementing policy somewhere small or smaller, close or closer, low or lower. The local is indefinite in the abstract but becomes definite when contrasted with that which is not local.

Localism is malleable. Most of the cases of localism that interest us are about neighborhoods, towns, and cities, but the idea can be extended downward, so to speak. If a neighborhood grows to the point where it becomes impersonal and unwieldy, localism may recommend a division of the neighborhood into two smaller pieces, or even a new, heretofore unnamed, organization or association below the neighborhood—smaller than it.

It can be extended upward, too. "At eight o'clock on Thursday morning," Arthur Dent, the protagonist of the *Hitchhiker's Guide to the Galaxy*, "woke up blearily, got up, wandered blearily around his room, opened a window, saw a bulldozer, found his slippers, and stomped off to the bathroom to wash."[45] From there his "shaving mirror . . . reflected a second bulldozer through the bathroom window." At that very moment, he remembered a conversation from the evening before, "something about a new bypass he'd just found out about." "Fifteen seconds later he was out of the house lying in front of a big yellow bulldozer that was advancing up his garden path."

Sometime later Dent learned that plans for the new bypass had "been available in the local planning office for the last nine months." With his house now in ruins, "Arthur didn't notice that the men were running from the bulldozers." Mr. Prosser, an agent of the local council, "was staring hectically into the sky." He had noticed "that huge yellow somethings were screaming through the clouds."

A disembodied voice: "People of Earth, your attention please," it said, "This is Prostetnic Vogon Jeltz of the Galactic Hyperspace Planning

Council. . . . As you will no doubt be aware, the plans for development of the outlying regions of the Galaxy require the building of a hyperspatial express route through your star system, and regrettably your planet is one of those scheduled for demolition."

Arthur Dent, Mr. Prosser, the demolition men, and everyone else on Earth erupted in panic. The voice: "There's no point in acting all surprised about it. All the planning charts and demolition orders have been on display in your local planning department in Alpha Centauri for fifty of your Earth years, so you've had plenty of time to lodge any formal complaint and it's far too late to start making a fuss about it now."

The local is relative. Arthur Dent just happened to find himself in the crosshairs of two local planning boards at once, one terrestrial, the other extraterrestrial. That one was located down the road and the other near Alpha Centauri did not change the fact that both were local. As Ursula Heise explains, "the language of the alien technocrats derives much of its humor for the reader from the way it redefines the meaning of the word 'local,' which here encompasses not just all of Planet Earth but also distant solar systems where humankind has not even yet set foot."[46]

It bears repeating that we can't tell whether a particular place in space is local until we know its referent. A town is local relative to a province, the nation-state, or the galaxy, but it is not, relative to a neighborhood.

Now that we've got a handle on the *local*, let's move on to *more locally*. Something can be done more locally in two different senses; one pertains to size, the other to scale. With respect to size, something is done more locally when it is done someplace smaller than before. Because neighborhoods are found within cities and cities are found within provinces, neighborhoods are smaller than their cities and cities are smaller than their provinces. Which is not to say that neighborhoods are smaller than cities as such.

I don't think it matters whether by smaller we mean area or population, as long as we stick to one or the other. Doing something in Washington Heights, a neighborhood in Manhattan, rather than in New York City, is to do it more locally because Washington Heights is smaller, both in population and area, than New York City. But doing something

FIGURE 2-1. **Matryoshka Dolls**

in Rapid City, South Dakota (population 74,703)[47] rather than Manhattan Community District No. 12 (Washington Heights and Inwood, population 195,302)[48] is not doing it more locally. Doing something more locally is to do it someplace smaller within something else of which it is, or could be, a part.

With respect to scale, something is done more locally when it is done someplace lower in a hierarchy of jurisdictional scales. Geographers like to point out that scale is "a 'vertical' differentiation in which social relations are embedded within a hierarchical scaffolding of nested territorial units stretching from the global, the supra-national, and the national downwards to the regional, the metropolitan, the urban, the local, and the body."[49] In this passage, the local is included as one of the scalar levels, but if I am correct in what I've said so far, this is a mistake. It's easy to point to regions, metro areas, urban centers, and bodies but not "the local." Some scholars reject the vertical conception of scale, but for reasons we don't need to get into. The matryoshka doll conception of scale works just fine for our purposes.

The neighborhood is local with respect to the city because the neighborhood is lower in its jurisdictional hierarchy. Unlike local as it pertains to size, local as it pertains to scale depends on socially constructed hierarchies. Jurisdictions do not exist in the natural world. Not every jurisdictional hierarchy has the same scales; the United States has states and counties (parishes in Louisiana; Alaska has boroughs), while France has régions and départements.

This fact, that hierarchies of scale are socially constructed, has interesting consequences. Sometimes, the locality in question does not, strictly speaking, exist. Neighborhoods, for instance, are local with respect to cities, but they may not have jurisdictional status—they may not have a recognized position within their jurisdictional hierarchy. But they could, in principle.

Doing something more locally, then, means doing it someplace small or smaller than before, or someplace low or lower within a jurisdictional hierarchy. Let me reiterate that our definition thus far is descriptive. It refers to things being done in the world—to activities or processes: prioritizing the local by making decisions, exercising authority, or implementing policy locally or more locally.

"Il y a politique de l'espace, parce que l'espace est politique." There is a politics of space, because space is political, the French philosopher Henri Lefebvre once proclaimed.[50] How is space political, and why would that matter?

To summarize a massive literature in critical political geography, space is political because people can do things with space. The study of politics, as Harold Lasswell once put it, is the study of who gets what, when, and how; Lasswell forgot *where*.[51] Where things are done affects who gets what, when, and how.

For an example, consider the "doctrine of popular sovereignty" in the antebellum United States. Stephen Douglas, most famous for debating and then beating Abraham Lincoln to maintain his seat in the United States Senate, argued that fledgling United States territories (not yet states) should decide the status of slavery (legal or illegal) within their borders. Northern Democrats, Whigs, and Republicans argued, in contrast, that the United States—the whole country—should decide, seeing as the territories were under its jurisdiction.

The two sides disagreed about where, and consequently by whom, the decision should be made: locally, in the territories, or by the national government. That decision mattered. If it were made nationally, slavery would have been prohibited; majorities in the United States opposed the extension of slavery. If the decision were made locally, in the territories, it was anyone's guess. As Lincoln insisted in his famous Peoria speech:

> If there is ANY THING which it is the duty of the WHOLE PEOPLE to never entrust to any hands but their own, that thing is the preservation and perpetuity, of their own liberties, and institutions. And if they shall think, as I do, that the extension of slavery endangers them, more than any, or all other causes, how recreant to themselves, if they submit the question, and with it, the fate of their country, to a mere hand-full of men, bent only on temporary self-interest.[52]

Douglas won the day, however. Kansas subsequently erupted into a quasi-civil war, with pro-slavery and anti-slavery forces battling to control the territory's government.

He who controls where decisions are made makes the rules. Where decisionmaking authority is assigned within a jurisdictional hierarchy is therefore a political question. Critical political geographers like to say that space and scale are "socially constructed."[53] What they mean is that space and scale, or at least the ways in which they are conceptualized, can be made and remade. Anything that can be made can be unmade or remade. Space and scale are not natural, neutral, or inert—they are political. Claims to the contrary are political, too.

I'm mentioning all of this because localism does not exist in an ideological vacuum. Prioritizing the local, or claims that we should make decisions, exercise authority, or implement policy locally or more locally are normative or ideological, though not necessarily in the Marxist sense. Localism has a second, normative (moral or ethical) definition. In the normative sense, localism is the claim that we *should* prioritize the local by making decisions, exercising authority, or implementing policy locally or more locally.

It's no coincidence that localism in the descriptive sense lines up with the noun of action, *localism*, formed by combining the verb *localize* and the suffix *-ism*.[54] Localism in the normative sense, by contrast, lines up with the noun *local* combined with the suffix *-ism*, "forming the name of a system of theory or practice, religious, ecclesiastical, philosophical, political, social, etc." That is, localism as theory, ideology, or doctrine.[55]

The two definitions, descriptive and normative, are intimately related. Normative localism expresses approval for descriptive localism. It says that there is this phenomenon in the world—prioritizing the local by making decisions, exercising authority, or implementing policy locally or more locally—and it's a good thing. We should do it or have more of it.

The two definitions are intimately related but distinct. The distinction is critical for this book. My objection is to normative localism, not descriptive localism per se. In fact, I think there is nothing wrong, in some cases, with prioritizing the local by making decisions, exercising authority, or implementing policy locally or more locally. Whether that's a good thing depends on the facts of the case—the circumstances, the context.

This book develops a case against normative localism, that we should, generally speaking, prioritize the local by making decisions, exercising authority, or implementing policy locally or more locally. We shouldn't. Let me repeat that I have nothing against localism in the descriptive sense. This book is about the reasons for and the arguments in favor of normative localism. My overarching claim in this book is that the arguments made by scholars, officials, commentators, pundits, and ordinary people in favor of prioritizing the local by making decisions, exercising authority, or implementing policy locally or more locally aren't convincing.

In chapters 3 through 8 of this book, I shine a light on a series of arguments for normative localism, the claim that we should prioritize the local by making decisions, exercising authority, or implementing policy locally or more locally. Some are better than others of course, but I want to emphasize here, and again and again, that my objection is to the arguments, not where they would lead were they convincing. I reject localism not as a matter of principle but because virtually every argument in its favor is weak, misguided, misleading, or dangerous.

It is important to recognize, in this regard, that I do not consider every argument for localism, and not even every argument I know about. I've tried to be comprehensive without being exhaustive; readers will see what I'm up to and will be able to extend the logic to the remaining arguments themselves.

That said, it's possible that there are arguments I don't know about that count strongly in favor of localism. I doubt it, but it's possible. If there are, I'm happy to eat my words. As I've suggested, my case against localism isn't dogmatic; at least I hope not. I simply wish to show that the arguments we have for localism at present are much weaker, given what we know, than is usually thought.

I'm not so naïve as to believe I'll convince everyone. I've become convinced that localism is misguided, but I'll have accomplished my objective in this book if it encourages proponents of localism to take a hard second look. In this way, these pages are a contribution *to* localism as well as a critique *of* localism. If proponents of localism, in response to my prodding, develop new, stronger arguments for their position, I'll be satisfied. Because localism has consequences, however, we owe it to ourselves to proceed with localism, if we must, with its best foot forward.

What It Excludes

Descriptive localism is prioritizing the local by making decisions, exercising authority, or implementing policy locally or more locally. Normative localism is the claim that descriptive localism is something we should do.

Together, these definitions cover a lot—much, I believe, of what gets called localism—but not everything. Before making a few important distinctions between localism and some concepts in the same ballpark, I mention some things that get called localism that fall outside the scope of this book.

Most notably, this book is not about the Localism Act of 2011, passed by the Cameron-Clegg coalition government in the United Kingdom. It isn't about any specific policies, in fact. It's about the arguments people use to justify policies like the Localism Act. Hence you won't find a discussion of the details of the Localism Act or its implementation. This book is about ideas, how they work, and whether they are worth keeping.

Nor is the book about localism in telecommunications. In radio and television, localism is about maintaining local, as opposed to national, programming. Despite Donald Trump's support for localism in general, during his first year and a half in office, the Federal Communications Commission, under his leadership, "serially removed the policies that protected localism."[56] Strictly speaking, the claim that we should protect local programming is normative localism; it says we should prioritize locally produced content. However, as I've already mentioned, this book is about the arguments for normative localism. Although my claim is that those arguments are weak, generally speaking, it doesn't follow that there aren't good reasons for localism in this particular domain. Readers of this book who are familiar with the telecommunications industry are better equipped to decide.

Finally, this book is not about surf localism, the phenomenon in which surfers protect their local turf, sometimes violently, from interlopers. "Lunada Bay, a surf spot on the northern coast of the bucolic, affluent Palos Verdes peninsula in Los Angeles County, is . . . famously home to one of the most aggressive band of local surfers in the world: the Bay Boys," writes David Ferry. According to a lawsuit filed against them, the Bay Boys "confront, threaten to kill, assault, vandalize property, extort, and bring harm to other persons who live in, work in, or pass through the Lunada Bay area."[57] Although I don't wish to dwell on it, surf localism offers a glimpse of localism at its worst: petty, parochial, and downright mean.

Distinctions

Localism needs to be distinguished from several related phenomena and concepts: decentralization (and devolution), federalism, subsidiarity, community, and local autonomy.

Decentralization is the process in which power and authority is transferred away from central governments. Since decentralization typically transfers power and authority from the center to lower-level governments or jurisdictions, it's easily confused with localism. Indeed, localism and decentralization draw on many of the same arguments and intuitions. Proponents of localism and proponents of decentralization are natural allies.

As I see it, however, decentralization is a policy that is applied broadly throughout a country or territory, simultaneously in many places at once. Though demands for decentralization often come from the bottom, it is implemented from the top. It's a proposal to reform central governments by shifting some of their authority away from the center, toward the periphery.

Decentralization is broader spatially but narrower conceptually. Whereas localism easily captures the mania for local food—to "eat local" or "buy local" is to prioritize the local—decentralization does not. Eating local is not primarily about "decentralizing" food production (though it might also be about that); it's about eating food grown or raised near home. Moreover, it's possible to prioritize one's own local community without expecting others to do likewise. Localism, unlike decentralization, is sometimes isolated. People can favor localism without favoring decentralization.

I don't want to overstate the differences between localism and decentralization, however. Much of what I have to say about localism applies to decentralization, and much of what others have said about decentralization, especially Daniel Treisman in his book *The Architecture of Government: Rethinking Political Decentralization*, applies to localism.[58] But decentralization is narrowly political; it is about jurisdictions, power, and authority. As Gérard Marcou writes, in a report co-published by the World Bank and United Cities and Local Government, "it is preferable to reserve the notion of decentralization for the relations between the public powers, some of which are placed under the control of others, and not for the relations between the public powers and the economy or society in general."[59] Localism is concerned with jurisdictions, power, and authority, too, but also attitudes, feelings, and commitments. It is social as well as political. Decentralization is for academics and technocrats; localism is for the man on the street.

Federalism is like decentralization, except that lower-level governments in a federal state have independent authority.[60] A federal state is decentralized, but a decentralized state is not necessarily federal. Lower-level governments in federal states have constitutional status; they have authority that cannot be taken away by the center. Under decentralization, by contrast, the central government can take back the power it had given.

Much of what I said about the distinction between decentralization and localism applies to the distinction between federalism and localism. Federalism, like decentralization, is a theory that applies to the political system as a whole. Localism isn't necessarily. Moreover, it's possible to pursue or favor localism within a federal state. Localism doesn't have to result in constitutional status for localities, however.

According to the principle of subsidiarity, in its secular variant in the European Union, "in areas which do not fall within its exclusive competence, the Union shall act only if and in so far as the objectives of the proposed action cannot be sufficiently achieved by the Member States, either at [the] central level or at [the] regional and local level, but can rather, by reason of the scale or effects of the proposed action, be better achieved at [the] Union level."[61] Localism and subsidiarity clearly overlap. Nevertheless, subsidiarity is a principle that's supposed to determine where within a jurisdictional hierarchy authority should be exercised. As it is articulated here, subsidiarity has a presumption in favor of localism, but it doesn't require localism. Localism is in fact prohibited by the principle of subsidiarity if authority over a particular issue can be exercised more effectively or efficiently by higher-level governments.

Community is a vexing concept. Except for a short section in chapter 4 on belonging, I avoid the topic. Community is vexing because we often say "local community" when we're referring to localities or lower-level jurisdictions. That's verbal shorthand, however. Community is defined by relationships; the local is defined by space and scale. There's a reason we have two words, communitarianism and localism. Communitarianism is the theory, doctrine, or ideology of community. Normative localism is the theory, doctrine, or ideology of the local.

Communities are defined by relationships between and among individuals. Hence we can say "the Jewish community," "the Black community," and "the legal community." Communities may exist in localities, but they can also transcend them, as in the examples just mentioned.

Community, moreover, almost always has positive connotations.[62] Not so with the local or localism. "The local" is normatively neutral—unless, of course, you've already accepted normative localism. The local is just a place in space that means some things to some people and other things to others. Normative localism imbues the local with value, an imbuing I reject in this book.

As I will concede again and again, there are occasions when prioritizing the local by making decisions, exercising authority, or implementing policy locally or more locally (descriptive localism) works out well. It hardly follows that "the local" is valuable in itself. The local is valuable derivatively, one might say.[63] When the local is valuable, its value comes from the good it does when it does good, not because its value falls like manna from heaven.

Finally, consider local autonomy. Again, localism and local autonomy are similar without being the same. Gregory Clark, in his extremely helpful theory of local autonomy, distinguishes between two facets of local autonomy: initiative and immunity. Initiative "refers to the power of localities to legislate and regulate the behavior of residents."[64] Immunity refers "to the power of localities to function free from the oversight authority of higher tiers of the state."[65] Localities can therefore be autonomous in three different senses. They can have initiative but no immunity; immunity but no initiative; or immunity and initiative.

Because localism is prioritizing the local by making decisions, exercising authority, or implementing policy locally or more locally, localism usually requires the power of initiative. That said, localism does not specify how much initiative localities should have, just that they should have at least as much as they now have and probably more. And localism, at least according to the broad definition used in this book, is silent with respect to immunity. Muscular versions of localism may require immunity, but immunity is not required by localism as such, at least not conceptually.

Proponents of localism could argue (and some do) that making decisions, exercising authority, or implementing policy is all for naught if local decisions can be overruled by higher-level governments. Perhaps that's true. I should clarify, however, that immunity and initiative lie on a spectrum. Localism requires more initiative, and it may require some immunity. How much immunity localism requires is a serious and difficult question.

Localism has much in common with, but is not the same as, federalism, decentralization, community, local autonomy, or subsidiarity. Now, having identified localism and distinguished it from related concepts, we turn, in part II, to three arguments for localism that turn on controversial metaphysical, ideological, or ethical commitments: from tyranny, nature, and belonging.

PART II

Why Localism? Commitments

THREE

Tyranny

"Centralization is not only the death-knell of liberty," surmised Emma Goldman, "but also of health and beauty, of art and science, all these being impossible in a clock-like, mechanical atmosphere."[1] "Centralization as a system is inconsistent with a non-violent structure of society," Mahatma Gandhi declared in 1942.[2] In *The Road to Serfdom*, F. A. Hayek maintained that it was "no accident that on the whole there was more beauty and decency to be found in the life of the small peoples, and that among the large ones there was more happiness and content in proportion as they had avoided the deadly blight of centralization."[3] Aldous Huxley added, in his 1958 reflections on *Brave New World*, "democracy can hardly be expected to flourish in societies where political and economic power is being progressively concentrated and centralized."[4] "Centralisation is mainly an idea of order," E. F. Schumacher observed in *Small Is Beautiful*, "decentralisation, one of freedom."[5]

Even more damning than the charges levied by Goldman, Gandhi, Hayek, Huxley, and Schumacher is the alleged relationship between centralization and totalitarianism. "The effect of totalitarianism," Robert Nisbet writes, "whether in its Bolshevist or Fascist forms, is to impose upon the pluralism of traditional society the centralization which is native to the political state."[6] According to Glenn Frank, then the president of the University of Wisconsin, "there is one thing in common to all experimental governments of the time," by which he meant communism in the Soviet Union, fascism in Italy, and National Socialism in Germany, "and that is the assumption that the problems of this new age can be met by a new and intense centralization of power in the national government."[7] "Soviet-style communism was," according to Brink Lindsay, "but an extreme manifestation of a much broader vision that animated much of the history of the 20th century: the dream of centralized, top-down control over the course of economic development."[8]

Although none of these thinkers mentions despotism or tyranny (terms I'll use interchangeably[9]) explicitly, they capture a persistent, widespread, and generally horrified attitude toward centralization in the history of political thought. But what is centralization? For the purposes of this book, think of localism and centralization as two sides of the same coin, roughly opposites.[10] Localism, as we've seen, is the claim that we should prioritize the local by making decisions, exercising authority, or implementing policy locally or more locally. Centralization, then, is the claim that we should make decisions, exercise authority, or implement policy centrally or more centrally. Stripped to its essentials, the argument for localism grounded in the fear of tyranny says that because centralization is bad, evil, despotic, foolish, tyrannical, and so on, and because localism is the opposite, obverse, or antithesis of centralization, localism is good or necessary. This is a bit simplistic, I admit; real world arguments are more nuanced—and I certainly do not want to erect straw men. But this is the basic intuition, and a decent place to start.

The Arguments

From the history of political thought, the Baron de Montesquieu, Publius (Alexander Hamilton, James Madison, and John Jay), and Alexis de

Tocqueville, each in their own way, have advanced arguments for localism grounded in the dangers of tyranny. They are considered here as representatives of a tradition.

We begin with "the celebrated Montesquieu,"[11] whose fundamental claim is that unmediated power constitutes tyranny: "When legislative power is united with executive power in a single person or in a single body . . . there is no liberty."[12] Despotism, he adds, " is uniform throughout."[13] Liberty would be lost if the same group or individuals "exercised these three powers: that of making the laws, that of executing public resolutions, and that of judging the crimes or the disputes of individuals."[14] For example, "among the Turks, where the three powers are united in the person of the sultan, an atrocious despotism reigns."[15]

For Montesquieu, centralization is tyrannical because it unites all political authority in the central government. When the authority exercised by lower-level institutions is withdrawn and then concentrated in the center, the latter rules unimpeded. Absent a division of power among multiple levels of government, the center rules, like an Oriental despot, according to his own "wills and caprices."[16]

Viewed from a slightly different angle, the problem with centralization is its tendency toward immoderation (which, for Montesquieu, is obviously dreadful). To retain a moderate government, Montesquieu says, "power must check power."[17] To govern moderately, according to fundamental law, power must flow through "mediate channels."[18] This mediating power counterpoises the power of the ruler, preventing him or her from governing as a tyrant. Without "intermediate, subordinate, and dependent powers,"[19] and without "the prerogatives of the lords, clergy, nobility, and towns," tyranny rules.[20]

The necessary checks on moderate government that distinguish it from tyranny are both *vertical* and *horizontal*.[21] Separation of legislative, executive, and judicial powers supplies horizontal checks *within* the central government, whereas towns and *parlements* supply vertical checks *against* the central government. The latter are territorial or geographical, for example, localities, whereas the former are functional, what we today call the branches of government.

The Federalist, written as a series of newspaper articles in 1787 and 1788 by Alexander Hamilton, James Madison, and John Jay, pilfered Montesquieu's separation of powers theory, and expressed its implications more forcefully: "The accumulation of all powers legislative, executive and judiciary in the same hands . . . may justly be pronounced the very definition of tyranny."[22] Thomas Jefferson concurred: "All the powers of government, legislative, executive, and judiciary, result to the legislative body. The concentrating these in the same hands is precisely the definition of despotic government."[23]

In *Federalist* No. 51, Publius argued that a "single republic" guards against usurpations "by a division of the government into distinct and separate departments," that is, branches.[24] He then distinguished between a single republic and a "compound republic," in which "the power surrendered by the people, is first divided between two distinct governments, and then the portion allotted to each, subdivided among distinct and separate departments."[25] Dividing power "between two distinct governments" supplies vertical checks whereas dividing power "among distinct and separate departments" supplies horizontal checks. Combining vertical and horizontal checks, according to Publius, provides "a double security . . . to the rights of the people."[26]

Tocqueville's discussion of centralization is more famous—or perhaps more infamous—and more complicated. It helps that he, unlike Montesquieu and Publius, actually used the word *centralization*.[27] His account is notorious for its harrowing description of life and liberty under centralization's yoke. A degree of localism becomes, for Tocqueville, a necessary condition of freedom and public virtue.

Tocqueville distinguishes between administrative and governmental centralization.[28] Governmental centralization is concentrating power to direct "the enactment of general laws . . . common to all parts of the nation" whereas administrative centralization is concentrating power to direct that which is "special to certain parts of the nation: local projects, for instance."[29] Perhaps surprisingly, given Tocqueville's starring role in this chapter, he believes that governmental centralization is absolutely essential; without it a nation cannot "endure, much less prosper."[30]

Centralization is only dangerous, Tocqueville argues, when administrative centralization is *united* with governmental centralization.[31] Administrative decentralization, especially local government, is necessary because "organized forces" repel tyranny and despotism: "How can tyranny be resisted in a country where individuals are weak and no common interest binds them together?"[32] For Tocqueville (an aristocrat himself), aristocracies tend to avoid tyranny because the aristocracy is itself an organized force, but democracies need "provincial institutions," which are "useful to all peoples," but necessary "among those whose social state is democratic."[33]

Tocqueville is clear about why "organized forces" like local government are needed to resist tyranny. He is less clear, however, about why resistance is needed in the first place—about how tyranny is born and persists. His claim is that "when all the prerogatives of government are already vested in a single power, it is difficult for that power to refrain from entering into the details of administration, and over the long run there will be no shortage of opportunities to do so."[34]

In the chilling conclusion to *Democracy in America*, we learn that "equality of conditions" and the taste for political independence it engenders *cause* centralization, and eventually tyranny. Tocqueville suggests that "if men in centuries of equality readily perceive the idea of a great central power, there can be no doubt that their habits and sentiments also dispose them to recognize such a power and lend it a hand."[35]

Although on its face, Tocqueville's argument is causal—that centralization causes tyranny—I believe that deep down, it's conceptual. It's not that centralization *causes* tyranny, it's that tyranny simply follows, by its very nature, from centralization. Consider the concluding paragraph of part IV, chapter 4, volume 2 of *Democracy in America*: "The most important, and in a sense the only necessary, condition for centralizing public power in a democratic society is to love equality or to make a show of loving it. Thus the *science of despotism*, once so complicated, is made simpler: it can be reduced, as it were, to a single principle."[36]

My suspicions are supported by Tocqueville's suggestion that centralized power well-administered is merely despotism delayed: If the central power "should happen to represent [the people's] interests faithfully and reproduce their instincts precisely, their confidence in it will be virtually without limit, and they will believe that whatever they grant to the central power is something they accord to themselves."[37] If centralization that represents the people's "interests faithfully" leads to tyranny, then what doesn't?

Problems

In what we just saw, Tocqueville intends to argue that the relationship between centralization and tyranny (and therefore freedom) is causal—centralization causes tyranny. But without meaning to he implies that the relationship between centralization and tyranny is logical or conceptual. What I mean by a logical relationship between tyranny and centralization is that the connection between those two ideas is so tight that centralization either implies or entails tyranny (in the logical sense) or necessarily causes tyranny. In both senses of tight (we can use entailment to describe both[38]), it's impossible to have centralization without despotism.

My position in this book resists any claim that makes the connection between centralization and tyranny so tight that localism—as the rough opposite or antithesis of centralization—simply *follows*, logically, from our justified aversion to despotism. That's just too easy. Not only is the claim too easy, it's uninteresting. If localism simply follows from our noble desire to avoid despotism, tyranny, and totalitarianism, there is no need to make a fuss about it, and no need to argue for it. So if it's just true that centralization and tyranny go together, in either sense of tight mentioned above, I encourage the reader to skip the remainder of this chapter.

Let me pause for a (philosophically) technical point. Even if centralization entails tyranny, it does not follow that localism (as the negation of centralization) entails the negation of tyranny—whatever that is. To conclude otherwise is to commit a logical fallacy called affirming the consequent. To see why, suppose it's true that if the blinds are closed, the room is dark. Can we conclude, if the room is dark, that the blinds are closed? Of course not. It could be dark outside. The same goes for tyranny and centralization. If you see tyranny, centralization does not follow. Many other things could have been responsible for the tyranny you've observed, localism included!

One of the most popular expressions of the logical claim we just encountered—centralization implies or entails tyranny—is mistaken because it implicitly conflates two different concepts: centralization and concentration; centralization and absolutism. To see why, recall Publius: "The accumulation of all powers legislative, executive, and judiciary in the same hands . . . may justly be pronounced the very definition of tyranny." And Jefferson: "All the powers of government, legislative, executive, and judiciary, result to the legislative body. The concentrating these in the same hands is precisely the definition of despotic government." Publius and Jefferson claim, in essence, that concentrating all power in the same hands is the definition of tyranny: concentration entails tyranny.

While it may be true that concentration of all power in the same hands is the definition (or a definition) of tyranny, concentration and centralization are not equivalent. It is easy to conflate them because they both imply a collection or an accumulation of functions, powers, or authority around a *node*, where a node is a site from which power or authority emanates. Concentration and centralization can be distinguished by reference to the *kinds* of nodes around which authority is collected in each case. Concentration refers to nodes of authority of any kind, whereas centralization refers to spatial or scalar nodes. In other words, centralization is the collection of authority in one place in space (spatial) or in one level of government (scale). Concentration is the more general notion; centralization is one of its instances. Centralization is a special kind of concentration, namely concentration around spatial or scalar nodes.

The implication of this distinction between centralization and concentration is that power in a society can be centralized without being
concentrated. As long as power is spread among several nodes, power
is not completely concentrated, and the society is not tyrannical or
despotic. The logic of the argument against concentration doesn't say
how power should be separated, just that it should be. The worry is
about all power being exercised by the same person or group, because
tyranny is power exercised without limits.

As a matter of fact, the traditional separation of powers argument
advanced by Montesquieu, Publius, and Jefferson recommends distribution of power among functional nodes rather than spatial or scalar
nodes. Both Publius and Jefferson refer to powers of government *"legislative, executive, and judiciary."*[39] Montesquieu, too, said that "when legislative power is united with executive power . . . there is no liberty."[40]
The traditional argument, therefore, is about what we encountered
earlier as horizontal separation of powers.

This is not to say that Montesquieu and Publius were uninterested
in vertical separation of powers. I've shown above that they were. But
for them, functional separation of powers rather than spatial or scalar
separation of powers was paradigmatic.

Publius's treatment of the issue in *Federalist* No. 51 is telling in this
regard. A brief digression on the historical context will help explain why.
In *The Federalist*, Publius is, in essence, defending the Constitution
signed in Philadelphia at the close of the Constitutional Convention in
September 1787, not the plan he would have wanted. Hamilton and
Madison defended the document despite having been outvoted on several critical issues at the Convention. What this means is that some of
Publius's arguments, including some of the most famous, can and should
be read as post hoc rationalizations. Hamilton, Madison, and Jay decided
to defend the Constitution over their own objections and to look for
merit wherever merit could be found.

We can read Publius's famous remark (quoted above) in this light:
"In the compound republic of America, the power surrendered by the
people, is first divided between two distinct governments, and then the

portion allotted to each, subdivided among distinct and separate depart-ments. Hence a double security arises to the rights of the people." Madison wrote this despite the fact that Hamilton and Madison were among the most ardent nationalists at the Constitutional Convention.[41] Madison, for instance, wanted the national Congress to have the power to veto state laws. In "Vices of the Political System of the United States," written in April 1787, Madison blamed the state governments, which he would later argue provide a "double security," for the failure of the Ar-ticles of Confederation.[42]

It is certainly possible, therefore, that Madison did not really believe that dividing power between the national and state governments would provide any extra security "to the rights of the people." What he un-doubtedly knew was that the Constitution was threatened by detractors who believed otherwise. He thought separation of powers would pro-vide plenty of security "to the people," but also that it would do no harm to play up an extra layer of security he thought superfluous.

In fact, Madison's use of the "double security" idea clearly demon-strates that he was aware of the distinction between centralization and concentration of power. He understood that the division of power between "two distinct governments" was different than the division of power between "distinct and separate departments." Because he thought the states were nothing less than noxious, his "double secu-rity" argument is a rhetorical sleight of hand rather than a theoretical commitment.[43]

I wish to add that if Madison believed that the second layer of security—dividing power between national and state governments—was a harmless addition, he was mistaken. If one layer of security—horizontal separation of powers, for example—is *sufficient* protection against tyr-anny, any costs associated with the second layer are borne needlessly.

Thus far we have considered the claim that centralization implies or entails tyranny. We've seen that even if concentration of power entails tyranny, centralization does not. Let's move on to the relationship be-tween centralization, tyranny, and *uniformity*, which I mentioned briefly in our discussion of Montesquieu. The argument goes like this: Centralization is tyrannical because centralized governments impose uniform legal standards, wiping out local customs and traditions in the process.

Indeed, there is a perfectly reasonable sense in which centralization is a necessary condition of legal uniformity. By legal uniformity, I mean that the same laws apply to everyone and everything within a particular domain, usually a particular territory. Although it is possible for several different lawmakers to impose the same set of laws—that is, uniformity by accident—this seems unlikely and irrelevant. Genuine uniformity is when the same laws emanate from the same source, the same lawmaker. When there is only one node of authority, power is concentrated and centralized. Thus uniformity requires centralization.

Uniformity requires centralization, perhaps, but centralization does not require uniformity. Centralization is a necessary but not a sufficient condition of uniformity. That's because a centralized lawmaking body can divide its domain into multiple jurisdictions, applying different laws to each.[44] This is a prerogative of sovereignty. A single lawmaking body can adapt its laws to local conditions, and even can apply different sets of laws to different people within the same territory. Segregation is an obviously pernicious example of the latter.

Daniel Treisman argues this point quite convincingly in *The Architecture of Government*: "Central governments in heterogeneous countries both can and do differentiate their policies geographically."[45] Even highly centralized states, the former Soviet Union, for instance, vary policy geographically. Most importantly, "any differentiation that local governments would themselves generate under decentralization could be reproduced precisely under centralization."[46]

If adapting policy to local conditions is effective, any effective government would do so, even centralized governments. Only ineffective or despotic centralized governments would impose uniformity hamhandedly or unthinkingly. Yet the problem with dysfunctional or tyrannical governments is not that they impose uniformity, but that they are dysfunctional or tyrannical.

Critics of centralization tend to think government is more likely to be dysfunctional when it is centralized, and that this counts in favor of localism. But without a detailed explanation specifying the relevant mechanisms—how centralization makes governments dysfunctional—I see no reason to think governments are more or less pathological simply because of the level in which their authority is exercised.

Notice how the ground has shifted. The claim we were considering was that centralization is tyrannical because the centralized state imposes uniformity on its citizens. That centralized states have unique pathologies is a different claim, one that applies to governments of all kinds, at every level. We haven't yet seen why the pathologies of centralized government are despotic or tyrannical in nature. The evil that critics of uniformity have identified is that of needlessly eliminating valuable local customs and traditions, which I am happy to call tyranny or despotism, but not uniformity or centralization.

Thus far in this chapter, we've assessed several different *conceptual* arguments—each a variation of the claim that it is in the nature of centralization or that it is part of the concept of centralization to be tyrannical or despotic. A major and no doubt foreseeable problem with conceptual arguments is that they do not provide an account of how centralization leads to tyranny. The argument for localism grounded in the dangers of tyranny needs a mechanism, in part because identifying a mechanism is a first step toward providing evidence. My worry, however, is that the plausibility of each argument offered is inversely related to how well its proposed mechanisms are fleshed out. The closer one looks, the less plausible each claim appears.

To my surprise, much of the literature on the "perils of centralization," the "ratchet effect," big government, the Leviathan state, and so on, where one would expect to find the mechanisms we are looking for, is concerned with *processes* of centralization, concentration of power, the growth of the state, etc., rather than how these processes actually generate tyranny or despotism. It should be clear by now that unless the relationship between centralization and tyranny is conceptual, this line of argument is incomplete. We need to see *how* centralization leads to tyranny or despotism.

One attempt to flesh out the relevant mechanisms, influential in the field of public choice, assumes that states are unitary actors who "maximize revenues from whatever sources of taxation are made available to them constitutionally."[47] Geoffrey Brennan and James Buchanan call this the Leviathan assumption. Unconstrained, Leviathan maximizes tax revenue, tyrannically extracting social surplus.[48]

Motivating assumptions in rational choice models are not causal mechanisms, however. Brennan and Buchanan admit as much: "The monopoly-state model of government" is not useful because it predicts how governments work, "but because there are inherent tendencies in the structure of government to push it toward that sort of behavior implied in the monopolistic model."[49] "Inherent tendencies" do not constitute mechanisms; they are the conceptual argument in disguise.

Another mechanism through which centralization could lead to tyranny has been attributed to Adam Smith in *The Theory of Moral Sentiments*:

> The man of system . . . is often so enamoured with the supposed beauty of his own ideal plan of government, that he cannot suffer the smallest deviation from any part of it. He goes on to establish it completely and in all its parts, without any regard either to the great interests or to the strong prejudices which may oppose it: he seems to imagine that he can arrange the different members of a great society with as much ease as the hand arranges the different pieces upon a chess-board.[50]

James Otteson, a political economist who studies Smith, has argued that "Smith's criticism here is directed at centralized legislators."[51] Note, however, that Smith does not mention centralization at all in this passage or in the book—the term did not enter the English language until 1797.[52]

One way to reconstruct the argument implied by Otteson, connecting Smith's "man of system" to centralization and tyranny, is that the man of system is enamored with and so demands centralization, and then uses centralized power to tyrannically impose his plan over any and all objections, using force if necessary.

But a much more plausible—and far less ideological—reading of Smith suggests that the really dangerous men of system are *already* tyrants; they do not somehow become despots upon realizing what they can do with centralized power. In fact, Smith argues (four sentences later) that "Some general, even systematical, idea of perfection . . . may no doubt be necessary for directing the views of the statesmen."[53] Smith's distinction between statesmen and men of system is their attitude toward centralization, not their willingness to use it. Men of system are enamored with centralization; statesmen are more level-headed. This argument, then, is not so much an argument against centralization or for localism as an argument for character and against empowering men of system.

What if the "spirit of system" is ubiquitous, governments inevitably centralize, and do so tyrannically? I personally doubt that the "spirit of system" is ubiquitous or widespread—the spirit of keeping one's head above water is far more common. Far more likely is that men and women of system comprise a very small minority of the population and they, like everyone else, want to put their special talents to good use. It's conceivable that governments, especially higher level governments, attract men and women of system because they provide opportunities to play chess. (I note in passing that Robert Moses, a notorious man of system, worked at the state and metropolitan level.[54]) Suppose, furthermore, that those less enamored with system are less likely to enter the public sector and that men and women of system hire from within their ranks. Under these conditions, governments will be staffed by a greater proportion of men and women of system than that found in the general population. Men and women of system will then band together to overrule their opponents, centralize power, and impose it tyrannically.

This interpretation of the connection between the man of system, centralization, and tyranny has the virtue of coherence. It supposes, however, that the unsystematic among us are either unaware of men of system or that we are content to let them run amok. Both seem implausible. This is why bureaucracies have rules and oversight and democracies have elections, and why some governments have established special schools to train civil servants, the *École nationale d'administration* in France, for instance. These rules don't work perfectly, but they don't work terribly either. There's a reason it's news when they fail.

Another possibility is that governments *make* men and women of system. Merely having power within one's grasp is enough for ordinary people to catch the spirit of system; and then there is no turning back. A weaker form of this hypothesis, one that suggests that power stimulates the spirit of system, is quite plausible, but banal. "All power tends to corrupt," Lord Acton tells us. Power exists independently of centralization, however, and the problem of corruption is not unique to centralization.

From Smith's man of system, we have finally identified a mechanism that connects centralization and tyranny: first, governments attract or make men and women of system; second, men and women of system centralize power to implement their "ideal plan of government"; and third, men and women crush all opposition and tyrannize. The problem with this mechanism in an argument for localism is that this is precisely the mechanism that animated Montesquieu and Publius: concentration of power. And recall that the remedy for concentration of power is to de-concentrate power, not necessarily decentralize it.

In our search for mechanisms, we identified two. The first, the Leviathan assumption, turned out not to be a mechanism at all. The second, the man of system, did not generate a plausible argument for localism or against centralization. Our purpose in the discussion of mechanisms was simply to clarify what normally remains opaque in critiques of centralization. I'm sure there are other mechanisms I've neglected; they should be scrutinized as I've done with these. The point is that if centralization causes tyranny, it does so by identifiable mechanisms, not by magic. And once a causal mechanism has been identified, one can begin thinking about the likelihood of despotism, given centralization.

In my view, the most sensible interpretation of the relationship between centralization and despotism, tyranny, and totalitarianism is probabilistic. Greater centralization makes tyranny more likely. An increase in centralization of a certain magnitude increases the probability of tyranny by a certain amount, where the latter is a function of the former (with some noise). For the time being, I'm assuming that all tyrannies are equally tyrannical. Although we probably think some despotisms are worse than others, we think that all tyrannies—the really bad and the really, really bad—should be avoided.

One wonders, however, whether the function just mentioned—tyranny as a function of centralization—is monotonic; that is, never decreasing. Perhaps I am playing fast and loose with the concept of tyranny, but it's conceivable that at very low levels of centralization, anarchy for instance, increasing centralization actually *reduces* the probability of tyranny. This assumes, of course, that anarchic violence is comparable to tyranny. Roving bands of marauders pillaging the countryside may not be tyrannical in the narrow sense, but I am sure their terrorism feels as bad as tyranny.

Assume, furthermore, that anarchic violence and despotism are comparable—that they can be treated together as a form of general badness. If the function relating general badness and centralization is decreasing at lower levels of centralization and increasing at higher levels of centralization, it will have a local minimum. There will be a level of centralization that minimizes general badness. Locating that level is difficult; I have no idea how to find it, or even how to go about finding it.

Uncertainty about the optimal level of centralization is not just a theoretical problem. If a society's current level of centralization is above the optimum, decreasing centralization—injecting some localism—will lead to reductions in general badness. This is a core intuition behind the argument for localism derived from the evils of tyranny. But if a society's current level of centralization is below the optimum, injecting localism will generate more general badness. Unless more centralization is always bad, localism is good only when the society is already too centralized. If the society is not centralized enough, localism causes harm.

Doesn't the fact that a degree of localism is beneficial in an overly centralized society damage my case against localism? It does not. I have

not argued, nor will I argue, that prioritizing the local by making decisions, exercising authority, or implementing policy locally or more locally is always bad. What I have argued, and will continue to argue, is
that doing so is not always or even dependably salutary.

I've mentioned already my befuddlement about the optimal level of
centralization. This is actually a point in favor of my position in this book.
Many proponents of localism whose argument is premised on the dangers
of tyranny simply assume that societies are overly centralized. Yet I haven't
encountered a satisfactory argument to justify this assumption.

It is not enough to say that contemporary societies are much more
centralized than they once were. In making this claim, critics of centralization in the United States tend to use the size of government (in
dollars spent) as a proxy for centralization, which is reasonable enough,
although not ideal, for reasons that will become clear. Critics note that
central government spending as a percentage of GDP has grown from
3 percent in 1929 to 22 percent in 2019 to (as a result of the coronavirus
pandemic) 33 percent in 2020.[55]

Much of this growth, however, is in the form of transfer payments.
For instance, if you subtract transfer payments from federal government
expenditures (both as a percentage of GDP), nontransfer government
spending has grown from 2 percent in 1929 to 8 percent in 2017 to
12 percent in 2020. Much of this is just the New Deal in the 1930s and
the response to the coronavirus pandemic. Government spending less
transfers was 7 percent of GDP in 1939 (before the Second World War),
30 percent in 1945, and 11 percent in 1948, after demobilization but before the Korean War.[56] It's hard not to conclude that complaints about
the "growth" of the national government are nothing more than a rear-
guard action against the New Deal. One can criticize the New Deal, of
course, but it obfuscates to do so by objecting to growth in the abstract.

In 2020, roughly 13 percent of federal expenditures, or 4 percent of
GDP ($881 billion), went to states and local governments.[57] While much
of this comes with strings attached, one could argue that spending
money in this way is less centralized than the alternative. According to
Robert Doar, a poverty expert for the right-leaning American Enterprise Institute, "in virtually every instance of interaction between the

agency providing and the citizen receiving benefits from Supplemental Nutrition Assistance Program or Medicaid—our two largest programs—the administering official is a state, county, or city agent."[58] A good chunk of the growth of the national government consists of a computer writing checks or better yet, initiating electronic transfers. I doubt this is what critics of centralization have in mind when they worry about bureaucracy and concentration of power.

Even if governments are much bigger than they once were, and therefore much more centralized, it does not follow that they are too centralized. You could just as well think that for the vast majority of human history societies weren't centralized enough. As Franklin Roosevelt put it (in a passage I'll use more than once): "The growth of the national governments of Europe was a struggle for the development of a centralized force in the nation, strong enough to impose peace upon ruling barons. In many instances . . . the creation of a strong central government . . . was a haven of refuge to the individual. The people preferred the master far away to the exploitation and cruelty of the smaller master near at hand."[59] This could be taken as a conceit of a rabid centralizer or a man of system, but to do so would be to confuse Roosevelt, a man who yearned for balanced budgets until 1937, for a dogmatic centralizer.[60] Roosevelt was no Le Corbusier.

I do not hesitate to grant that at certain times and places, and in certain areas of human life, societies have become or are becoming too centralized. In these cases, some localism could help correct the imbalance. But we need good evidence, or decent arguments, to support particular claims of excess centralization. I am skeptical of arguments from the hip or from the gut. Absent good reasons to believe that societies are, in general, too centralized, I prefer the epistemically humble approach. Let's see the evidence.

Suppose the relationship between centralization and tyranny is tight, in the sense of *tight* introduced earlier. Or suppose that centralization increases the probability of despotism or tyranny. What then follows?

As usual, it depends. If efforts to avoid tyranny and despotism were costless, it would follow that we should do everything we can to minimize tyranny. But since mitigating tyranny requires distributing power among multiple nodes (assuming the conventional view), it is not costless. To divide power is to trade security against tyranny for what Hamilton called "energy" and "dispatch," speed and capacity.[61] Centralization can facilitate great good as well as great evil. Localism guards against great evil but also thwarts great good.

The costs of localism are borne needlessly if power could be divided among functional nodes rather than spatial or scalar nodes. Localism is a blunt instrument. It divides authority geographically, or among levels of government, when other divisions might work just as well or better.

When evaluating arguments for localism grounded in the dangers of tyranny, it is important to resist the allure of sacrifice. The importance of sacrifice to maintaining liberty is a common trope in liberal political thought. Tocqueville said: "Men cannot enjoy political liberty without making sacrifices to obtain it, and it has never been won without great effort."[62] Although it is often necessary to sacrifice something to get what you want—the idea of opportunity costs in economics makes this abundantly clear—it does not follow that because sacrifice is sometimes necessary that sacrifice is always necessary or, for that matter, sufficient. We sacrifice something in order to get something more valuable; sacrificing the wrong thing, or too much of the right thing, is needless sacrifice. Sacrificing state capacity for the sake of liberty is needless sacrifice if liberty can be obtained or maintained by other means. The argument for localism from the concern with tyranny needs to show that dividing authority among spatial or scalar nodes protects against tyranny at least as well as other divisions of power, at a lower cost.

The argument for localism also depends on how bad despotism and tyranny are—relative to chaos and anarchy. It depends on the probabilities too, but set that aside for a moment. I'm also setting totalitarianism to one side, since part of the utility of that concept is to invoke unimaginable horror. Totalitarianism is particularly useful as an argumentative trump card and tends to cloud our judgment.

Simply put, the argument for localism from the concern with excessive centralization fails if the probability weighted evils of excessive fragmentation—chaos and anarchy—exceed the probability weighted evils of excess centralization—tyranny and despotism. I've already suggested how difficult it is to estimate the probabilities of these two worst-case scenarios.

That said, consider the problem with relying on intuitions. Human beings are notoriously bad at estimating probabilities. Confirmation and availability bias wreak havoc. The latter is "a cognitive heuristic through which the frequency or probability of an event is judged by the number of instances of it that can readily be brought to mind."[63] The former is self-explanatory.

Despotism and tyranny, because they are so nasty, are especially salient in the historical imagination. Periods of peace and prosperity are blissfully dull and easily forgotten. Availability bias suggests that we tend to overestimate the probability of tyranny or despotism. And because many people already believe that despotism and tyranny are common occurrences, confirmation bias suggests they will use the occasional example to confirm their suspicions. I want to be clear that I am not trying to say that despotism and tyranny never happen, or that they are benign, just that accurately estimating probabilities requires that we adopt a skeptical attitude toward our intuitions.

Matthew White, author of *The Great Big Book of Horrible Things*, has done precisely that. He has compiled a list of the 100 worst atrocities in human history, measured by body counts. Compiling a list of atrocities is helpful, White says, because "if we study history to avoid repeating the mistakes of the past, it helps to know what those mistakes were, and that includes *all* of the mistakes, not just the ones that support certain pet ideas."[64]

Some readers may balk at the idea of using body counts, since there are fates worse than death. Body counts have the advantage of rough neutrality, however. While all may agree that there are worse fates than death, I doubt we agree on what those are. Violent death is a useful common denominator, as it is exceedingly difficult to realize one's highest ideals while rotting in the grave.

White introduces the atrocities with some general lessons, the first of which strikes at the heart of the issue at hand: "Chaos is deadlier than

tyranny. More of these multicides result from the breakdown of authority rather than the exercise of authority."[65]

Drawing on Norbert Elias's *The Civilizing Process*, and echoing
Roosevelt, Steven Pinker has argued that the first major decline in violence in human history corresponds with the formation of the earliest
states. Stateless societies in the period from 14,000 B.C.E. to 1770 C.E.
had an average war death rate of 15 percent, whereas the corresponding
rate for the first half of the twentieth century (including both world
wars) was 3 percent. With the formation of states "came a reduction in
the chronic raiding and feuding that characterized life in a state of nature and a more or less fivefold decrease in rates of violent death."[66]

My point here is that even if one accepts, over my objections, the
claim that centralization leads to tyranny or despotism, centralization
might well be worth the risk if the alternative is a return to raiding and
feuding. Consider, for example, the period in English history, often referred to as "the Anarchy," during the reign of King Stephen (roughly
1135–1153), in which rival claimants to the throne led England to fall
"spectacularly from the strictly administered harmony of Henry to the
bloody purgatory of Stephen."[67]

Perhaps I'm being unfair to localism, which neither entails nor causes
anarchy, after all. But neither does centralization entail despotism.
Localism does not necessarily cause chaos, but centralization does not
necessarily cause tyranny. Centralization increases the likelihood of
despotism; localism increases the likelihood of anarchy. Anarchy and
tyranny are both worst-case scenarios. I see no good reason to posit anything other than symmetry between them. If concerns with the dangers
of centralization support localism, concerns with the dangers of localism
support centralization. And if we are forced to choose, and I don't think
we are, there are decent enough reasons—namely, life—to choose tyranny over chaos.

Even if we accept that centralization entails or causes tyranny, our judgments about which regimes count as tyrannical or despotic will depend, in part, on political judgments. What one person calls tyranny
another might call justice; tyranny is in the eye of the beholder.

This is not idle speculation. Radical skeptics of the state, including some anarchists and some libertarians, sometimes argue that concentrations of power are evil in themselves. For his part, Tocqueville occasionally writes as though centralization in accordance with the people's wishes is a particularly insidious variety of tyranny, the despotism of a state that "works willingly for their happiness . . . provides for their security, foresees and takes care of their needs, [and] facilitates their pleasures . . ."[68]

If a substantial majority of the people want a generous welfare state, for example, and if centralization is required to get it, is that really tyranny? We human beings are disagreeable creatures who use language to get what we want; we're happy to call any regime where we don't get what we want tyrannical. The fact that a small but vocal and erudite minority on the losing side scorns the desires of the rabble and sees the centralized state as a tyrant does not make it so, however. Perhaps localism is rhetorically useful for those who desire a smaller, less active government, but its utility in this regard should not be confused with an argument.

The argument for localism from the justified fear of tyranny is actually older than localism itself. It is at least as old as liberalism. Wherever and whenever people have feared excessive concentrations of power, they have tried to divide it up and distribute it widely. Nevertheless, in this chapter, we have seen that localism is best understood as a response to centralization, a special kind of concentration of power, not concentration as such.

Centralization, moreover, is not necessarily tyrannical; at most, centralization facilitates tyranny, or makes it more likely. Despotism and tyranny can be resisted without recourse to localism, which is fortunate, because localism can do more harm than good. Power ought to be checked, but not in such a way as to needlessly incapacitate public power pursuing the public good. Localism is a check on tyranny, despotism, and totalitarianism, but not the only one, and it's a particularly costly one at that.

FOUR

Belonging

The argument for localism from belonging, attachment, or affection is perhaps the most profound but also, and partly for that reason, the most difficult to evaluate clearheadedly. It is romantic, poignant, rooted, nostalgic, and sensibly obvious. We should prioritize the local by making decisions, exercising authority, or implementing policy locally or more locally because that is where we live, work, love, play, and someday die: "people tend to prefer more localized governance" because local governments are closer to home.[1]

Before going any further, we need to clarify that belonging operates in two different ways in the argument for localism: directly and indirectly. These should not be confused. Belonging operates *directly* when our feelings and beliefs about particular places justify or ground localism. Because our local places matter to us and give our lives meaning, we are morally or politically justified in taking steps to bring decisionmaking closer to home.

Belonging works *indirectly* (or instrumentally) when the claim is that prioritizing the local by making decisions, exercising authority, or implementing policy locally or more locally facilitates useful attitudes, actions, or dispositions, and those attitudes, actions, or dispositions produce good results. Because localism produces good outcomes (makes people's lives go well), we are justified in choosing it. Strictly speaking, the indirect arguments belong in part II on consequences; they are considered here to maintain thematic consistency.

It is worth distinguishing these two roles for belonging—direct and indirect—because they figure into radically different arguments for localism. When belonging operates directly, facts about us and our psychology ground localism on their own, so to speak. When belonging operates indirectly, on the other hand, the case for localism is built on causal mechanisms, namely that localism puts facts about us and our psychology to good use.

The Facts

Since 1972, when Gallup began asking Americans how much "trust and confidence" they had in their local governments, 63 to 77 percent expressed a "great deal" or a "fair amount."[2] During the same period, 51 to 80 percent voiced a "great deal" or a "fair amount" of confidence in their state governments. In international affairs, 39 to 83 percent trusted the "federal government in Washington." Only 35 to 77 percent were confident in the national government in domestic matters.[3]

Confidence in local government has trended upward since 1972, while trust in the national government and the state governments has fallen. Americans' trust in local government is high and consistent; in the federal government, lower and falling. In the most recent survey in which all three levels of government were evaluated (September 2021), 66 percent of Americans expressed confidence in their local governments, 57 percent in their state governments, and only 39 percent in the federal government "when it comes to handling domestic problems."[4] Twenty-one percent of Americans had a "great deal" of confidence in the local governments, while only 6 percent had the same level of confidence in the national government in domestic affairs.

Since the Pew Research Center began asking similar questions in 1997, 60 to 78 percent of Americans' "overall opinion" of local government has been "favorable." The corresponding figure for state government is 50 to 77 percent, and for the federal government, 28 to 82 percent. Excluding the November 2001 outlier (82 percent), the federal government's favorability has not topped 73 percent, and fell to 28 percent in March 2013. The Pew data therefore corroborate the Gallup numbers, although with slightly less favorable ratings for governments across the board.[5]

The Heartland Monitor Poll, sponsored by Allstate and Atlantic Media, has asked more detailed questions about local communities and local politics. From February 2015 to June 2016, 56 to 64 percent of Americans said that more progress was being made at the state and local level while only 24 to 26 percent said that more progress was being made at the national level.[6] In June 2016, 68 percent said that "new ideas and solutions are more likely to come from . . . state and local institutions like government, businesses, and volunteer or community organizations because they are closer to the problems, are more adaptable, and have more at stake in finding solutions."[7] Only 23 percent said that more progress was being made by "national institutions like the federal government, national businesses, and major non-profit organizations because they have more financial resources, experience, and long-term stability."[8]

In February 2015, majorities said that state and local institutions would do a better job than national institutions in "making neighborhoods more attractive places to live" (89 percent), "improving the way we educate young people" (66 percent), "finding new ways to provide more opportunity to poor people" (63 percent), "developing new products and services that create new jobs" (63 percent), "improving wages and living standards for average families" (57 percent), and "ensuring that businesses are regulated fairly and consistently" (51 percent). In only one area did a majority think national institutions would do better: "finding new ways to save energy and improve the environment" (51 percent).[9]

Two-thirds said their "local area . . . is headed in the right direction" and 60 percent approved of their local leaders' performance.[10] In contrast, only a third of those questioned said the country as a whole was headed in the right direction, and only 44 percent approved of President Obama's performance.[11] Asked what they could do—personally—that would "have the biggest impact to improve life" in their local area, 47 percent of respondents said "buying from local and small businesses."[12] Finally, 9 percent said their area's quality of life would improve with more people, 23 percent said with fewer people, and 64 percent said that population size would "make no difference."[13]

The Direct Argument

We know that people, Americans at least, prefer their local governments and feel a great deal of affection for their local communities.[14] These are facts. I now want to ask how these facts fit into the argument for localism. What follows from our feelings of belonging? It's not obvious. It's a tricky question, in fact, that turns on deep and controversial moral questions.

I'll start with a flat-footed version of the argument: Because we feel we belong in our local communities, because we value them and find meaning in them, it is permissible, or perhaps even obligatory, to prioritize them. Therefore we should make more decisions and exercise more authority in the localities that matter to us most. This version of the argument appeals to the intrinsic value of local communities. *Intrinsic*, at least the way philosophers use it, is jargon for "valuable for its own sake." Something is instrumentally valuable when it is valuable for the sake of something else. Pleasure is intrinsically valuable—when it is valuable—because we don't seek pleasure for the sake of something else. Money is instrumentally valuable because it gets us other things we want.

The direct argument seems eminently reasonable at first blush. When framed slightly differently, however, it can look pretty *unreasonable*. Note that we feel attachment to our local communities, we find meaning and value in them, not entirely because of features about them but because they are ours. Some of us value community in general—we think it's good that people have special relationships with their neighbors—but I very much doubt we have strong attachments to locales we've never even seen. Whether you feel attachment toward a locality crucially depends, then, on whether it's yours.

The argument I have been describing thus far has a great deal in common with a problem that moral philosophers have been arguing about for centuries: the problem of special obligations. Special obligations "are obligations owed to some subset of persons, in contrast to natural duties that are owed to all persons simply *qua* persons."[15] The paradigmatic special obligations are those to friends and family. The kinds of special obligations I am interested in here are *agent-relative*: the persons to whom obligations are owed stand in a special relationship *with the agent*. The friends I am permitted to favor are my friends, not someone else's. Similarly, the neighbors I am permitted to favor are my neighbors, not neighbors in general. Special obligations are a problem because, according to some well-respected moral theories, it's wrong to treat different people differently under identical circumstances.

Utilitarianism, according to which an action is morally right if, and only if, it produces the most utility, welfare, or goodness, has no place for special obligations. Each person's utility, welfare, or happiness counts equally, so it is wrong to prefer friends and family if doing otherwise would produce more utility. According to utilitarianism, we are morally required to do the thing that produces the most good; if helping a stranger produces more good than helping a friend, you should help the stranger. The fact that your friend is *your* friend makes no difference.

Some people think this is a count against utilitarianism; they say it conflicts with commonsense morality: "if a moral theory says I shouldn't prefer friends to strangers, it must be wrong!" I'm skeptical that we ought to reject moral theories when they don't corroborate commonsense morality, however. For a moral theory to have critical purchase, it can't simply be measured against what common sense demands. Some distance between our moral theories and commonsense morality is a condition of moral progress.

Utilitarianism rejects special relationships because it contains a strong dose of impartiality. The reasons we have to do one thing rather than another have to be *agent neutral*. The bit about each person's utility, welfare, or happiness counting equally is how utilitarianism registers impartiality and agent neutrality. And the idea that no one counts more than anyone else has a great deal to be said for it. It is a fundamental commitment of modernity.

We don't actually need to be utilitarians to care about impartiality, however. Rather, it is helpful to use utilitarianism's impartiality requirement as a starting point. It's not that there are no special obligations; it's that special obligations require justification. We all feel a tinge of moral discomfort, or we should, when we choose to help a friend when helping a stranger would do more good.

Intrinsic value is a good place to start. If the relationships that are thought to generate special obligations have intrinsic value, there are good reasons to cultivate them—good moral reasons. Alternatively, if cultivating special relationships, which sometimes requires prioritizing friends or family over strangers, makes people's lives go better overall, then special obligations might be justified (instrumentally).

This matters for the argument for localism because the permission or obligation to favor one's own locality is *special*. Localism picks out a subset of persons, namely those in one's own locale, for special treatment. Strict impartiality would require treating neighbors no differently than strangers.[16]

The argument for preferential treatment toward locals, because it recommends a departure from impartiality, requires justification. Notice how this way of framing the problem puts pressure on the argument. We began the chapter with the observation that people feel attachment and affection toward their local communities. That was supposed to ground the argument for localism; we said that we are permitted to prioritize our localities because we feel attachment or affection toward them.

But now I'm suggesting there is a straightforward reason to reject the inference from belonging to permission or obligation, namely that it violates impartiality. The fact that we are attached to our localities is just a fact, and it remains to be seen whether it is a morally relevant fact.

We'll consider the matter by comparing relationships among co-locals to friendship and kinship. Many people think prioritizing friends and family is morally justifiable. The argument for localism, then, needs a justification at least as persuasive as those for prioritizing friends and family. My suggestion, for the time being, is that prioritizing co-locals is going to be much harder to justify than prioritizing friends.

For the record, I am skeptical that things like friendship are intrinsically valuable. Sometimes saying something is intrinsically valuable is to refuse to say *why* it's valuable. I think friendship is good because having friends, and doing the things friends do, contributes to human flourishing. Friendship can look intrinsically valuable because we refuse to call relationships that detract from human flourishing friendships. Flourishing is built into the very concept of friendship. Nevertheless, it does not follow that because friendship is *always* valuable that friendship is *intrinsically* valuable. But I'm happy to accept that friendship is intrinsically valuable, for the sake of argument.

Kinship, unlike friendship, is nonvoluntary. Also unlike friendship, we continue to call relationships among kin that detract from human flourishing kinship. We could say that kinship relationships that contribute to human flourishing are valuable intrinsically; it's more natural to say, however, that kinship offers opportunities for a unique kind of human flourishing: one that can't be had in other ways. It also threatens a unique kind of human misery.

Relationships among co-locals are closer to kinship than friendship. They are voluntary in some respects, involuntary in others. People can choose a locale by moving, but they can't pick and choose their future neighbors, one-by-one. Like kinship, relationships among co-locals can contribute toward, or detract from, human flourishing. We tend to call locales that contribute to human flourishing *communities*, and co-residents who help us flourish *neighbors*. In some cases, we call locales that detract from human flourishing *ghettos*, and co-residents who do likewise *disturbances*.[17] Ferdinand Tönnies, who we'll discuss in greater detail in the next chapter, remarked that "'bad community' makes no sense in our language."[18] This is why I avoid, wherever possible, using words with positive connotations, like *community* and *neighbor*, to refer to generic people and places.

If there is a plausible argument for the intrinsic value of relationships among co-locals, one that could ground the permission to prioritize one's own locale, I believe it will appeal to community. We sometimes use *community* as a synonym for *locale*, but I doubt that communities in that sense are intrinsically valuable. Locales provide meaning for people, but not invariably a meaning they endorse. There is such a thing as a bad meaning, a meaning one would repudiate if one could. As pieces of nature, locales might have intrinsic value but not the kind that would ground a permission to prioritize one's own locale. Now I think an argument can be made that communities understood as locales that contribute to human flourishing are intrinsically valuable. (I'd prefer to say that their value is derivative, but I won't insist on it.) We could just as well say: community is intrinsically valuable.

Can the intrinsic value of community justify the permission to prioritize one's own locale? Only, it seems, if one's locale is a community. Prioritizing one's own locale, if that locale is not a community, is prioritizing something that detracts from human flourishing.

Perhaps by prioritizing one's locale, when that locale currently detracts from human flourishing, one can turn it toward community. Deficient locales need extra help; flourishing communities don't. You are permitted or even obligated to favor your own locale if it is deficient, but not if it is flourishing.

This isn't a crazy thought. The practice of prioritizing one's own locale, when it is already flourishing, could be called "opportunity hoarding."[19] Social justice might then require that residents of flourishing communities *disfavor* their own communities and instead favor struggling locales. Connecticut's "Education Cost Sharing" program provides an example. In the United States, primary and secondary public schools are typically funded by local property taxes, so rich school districts have more money to spend than poor school districts. In Connecticut, however, rich districts are required to contribute a proportion of their property tax revenue to a statewide kitty that helps fund poorer schools.

While this might sound reasonable—I think we ought to do it—it is decidedly not an argument for prioritizing one's own locale *because* localities are intrinsically valuable. The argument actually says that because communities are intrinsically valuable, one should try to turn deficient locales into communities. The permission to prioritize one's own locale is doubly contingent, then. First, whether prioritizing one's own deficient locale will help turn it into a community is an empirical matter. If the locale is deficient because its residents lack social, financial, and cultural capital, it's hard to see how localism will help. Second, the permission to favor one's own locale applies *only* to residents of deficient locales. Residents of flourishing locales are permitted and perhaps obligated to favor *other* locales, not their own.

Since I will return to indirect arguments like this one later in the chapter, I leave the matter there. Community might be intrinsically valuable, but that does not mean we are permitted to prioritize our own locales.

One important difference between the justification for localism and the justification for prioritizing friends and family is that the *self* is included in one's own locale. The self is a member of the subset of persons being granted special treatment. Prioritizing one's locale is therefore closer to self-interest than to prioritizing friends or family. Special treatment toward friends and family can be altruistic; special treatment toward one's own locale less so.

Justifying preferential treatment toward the self is somewhat different than justifying preferential treatment toward friends and family. Most people think that if there is only one life jacket for two people (and if they try to share, both will drown), it is permissible to take it rather than give it to a stranger. The question is whether this intuition scales up to justify preferential treatment toward one's own locale.

This lets us pick up a loose thread from earlier. While we were exploring whether locales were intrinsically valuable, I neglected the fact, established at the very beginning, that we value them. Some followers of the philosopher Immanuel Kant believe that rational agents can confer value on things by valuing them. Less formally: because *human beings* are valuable, the things they value are valuable. Perhaps, then, the fact that people's localities are valuable *to them* is sufficient for the argument to work.

We don't ordinarily think it's okay to prevent people from pursuing the things they consider valuable unless there are very good reasons. So if people value their locales, and if they value them by prioritizing them, then they are permitted to, or required to, favor their locales. It's a splendidly simple argument.

The argument works if we are in fact permitted to favor what we value. Another influential critique of utilitarianism helps explain why we might be. Bernard Williams writes of the "evident fact that among the things that make people happy is . . . being taken up or involved in any of a vast array of projects or . . . commitments."[20] Commitments are projects "with which one is more deeply or extensively involved or identified."[21] The problem with utilitarianism, according to Williams, is that it treats an agent's commitments as though they were garden-variety projects that must be sacrificed for the sake of others' projects, if doing so would produce greater happiness. Sacrificing one's commitments for others' projects in this way is an affront to one's identity and sense of self-worth or, as Williams puts it, one's integrity.

Williams thinks it would be "absurd" if it were impermissible to favor one's own commitments.[22] The permission to favor one's own commitments is special in the sense mentioned earlier. Since prioritizing one's own commitments is a departure from impartiality, it demands justification. This is what integrity is supposed to provide. It is permissible to favor one's own commitments because doing so is part of what it means to be a human being rather than a conduit for other people's happiness.

If our attachments and affections for our own locales are like commitments, then there may be a respectable argument for localism grounded in integrity. We want to prioritize the local by making decisions, exercising authority, or implementing policy locally or more locally because that is how we further our commitments to our locales.

While I recognize the force of Williams's argument, I am skeptical that it translates cleanly into an argument for localism, for two reasons. First, the permission to favor one's own commitments is not unqualified, even according to Williams's view. He mentions the "maximally harmonious realization" of people's projects.[23] Even if maximization is not required, incompatible commitments cannot, by definition, be satisfied simultaneously, and we need to determine whose commitments should win out. It's impossible to avoid making judgments about people's commitments, however. It seems to me that commitments that make numerous others' commitments difficult to pursue should be the first to go.

In this regard, what's interesting about localism is that it prioritizes commitments that can be pursued locally over those that can be pursued only extra-locally. In the largely abandoned quest for school desegregation, for example, one of the most effective ways to pursue the commitment to racial equality is to enact school assignment policies that cross jurisdictional boundaries. By contrast, the most effective way to pursue the commitment to local control and local autonomy is to disregard other jurisdictions entirely. In cases like these, one kind of commitment—local autonomy—impedes and excludes the other—racial equality.

Second, the commitment to one's own locale is not universally shared. While it is possible to imagine that some personal commitments can be pursued without affecting or implicating others, pursuing a commitment to one's own locale through localism *necessarily* implicates others. Localities are plural subjects. To choose to prioritize the local by making decisions, exercising authority, or implementing policy locally or more locally is to choose on behalf of others. And I doubt that integrity is threatened in precisely the same way when the commitments being respected interfere with the commitments of others. In the religious context, do we say that evangelists' integrity is threatened when they are asked to sacrifice their commitment to universal conversion for the sake of others' worldly commitments?

The fact that people value the places where they live and work does not settle the matter. I started this branch of the discussion with the Kantian claim that valuing generates value. Kantians do not believe that valuing generates intrinsic value, however. Rational agency, and rational agency alone, is intrinsically valuable, and this is what *makes* the things rational agents choose to value valuable. The Kantians, like Williams, have a way to evaluate and adjudicate between what people value: by reference to rational agency. But I doubt that the intrinsic value of rational agency gets us to localism. Neither the intrinsic value of rational agency nor the intrinsic value of some locales generates a general permission to prioritize one's own locale. The argument for localism from belonging will have to be indirect.

The Indirect Argument

I fear I've dragged the reader through some formidable weeds: but for a purpose. Claims that we should prioritize the local by making decisions, exercising authority, or implementing policy locally or more locally merely because we feel a certain way toward our locales are and should be morally suspect. We are not *entitled* to beggar thy neighbor.

One of the most compelling indirect arguments for localism recognizes that making the world a better place requires investment—not investment in the abstract, but investment in particular communities. Speaking crudely, people do not make investments purely out of the goodness of their hearts; they are looking for a return on their investments. To make their investments in particular communities worth the effort, they need to be able to see or feel results. They are most likely to see results in the communities in which they live or work and in which they have invested time and energy. "The New Englander is attached to his town not so much because he is born there as because he sees the town as a free and powerful corporation of which he is a part and which it is worth his trouble to seek to direct," as Tocqueville put it.[24] They also want the benefits of their investments to redound *to them*. Investments in which the return redounds elsewhere produce social value, but this is usually not what investors have in mind.

If people are less likely to invest in particular communities when they do not expect to see or feel results, and if investment in particular local communities makes those communities better places to live, we have good reasons to do what we can to make it easier for people to see a return on their investments. Localism is an obvious solution. Prioritizing the local by making decisions, exercising authority, or implementing policy locally or more locally makes it easier for people to see and feel the results of their hard work.

Arguments like this abound in the history of political thought, so for the sake of brevity, I'll recount those of David Hume and Adam Smith. In *An Enquiry Concerning the Principles of Morals*, Hume wrote: "It is wisely ordained by nature, that private connexions should commonly prevail over universal views and considerations; *otherwise* our affections and actions would be dissipated and lost, for want of a proper limited object. Thus a small benefit done to ourselves, or our near friends, excites more lively sentiments of love and approbation than a great benefit done to a distant commonwealth."[25] Smith put it even more pointedly: "That wisdom which contrived the system of human affections . . . seems to have judged that the interest of the great society of mankind *would be best promoted* by directing the principal attention of each individual to that particular portion of it which was most within the sphere both of his abilities and of his understanding."[26]

Human psychology is structured so that we promote the good of humankind *by* focusing on what we care about most. Hence the argument is indirect. Here belonging does not justify localism directly; belonging now operates as an instrument.

Smith makes an analogous argument in a famous passage in the *Wealth of Nations*: "It is not from the benevolence of the butcher, the brewer, or the baker, that we expect our dinner, but from their regard to their own interest."[27] In market economies, self-interest is an instrument of the public good. Hume, Smith, and Edmund Burke would have agreed, likewise, that prioritizing one's own locality could produce general benefits.

It is not obvious that either Hume or Smith is happy about this feature of human psychology, however. The passage from Hume continues, "But still we know here . . . to correct these inequalities by reflection, and retain a general standard of vice and virtue, founded chiefly on general usefulness."[28] Hume thinks we need to use reason to compensate for destructive bias in our affections.

Matters are less clear for Smith. Fonna Forman-Barzilai, a Smith scholar, claims that "localism served for Smith as a sort of *desirable* middle terrain between" selfishness and cosmopolitanism.[29] I have difficulty, however, squaring Forman-Barzilai's reading with Smith's insistence that the "wise and virtuous man is at all times willing that his own private interest should be sacrificed to the public interest of his own particular order or society. He is at all times willing, too, that the interest of this order or society should be sacrificed to the greater interest of the state or sovereignty of which it is only a subordinate part."[30] It's true that Smith warns that "care of the universal happiness of all rational and sensible beings . . . can never be an excuse for his neglecting the more humble department,"[31] but the critic of localism hardly demands "neglect."

People are less likely to get involved when decisions are made, authority is exercised, or policy is implemented far away, or by higher-level governments because some, or perhaps most, of the expected benefits will accrue elsewhere, out of sight. It takes a level of dedication far beyond what can ordinarily be expected to expend time, money, and emotional energy on projects whose benefits are diffuse or distant.

The principal objective of focusing on one's "humble department" with local investment and development is to produce what economists call quasi-public goods. Pure public goods are non-excludable—that is, once the good is produced, it's impossible to prevent anyone from consuming it—and nonrivalrous—that is, one person's consumption of the good does not diminish consumption opportunities for others. Many of the goods produced by local communities are *quasi*-public because outsiders typically cannot be prevented from consuming them (nonexcludable), but opportunities for consuming them diminish if they are overused (rivalrous).

This is all very abstract, so consider a fictional example.[32] A local business organization has decided to build a new skate park for troubled local youths. The kids can't afford an entry fee because they're down on their luck. Everyone agrees it's better for them to skateboard in the park than on the railings in front of local businesses. The kids flock to the facility once it's completed, have a wonderful time, and leave local businesses alone.

One of the kids has a cousin visiting from a neighboring community. When the cousin returns home, he tells all his friends, who tell all their friends, and eventually they all turn up at the new skate park. Skateboarding is no fun if you don't have enough room to gather speed unimpeded, however. When enough kids show up, the skate park is effectively ruined, and some of the kids go back to the railings, and decide—frustrated that their skate park has been taken over by outsiders—to terrorize local business owners and their customers.

Local business owners ended up spending a lot of time, money, and effort to make the problem worse. As good businesspeople, they have learned their lesson: investments in the local community don't pay. That's not quite right, though. The investment would have paid had it been possible to keep some of the kids out. Business owners don't want to charge a fee, which is the easiest way to keep kids out, because the kids terrorizing their businesses are poor. A simple quota won't do, because the local kids are especially lazy and always get to the park too late to get in. The next best thing is to impose a residency requirement: to use the park, you have to live in the neighborhood. The business owners discover that this works perfectly, at least until one of the outsiders complains to his parents, who complain to the city. The city, of course, says that the business owners can't exclude anyone from the skate park; it's a public good after all!

The business owners are either annoyed or chastened, but they eventually wonder why this faceless city bureaucrat gets to decide how they run their skate park. And they become localists. They now see, ever so clearly, the merits of prioritizing the local by making decisions, exercising authority, or implementing policy locally or more locally.

The argument here is indirect because the claim is not that prioritizing the local by making decisions, exercising authority, or implementing policy locally or more locally is good on its own; rather, it's that unless decisions are made, authority is exercised, or policy is implemented locally or more locally, people like the concerned business owners won't invest in their communities. An economist would say that quasi-public goods are undersupplied for the same reason that pure public goods are undersupplied: externalities undermine producers' incentives. Some of the benefits, all of which were intended for the local community, have leaked out.

In this case, however, localism provides an institutional mechanism for internalizing the externality. When decisions are made and authority is exercised locally, benefits can be restricted to local residents. Localism makes local investment pay. Localism is good insofar as and because it encourages local investment. Localism is *contingently* good because localism might not encourage local investment, or might discourage other kinds of investment.

As I will have reason to repeat on several occasions, arguments for localism like this one, which rely on empirically contingent premises, need to be subjected to something akin to what economists call general equilibrium analysis. The hypothesized first-order effect of localism is to increase local investment, but second-order effects, which could be negative, need to be considered as well.

Under ordinary conditions higher-level governments invest considerable financial resources in lower-level governments. In 2019, local governments in the United States received $570 billion from state governments and $22 billion from the federal government (39 percent of current receipts).[33] It is quite plausible to assume that when local governments take greater control over particular tasks and functions, higher-level governments retract some fiscal support, especially for the tasks and functions in question. One can imagine a higher-level governmental official saying, "You want to run the parks on your own? Fine. It gets them off my plate. But don't expect me to foot the bill!" If countervailing second-order effects on local investment exceed the first-order effects, the goal of increasing local investment won't be served by localism.

General equilibrium analysis is important for another reason. When localities invest, they pursue what Paul Peterson calls developmental policies: "those local programs which enhance the economic position of a community relative to others. They strengthen the local economy, enhance the local tax base, and generate additional resources that can be used for the community's welfare."[34] Those skeptical of economic criteria can focus on the last clause in this passage. Economic growth generates additional resources that can be spent on parks, museums, theaters, and festivals. Economic growth also, by making citizens better off, drives out crime, improves students' test scores, and so on.

However, much of what localities do is allocational or redistributive rather than developmental, according to Peterson's typology. Developmental policies are developmental because they improve the economic position of the locality. Redistributive policies help the needy, "but at the same time negatively affect the local economy," by making it less competitive.[35] Allocational policies are those with neutral economic effects.[36]

I mention these categories because developmental, but not allocational or redistributive, policies count as investing in or prioritizing a locality. When people say they want to prioritize the local because doing so will make the community better off, they have developmental policies in mind. Redistributive policies make some residents better off, while making the locality less competitive; allocational policies make some residents better off and some worse off, with no net effect on the locality as a whole; only developmental policies make the locality unambiguously better off.

Developmental policies, with their objective of local economic growth, are not always successful. In fact, some "are purely wasteful; then there are policies which, while having some positive local impact are pure zero sum; and finally there are those that are capacity building, growth enhancing or adaptive."[37] Some developmental policies simply fail in terms of the locality's own interests. Many urban development projects in the mid- to late-twentieth century have been seen in this light. Despite spending millions of dollars, uprooting families, and effacing history, many communities were no better off than before. Other developmental policies make the locality better off "at the expense of other local communities."[38] Finally, some developmental policies make the local community better off while not making other communities worse off.

Only the latter are positive from a general welfare standpoint. Investments in infrastructure are most likely to be positive in this respect. Take the Delaware River Waterfront Corporation (DRWC), a nonprofit working to revitalize Philadelphia's waterfront.[39] In the summer of 2014, it decorated "a barely-used green space and sculpture garden" and "created a floating beach by connecting three barges, covering them in sand, and setting up beach chairs," in what is now Spruce Street Harbor Park.[40] Philadelphians certainly benefited, economically and culturally, but without robbing Peter to pay Paul. Some of the economic activity in Spruce Street Harbor Park is being drawn from neighboring communities, but some is entirely *new*. The DRWC is now working on the Spring Garden Connector, which will improve pedestrian access between the Northern Liberties neighborhood and Penn's Landing, bypassing Interstate 95.[41]

You don't need to be a localist to like positive-sum local development projects like those in Philadelphia. They add value to the world. Zero-sum local development projects, on the other hand, are vulnerable to the objections I've already raised. They make one locality better off at the expense of others. They reek of mercantilism.[42]

A lot of what we think of as local development turns out to be zero-sum at best, negative-sum ("pure waste") at worst. Consider the economic incentives used to lure businesses to local jurisdictions. Newark, New Jersey, Chicago, Illinois, and Montgomery County, Maryland, offered millions of dollars in tax incentives to win Amazon's second headquarters.[43] In a widely-cited meta-review (a literature review of literature reviews) of the economics literature in this area, Alan Peters and Peter Fisher conclude that "the best case is that incentives work about 10 percent of the time, and are simply a waste of money the other 90 percent."[44]

According to Daniel J. Wilson of the Federal Reserve Bank of San Francisco, "empirical studies tend to focus on the effects of policies within a jurisdiction and not on whether they adversely affect other jurisdictions," but in the few studies that have addressed this question, tax-incentives were "roughly" zero-sum.[45]

The logic is easiest to see with jobs. Unless local development projects affect *aggregate* national employment—which is highly implausible considering that so many local development projects fail to affect even local employment—no new jobs are created. Any effect on local unemployment comes at the expense of neighboring jurisdictions. Moreover, in general, firms "draw from metropolitan labor markets, not local ones," so some of the "new" jobs created in the jurisdiction will be filled by outsiders.[46] As the renowned urbanist Harvey Molotch puts it, "local growth does not, of course, make jobs: it distributes jobs."[47]

The point holds generally, and in the long run. In the short run, however, development projects that bring resources to the communities that need them most, or will be more productive in using them, contribute to the general welfare.[48] Projects of this kind can be economically efficient because they exploit inefficiencies in "sticky" markets. Nevertheless, one of the originators of the "new trade theory," where these insights were first developed, recommends against such policies because they are so easily manipulated and so often fail.[49]

Most importantly, the potential for welfare gains from selective local investment is not a point in favor of localism. Gains come from *targeted* local development, not from local development *everywhere*. Timothy Bartik, a cautious defender of local economic development, argues that "from a national perspective, we should applaud economic development policies to increase job growth when these policies are pursued by high-unemployment local areas, and *deplore* economic development policies to increase jobs when they are pursued by low-unemployment areas."[50] My earlier point about localism being defensible for struggling communities but questionable for prospering communities reappears.

One possible implication of the foregoing is that higher-level bodies—governmental or nongovernmental—have an important role to play in choosing which localities to target. Higher-level bodies have the perspective needed to evaluate multiple localities in terms of effectiveness and need. As Paul Cheshire and Ian Gordon put it, their "analysis of the wider welfare implications of territorially competitive policies provides good reasons for the competitive process to be regulated by higher levels of government."[51]

So it seems that the best possible case for localism from a local development standpoint recommends localism in some communities but not others, as well as extensive planning and oversight from higher-level governments or nongovernmental organizations.

Another place where the argument from belonging surfaces in contemporary civil society is in the injunctions to "support your local economy," buy local, and eat local. C. Clare Hinrichs and Patricia Allen call these practices "selective patronage."[52] Buying local is localism because it is to prioritize the local. Buying local becomes narrowly political when local governments use their scarce resources to promote the local economy or to encourage their citizens to patronize local businesses.

According to the Center for Community and Economic Development at Michigan State University, we ought to buy local because "local businesses hire locally, thereby creating jobs for the local community," and "buying from local businesses keeps money circulating in the local economy."[53]

Arguments of this kind depend on a questionable contrast between local and nonlocal businesses. Presumably local businesses are those owned by local residents. This is not quite right, however, because "buy local" advocates usually consider chain stores like McDonalds to be nonlocal, even when individual franchises are locally owned. Locally owned franchises are not local because some of their revenue flows to the franchising corporation. But even "genuine" local businesses often buy inventory and supplies from nonlocal companies, thereby sending revenue elsewhere. Truly local businesses would be those that get absolutely everything they use or sell locally. I wonder how many such businesses exist.

With that said, there is every reason to believe that buying local is zero- or negative-sum. If everyone everywhere bought everything from truly local businesses, money would just change hands *within* communities. "What is gained by a producer within the community is expended by other community residents," as Paul Peterson puts it.[54] Local growth would then depend upon increasing local capital stock or productivity gains. Unproductive and resource poor localities would be worse off than productive and resource rich localities. And every locality would be foregoing the gains from trade *between* localities.

In the real world, buy local campaigns encourage people to buy local when they can—not with every purchase. As with the discussion of jobs earlier, unless there are effects on national or international markets, buying something in one place means you are not buying it in another. The nonlocal business loses the sale that the local business gains.

I hope no one would deny that every business is local *somewhere*. Even Amazon.com, Inc. and Walmart Inc., public enemies no. 1 and 2 for supporters of the local economy, are local in Seattle, Washington, and Bentonville, Arkansas, respectively. This implies that buying locally is to choose one's own locality over someone else's. I don't need to repeat what I think about that.

Suppose I'm correct that buying local is zero-sum. Then if local governments or local organizations expend scarce resources convincing people to buy local, the whole affair is negative-sum. Local governments could do better by taking what they would have spent on a buy local campaign and distributing it to local residents.

One additional—and curious—feature of "support your local economy" campaigns is worth mentioning. Let's assume for a moment that those who wish to buy local also support growth from trade between communities. If they also support growth for their community, they must be hoping some people *don't* buy local. What they really want is for locals to shop local and nonlocals to shop nonlocally, namely *here* rather than *there*. Business from out of town is where growth has to come from. The whole "buy local" enterprise depends upon its apostates. The slogan should really be "support *my* local economy."

It should be said that these are not the only reasons to buy local. The Center for Community and Economic Development also suggests that buying local preserves variety in the marketplace. If tomato farmers in New Jersey called it quits, we'd lose the New Jersey tomato (people who like tomatoes tell me this would be tragic). Additionally, locavores say they support local food because they want to know how their food is grown and the people who grow it. Whatever their merits, these are not arguments from belonging, the subject of this chapter. Other reasons to prioritize the local are explored in subsequent chapters.

This chapter began with the suggestion that we should prioritize the local by making decisions, exercising authority, or implementing policy locally or more locally because that is where we live our daily lives. Although I do not contest that many people feel affection for and find meaning in their local communities, I deny that these feelings settle the matter, morally speaking. Localities are not intrinsically valuable; some contribute to human misery. The fact that some people value their localities does not mean that others do, or that they should.

Because one of the main reasons to prioritize the local—by making decisions, exercising authority, or implementing policy locally or more locally—is to extend partial treatment toward one's own locality, localism should be treated with suspicion on moral grounds. If extending partial treatment toward one's own locality makes everyone better off, locals as well as nonlocals, we should do it. I showed, however, that much of what passes for localism robs Peter to pay Paul. Furthermore, projects that generate net benefits and distribute them widely produce greater benefits when localities cooperate with—and are sometimes constrained by—other levels of government and nongovernmental organizations. Finally, I tried to show that "supporting your local economy" doesn't do quite what people tend to think it does. More on that later.

FIVE

Nature

In *Democracy in America*, Alexis de Tocqueville, whom we have seen twice before and will encounter again, claimed that "the locality (*commune*) is the only association that is so much a part of nature that wherever men come together, towns spontaneously arise. Communal society therefore exists among all peoples, regardless of their customs or laws. It is man who creates kingdoms and republics; the community seems to stem directly from the hands of God."[1]

According to the ancient Greek philosopher Aristotle, in book 7 of his *Politics*, "to the size of states there is a limit, as there is to other things, plants, animals, implements; for none of these retain their natural power when they are too large or too small, but they either wholly lose their nature, or are spoiled."[2] And as our friend the Baron de Montesquieu put it, "it is natural for a republic to have only a small territory; otherwise it cannot long subsist."[3]

Back in America, in a series of letters to friends and former rivals, Thomas Jefferson proposed a system of "ward republics," which were to be subdivisions of the county, roughly equivalent in size to a New England township, as Jefferson explained to his frenemy, John Adams.[4]

In a subsequent letter to Samuel Kercheval, Jefferson wrote: "the article . . . nearest my heart, is the division of the counties into Wards. These will be pure and elementary republics, the sum of all which, taken together, composes the state, & will make of the whole a true democracy as to the business of the Wards, which is that of nearest and daily concern."[5]

Far more recently, the novelist, essayist, and poet Wendell Berry has suggested that partisans of local community "know from personal experience—that the neighborhood, the local community, is the proper place and frame of reference for responsible work."[6]

Kirkpatrick Sale went further, arguing that "the existence of the anti-authoritarian, independent, self-regulating, local community is every bit as basic to the human record as the existence of the centralized, imperial, hierarchical state, and far more ancient, more durable, and more widespread."[7] He adds that it is obvious, in his view, that "for the two million years that humans have been on earth they lived in small clans and groups."[8]

According to David Popenoe, "the emergence of a society in which all semblance of tribalism," which he elsewhere equates with localism, "is gone poses a serious threat to social order and further human development because it mismatches with human nature."[9] Likewise, Michael Walzer argues that parochialism, like tribalism, is "permanent. It can't be overcome; it has to be accommodated, and therefore the crucial universal principle is that it must always be accommodated: not only my parochialism but yours as well, and his and hers in their turn. . . . our common humanity will never make us members of a single universal tribe."[10] Popenoe adds that "to improve the conditions for childrearing in America today, nothing may be more important than trying to protect and cultivate those natural, tribal- or village-like communities that still remain—communities which have families as their basic building blocks and in which a mix of people through free association and sets of relational networks maintain a common life."[11]

The passages I've just quoted are in no way peculiar; hundreds more like them could be produced on a moment's notice. Their ubiquity is not in doubt. What's less obvious is that they are all talking about roughly the same thing: the *natural* or *proper* size of human communities.

In the previous chapter, we considered the argument for localism from belonging, according to which we should prioritize the local because that is where we find meaning and where we can be motivated to do the most good. Here I take up the argument for localism grounded in nature, or more generally, propriety.

The argument is relatively simple. We should prioritize the local by making decisions, exercising authority, or implementing policy locally or more locally because local communities are the natural and therefore proper size: not too big, not too small, just right. According to this view, granting authority to higher and larger organizations and associations is contrary to nature.

Arguments from nature or propriety come in a variety of interesting flavors, as the passages above demonstrate. Tocqueville thinks localities are "a part of nature." Aristotle says that when human communities get too big or too small they lose their "natural power . . . or are spoiled." Jefferson believes ward republics—necessarily limited in size—are "pure and elementary." Berry uses the language of propriety directly, whereas Sale, one of the most enthusiastic localists, suggests that communities of a particular size are basic, ancient, durable, and widespread.

Size clearly matters for the argument. Most localists would not go as far as Sale to suggest that size "might well be regarded as *the* crucial variable in anything," but all localists think size matters and that smaller is better.[12] If they didn't think smaller was better, they wouldn't be localists. The arguments we encounter in this chapter go together for a simple reason: they all conclude, by different routes, that smaller is naturally better or that bigness naturally leads to badness. There is a particular size at which institutions and communities function well, and we can figure out how big is just right by looking to nature (ecology), human nature (biology, anthropology), or history (tradition, custom).

The notion that some forms of human community are natural and others are not is familiar to readers of Ferdinand Tönnies's *Gemeinschaft und Gesellschaft*. Like later communitarian thinkers, Tönnies insists that *Gemeinschaft* (community) has "real organic life" whereas *Gesellschaft* (society) is "a purely mechanical construction."[13] Moreover, "all kinds of social co-existence that are familiar, comfortable and exclusive belong to *Gemeinschaft*."[14]

Writing in the late nineteenth century, Tönnies is describing the epochal changes to the world around him. Nevertheless, like many of his successors, Tönnies cannot conceal his preference for *Gemeinschaft* over *Gesellschaft*, community over society. Community is good because it is traditional, familiar, and natural; society is not to be trusted because it is new, strange, and unnatural.

Of course the distinction between the simple, virtuous community and the complex, soul-manipulating society is not entirely about size. When pressed, communitarians will admit that what they care about is the character of people's relationships with one another in different settings, not size as such. But I think they are committed to arguing that the kinds of relationships they value are impossible in communities that exceed their natural limits, and the most important limits are physical and spatial. Thus, at least from the communitarian point of view, the argument for localism from nature hinges on possibility. One immediately recognizable problem with the view is that it can be refuted by reference to the facts; another is that it can be challenged by plausible hypotheses about how valued relationships are possible in large, complex, and heterogeneous forms of social organization.

Stated abstractly, the argument for localism from nature or propriety contends that the proper size of communities and political associations is a function of nonnegotiable features of the external world. This is a fancy way of saying that the size of communities can and should be determined by facts about nature, human nature, and the environment. Human beings are not supermen; they are constrained by their biological nature. Just as little Timmy falls flat on his face when he dons his new cape and tries to fly, human communities go splat when they exceed their natural limits.

Some of this makes a lot of sense. Human beings really *are* limited by nature and by their own nature in certain ways. Without fancy instruments, human beings can see only so far. More to the point is

"Dunbar's number," which is widely cited to prove that social networks have an upper limit of about 150 people.[15] According to Dunbar's followers, it's just not possible, cognitively speaking, to have meaningful personal relationships with more than about 150 people. Further evidence presented by Susan Pinker suggests that human beings really need face-to-face interaction to remain healthy and happy.[16] Phone calls, texts, Facebook, and Twitter aren't an adequate substitute for the real thing. Zoom meetings during the coronavirus pandemic add credence to her claim.

I'm happy to concede all of this. Social theorists and institutional designers should be aware of the facts. A word of caution, however. The study of human nature, like all scientific pursuits, is in flux; we are constantly learning new things, some of which contradict what we thought we knew for certain. There is an unavoidable danger in making grand pronouncements about how things have to be because of the way we are or have been. Later in this chapter, I'll recount some important discoveries in cognitive science, evolutionary biology, and anthropology which, taken together, suggest that human nature is rather different than localists typically assume.

Human nature is infinitely fascinating because our cognition is open-ended; it is in our nature to combine and recombine ideas in completely new ways. And it turns out that *Homo sapiens* have been organizing themselves into larger and larger groups for millions of years. Because of what Bernard Chapais calls "the deep social structure of humankind," anthropologists now believe that "human groups are always part of more inclusive social entities, which themselves belong to even more inclusive structures."[17] Human beings are the only species in nature whose capacity to form ever more complex social structures is limitless.[18] Joseph Henrich also has shown that because they develop more complex cultural toolkits, larger social groups tend to be more successful than smaller ones.[19]

The localist picture of human nature is contested by the latest science. These findings are fascinating, and I hope to give them their due, but they are not the main thrust of my argument in this chapter. My central claim is simple: Facts about human nature do not tell us how we ought to organize our social lives. Facts about human nature are empirical; questions about what we should do are normative (moral or ethical). Despite what critics of behavioralism in social science will tell you, the gap between facts and values is a chasm. Unsophisticated versions of the argument for localism from nature therefore commit what moral philosophers call the naturalistic fallacy: "moving from facts to values," or more technically, "defining values in terms of facts."[20] Facts about biology, custom, and tradition are useful, but it is up to us to decide what to do with them.

The Localist Thesis

But before getting to the science of social organization and the naturalistic fallacy, we need to get clear about what exactly localists are arguing. Localists who accept the argument from nature or the argument from propriety believe, more or less, that big communities are bad or that bad things happen when communities get too big. Bad things happen when communities get too big, moreover, because they are limited by their nature. Many localists would have us believe that critics of localism reject these insights entirely. But they don't need to and many don't. Sensible critics of localism do not worship at the altar of gigantism.[21] In fact, a sensible critic of localism accepts the claim that bad things can happen when communities get too big.

It's the conclusion drawn—that societies should prioritize the local by making decisions, exercising authority, or implementing policy locally or more locally because bad things naturally happen when communities get too big—that critics of localism question. Does it really follow that because bad things happen when communities get too big that we should keep communities small? When the question is phrased this way, the localist conclusion appears inescapable: smaller is better.

But let's dig deeper. Do bad things happen naturally, inevitably, when communities get too big? Are there not creative and clever ways for communities to get bigger? Do bad things happen, other bad things, when communities aren't big enough? By keeping communities small, do we not forego good things that are possible only in large communities? How bad are the bad things resulting from bigness? How good are the good things thwarted by smallness?

The fact that these questions can be asked indicates that it is not enough to say that bad things happen when human communities get too big. Bad things happen all the time. For the conclusion to follow, the localist would need to show that the costs of bigness exceed the benefits of bigness, or that the benefits of smallness exceed the costs of smallness. More precisely: that the net benefits of smallness exceed the net benefits of bigness.

Unfortunately, localists hardly ever frame the problem in this way. They direct our attention to the costs of bigness and the benefits of smallness, which of course leads directly to the localist conclusion. What happens when we direct our attention to the benefits of bigness and the costs of smallness? Perhaps this is how we got what E. F. Schumacher called the "idolatry of gigantism," which, if it ever existed, disappeared long ago. The reigning metaphor of contemporary society is *smart*, not *big*: smartphones, smart homes, smart cities, and so on.

What happens when we put both perspectives together—when we attend to the benefits and costs of bigness and smallness? We get something close to the frustrating position I am advocating in this book: it depends. Actually, if the intuitions of the partisans of smallness and the intuitions of the partisans of bigness could be formalized as mathematical functions, we would have a straightforward (but still difficult) optimization problem. After filling in some parameters, we could determine the optimal community size. Could this be what localists mean by "small is beautiful" or "politics on a human scale"?

I doubt it. If by human scale or small is beautiful localists mean optimal community size, anyone who thought through the problem would be a localist. Me too. It also would make localists' emphasis on smallness misleading. The localist preference for smallness would actually be contingent upon particular background conditions, namely suboptimal bigness. If we agree that communities have an optimal size, localism would be wrong in nearly half of the imaginable scenarios. Moreover, if conditions were different, localists would be committed to promoting bigness! In practice, of course, localists argue nothing of the sort. Localists neglect the possibility and dangers of suboptimal smallness.

Another issue: Suppose it's possible, in principle, to reduce intuitions about bigness and smallness to mathematical functions. (Incidentally, I suspect that the very idea of doing so makes localists uncomfortable; it smacks of rationalism and the man of system.) Determining the optimal size of human communities, then, would just take a little number crunching.

However, since the guiding intuition behind the argument for localism from nature is that the proper size of human communities can be determined by features of the world, which can be, in principle, registered as parameters in mathematical functions, optimal community size would be sensitive to shifting beliefs and circumstances. Unless one believes that the relevant parameters are forever fixed in time and space, optimal community size will be different for different communities, and different for the same community at different moments in time.

Once we let nature *determine* how large our communities should be, there is no reason to suppose that localism will be true in all times and places. Indeed, it would be extremely odd—contrary to experience—if every community were too big; none too small.

Imagine a world in which the argument for localism from nature succeeds. Communities have taken heed of localists' advice and are prioritizing the local by making decisions, exercising authority, or implementing policy locally or more locally than ever before. Are we to believe that we've gotten everything exactly right in all or even in most cases? It seems more likely that we'll have gone too far in some cases and not far enough in others, leaving some communities too small, some too big. In this world, the argument from nature would recommend making decisions, exercising authority, or implementing policy less locally at least sometimes.

It should now be clear that localists are not doing anything like a maximization problem, as I believe they should. I don't mean to argue that the problem must be solved using the economists' toolkit, with its functions and derivatives, however. Since the social world is replete with trade-offs, we *do* need some way to deal with them, however. Localists are instead driven by convictions about the evils of bigness and the virtues of smallness, not the full range of relevant considerations and the trade-offs between them.

So localists neglect the benefits of bigness, the costs of smallness, and the likelihood that considerations of human nature could count in favor of bigness rather than smallness in some cases. They also ignore the following: that the benefits of smallness might be combined with the benefits of bigness. Localists tend to see communities as undifferentiated, unstructured blobs. Communities, in this view, are autonomous and independent; relations with neighboring communities are of secondary importance. Organizations with complex internal structures belong to *Gesellschaft*, after all.

It is just a little ironic that one of the most famous examples of combining the benefits of bigness and the benefits of smallness comes from one of localism's heroes, the Baron de Montesquieu. In *The Spirit of the Laws*, Montesquieu made much of an institutional arrangement he called a confederate republic. He posited that "if a republic is small, it is destroyed by a foreign force; if it is large, it is ruined by an internal vice."[22] The only way to get the advantages of a large republic, Montesquieu argued, is for several republics to unite in common cause against hostile foreigners. By confederating, republics can stay small, internally, while acting as though they were large, externally. Apropos of the subject of this chapter, Montesquieu claimed that had *nature* taken its course, "men would have been obliged to live forever under the government of one alone."[23] Luckily humankind "*devised* a kind of constitution that has all the internal advantages of a republican government and the external force of monarchy."[24]

So even if nature dictates that communities should remain small, what's to stop us from devising a new kind of constitution in which communities remain small but unite to accomplish what they cannot accomplish separately? And aren't groups of united communities also *communities*? Like human beings in thought, human beings in society make clever use of nesting: one thought nested within another within another; one community nested within another within another. Perhaps, if the localists are right, the basic building blocks of any society can get only so big. But these basic units can be organized in a myriad of different ways for a variety of different purposes.

FIGURE 5-1. **Natural and Political Communities**

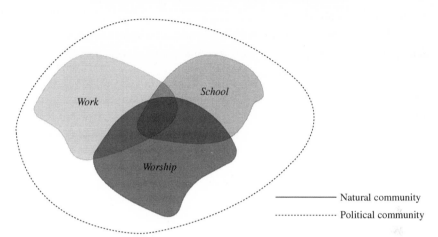

Work

School

Worship

——————— Natural community

·················· Political community

Nor is it obvious that the same basic units are basic in every situation. The neighborhood block might be basic for one set of issues (schools), the congregation for another (worship), and Local #2865 for yet another (work). In fact, the group of 150 people I can have meaningful relationships with according to Dunbar's number is a group only with respect to me. It's not as if the same 150 people have meaningful relationships with each other and no one else. The basic building blocks of society overlap and can be combined and recombined in an astonishing number of ways.[25]

This perfectly reasonable supposition—that there is not a single natural community for every aspect of our lives but rather many crisscrossing and overlapping natural communities, one for each domain of social life—has far reaching implications. It turns out that it is exceedingly difficult, perhaps even impossible, to demarcate a small, localized political community that does not sever at least one of its constituent (domain-specific) natural communities.

It's almost as if, according to the localist picture of social life, each natural community overlaps perfectly with all the others. As if the membership of each natural community is coextensive with the others, and each natural community occupies the same physical space. However, as figure 5-1 shows, if domain-specific natural communities are *not* coextensive, the only way for each natural community to remain whole within a political community is to make the latter big enough to include them all. Paradoxically, to respect the integrity of natural social units, we should allow the political community to extend its reach.

Let me briefly review our progress thus far. We've seen that bad things happen when communities get too big and other bad things happen when they're not big enough. We've also seen that good things happen when communities are big and other good things happen when communities are small. Unless, incredibly, communities are always too big, intuitions about the proper size of communities lend themselves to arguments against rather than for localism in particular cases. Most important, if natural social groups are numerous, overlapping, and crosscutting, to preserve their integrity, political communities will need to be big enough to include all of them.

Now, having clarified the structure of the argument for localism from nature, I turn to nature itself. Do the sciences of human nature corroborate or contradict localism's Lilliputian sympathies?

The Science of Human Nature

For a long time, I thought I would argue that there is no such thing as human nature. As Yuval Noah Harari puts the point I thought I would make, "heated debates about *Homo sapiens'* 'natural way of life' miss the main point. Ever since the Cognitive Revolution, there hasn't been a single natural way of life for Sapiens. There are only cultural choices, from among a bewildering palette of possibilities."[26]

Just because there isn't a single natural way of life, however, doesn't mean that human beings don't all share the same biology. Nor does it mean that all human cultures don't share certain general features, as Steven Pinker and Donald Brown have argued. Harari is right to mention the "bewildering palette of possibilities," but mistaken to imply that the possibilities are infinite or can be combined willy-nilly.

There are cultural choices, but all cultures deal with the same brain and the same body, and all cultures include a set of practices whose purpose is to advance more or less the same abstract ends. In *Human Universals*, Brown introduced an extensive list of "universals of behavior and overt language noted by ethnographers," helpfully reproduced as an appendix to Pinker's *The Blank Slate*.[27]

To be clear, I think Harari is right to imply that human groups are not nearly as constrained as many localists seem to believe. At the very least, however, all cultures deal with a similar set of challenges, one of which is to organize individuals into groups. If there are universal features of the human mind, the human body, or human relationships that militate against large groups, localism could be on to something. That is the question to which we now turn: If there is such a thing as human nature, what is it like? Does human nature put its thumb on the scales in favor of small, localized communities or large, complex, and heterogeneous societies? Here, I present one picture of human nature, not the whole picture; these matters are contestable and contested.

Imagine a band of *Homo sapiens*, millions of years ago, before agriculture, before machines, and before the state was even invented (and invented it was). What would they have been like? Scientists who try to answer this question are engaged in a speculative enterprise, as they would happily admit. Their method is that of triangulation: between distinct bodies of singularly inconclusive evidence. The direct evidence comes from paleoarcheology, mostly fossils of early humans and human ancestors. The fossil record is then pieced together using the tools of evolutionary biology, with evidence from contemporary hunter-gatherer societies (anthropology) and our closest living relatives, the great apes (primatology).

The genetic difference between common chimpanzees (*Pan troglodytes*) and humans (*Homo sapiens*) is approximately 1.2 percent, making chimpanzees our closest living relative.[28] Chimpanzees, like human beings, go to war with rival groups, and do so strategically. They use simple tools to collect food. Chimpanzee groups even have distinct cultural practices: different sets of tools depending on the group and its environment.

But male and female chimpanzees do not form pair bonds, as humans do, and this appears to make all the difference. Absent pair-bonding, male chimpanzees can never be sure which baby chimpanzees are theirs. Chimpanzees father children, but there are no chimpanzee fathers, so to speak. Male chimpanzees therefore do not invest time and energy in particular youngsters. In contrast, in many cases, human males *do* invest time and energy in their children, at least a little. Sometimes this means investing in the baby's mother, by providing food and protection, for example. With extra help from dad, female *sapiens* can invest additional resources, especially time, in their babies. This let human beings develop their big, powerful, brains.

Pair-bonding did something else. Because human fathers recognize their children and help care for them, children recognize their fathers as well as their mothers. If baby humans recognize their mothers *and* their fathers, they can recognize their brothers and sisters, not just their half-siblings. And if human beings can recognize their brothers and sisters, they can recognize their fathers' siblings and their mothers' siblings—their aunts and uncles. They can also recognize their maternal and paternal grandparents. Pair-bonding helps reveal "the underlying genealogical structure and create bilineal kinship."[29]

Combined with another feature of human mating practices—males and/or females (depending on cultural practices) leave their natal group upon sexual maturity—bilineal kinship ends up distributing "in-laws" (scientists call them *affines*) among several different human groups. Pair-bonding is what makes affinal relations possible. When humans, upon sexual maturity, leave their natal groups to join their mates, their children recognize their grandparents, aunts, and uncles in *both* groups. Similarly, grandparents, aunts, and uncles in one group recognize their relatives in other groups. More technically, "kin recognition in humans is bilineal and of unparalleled extent."[30] Moreover, unlike in nonhuman primate groups, many affines form lifelong bonds.

Bernard Chapais spells out the consequences: "from then on, a father, upon meeting another group, would recognize his daughter (if she transferred to it), and his grand-offspring, and refrain from attacking them. He would also recognize his daughter's preferential bond with her sexual mate (his 'son-in-law'), a factor alleviating conflicts between male affines. Similarly, grand-fathers, brothers and uncles would recognize their transferred kin and their affines, instigating a state of mutual tolerance."[31]

This is what Chapais calls the "deep social structure of humankind." Affinal ties generate dense networks of relationships among human groups: "the dramatic and fortuitous extension of kin recognition brought about by pair-bonding would have launched the evolution of supragroup social structures in which a large proportion of individuals were now distantly related."[32] Kin recognition, therefore, accounts for the multilevel, nested structure of human hunter-gatherer societies, the best source of evidence we have for our evolutionary history. Elsewhere, Chapais refers to "human societies as federations of multifamily groups."[33]

This account of the origins of human society fits with what I said earlier about the nested and overlapping characteristics of natural human communities. The latest scientific evidence suggests that "human groups are always part of more inclusive social entities, which themselves belong to even more inclusive structures. In contrast, the vast majority of primate societies are independent, single-group structures."[34] The localist conception of human groups, therefore, describes nonhuman primates better than *Homo sapiens*.

Now that we've seen that *Homo sapiens* form "federations of strongly bonded groups,"[35] we can turn to Joseph Henrich's work on cumulative cultural evolution. The details of Henrich's general thesis, that cumulative cultural evolution accounts for the stupendous success of Homo sapiens in the animal kingdom, need not concern us here. To make a long story short, Henrich argues that humans' evolutionary fitness depends on *both* biological and cultural factors. Culture matters because the best cultural practices, that is, the cultural practices that best facilitate survival and reproduction, are passed on from generation to generation.

An example: Groups of indigenous Americans who adopted peculiar cultural practices like throwing a bit of wood ash into their cornmeal as it cooked were more likely to survive and reproduce than groups that did not.[36] No one knew that throwing wood ash into the cornmeal during cooking releases niacin, an essential vitamin. We now know that without enough niacin people get a devastating disease, pellagra, the symptoms of which include delusions or mental confusion, diarrhea, nausea, inflamed mucous membranes, and scaly skin sores.[37] And death. Groups that adopted the cultural practice "throw wood ash into cooking cornmeal" were therefore more likely to survive and pass along their curious—and to an outsider, unappetizing—cultural practices.

Similarly, groups with the cultural practice "interact with neighboring groups and try their cultural practices," were more likely to survive and pass along their culture and genes to their descendants. Groups with the cultural practice "never interact with neighboring groups and stick with what we know" were comparatively disadvantaged.

Actually, it's hard to imagine human groups with such insular cultural practices surviving very long, as a couple of Henrich's examples demonstrate. Note that Henrich uses the "toolkits" of hunter-gatherer societies to explore cultural practices more generally. Now because it's difficult to imagine a group *adopting* insular practices—at least one that survives long enough to leave artifacts—the examples usually involve an external shock. Hunter-gatherers in Tasmania, which until quite recently was connected to the Australian mainland, have the least sophisticated toolkit ever observed.[38] Their closest genetic and cultural cousins on the mainland have a toolkit just as complex as the typical Australian aboriginal group. Archeological evidence suggests that the toolkits of Tasmanians, prior to Tasmania's separation from Australia, were just as complex as mainland toolkits.

Why, then, were Tasmanian toolkits so simple? Well, since the maintenance of cultural practices depends upon intergenerational transmission, if something prevents the transmission of the relevant knowledge and skills, the group is liable to lose the practice. When the group is small, a freak event—a fire, a war, an unexpected illness—might kill the only people with the relevant knowledge and skills before they can pass them on to the next generation. If the only bow maker knows how to make good bows, and if he dies before teaching an apprentice, knowledge of bow craftsmanship is gone forever.

Unless, of course, the group maintains connections with neighboring groups, each with its own master bow maker. Small groups embedded in a multilevel structure are relatively safe because, even if their experts die, they can relearn the skill from other groups' experts. The problem for Tasmanians was that rising oceans severed their connection with the mainland groups. Once a practice was lost, it was lost forever. Tasmanian toolkits, therefore, lost their complexity as the needed expertise was lost or forgotten.

Large, well-connected groups have complex toolkits for much the same reason that small, independent groups have more rudimentary toolkits. If a group develops a particularly useful cultural practice by chance, that group will be more successful than competing groups. The group will have lots of well-fed babies—a new generation ready to adopt the culture. Members of successful groups become attractive marriage partners for neighboring groups. Because of the network of ties generated through marriage, useful cultural practices are transmitted from one group to another. Less successful practices fall out of use.

Successful practices spread to neighboring groups through imitation, but also through group replacement. Unsuccessful groups lose members to more successful groups, or slowly die out. By whichever mechanism, successful cultural practices spread like wildfire if groups remain well-connected. It turns out, then, that the capacity to form larger and larger groups, composed of layer upon layer of smaller groups, was a condition of humanity's evolutionary success. Forming larger and larger groups is human nature.

This insight is not limited to hunter-gatherer societies in the distant past. Even today, larger groups develop more sophisticated cultural toolkits. As Henrich shows, languages with more speakers are more efficient. One language is more efficient than another if more information, and more specific information, can be conveyed in fewer words, or in less time. There are more words in English than in French, for instance, in part because English is an odd concoction of Anglo-Saxon and French, itself a dialect of Latin. (Notice the reason English has more words: the interaction between two groups, the Germanic speaking peoples of the British Isles and their Norman conquerors.) Because there are more words in English and each one is more precise, what takes several words in French might take only one in English. As Henrich puts it, "words are tools for communicating, and having the right words can increase the ease, speed, and quality of communication."[39]

I began this section by admitting that I was once skeptical of the whole idea of human nature. I thought localists were wrong that human communities were naturally small, not because I thought human communities were naturally large, but because I didn't think the size or structure of human communities was any of nature's concern. I had thought that nature gives us bodies and minds and that it is up to us to decide what to do with them. I thought it was up to human beings to decide how to organize themselves into political communities, communities of whichever size "shall seem most likely to effect their Safety and Happiness," in the words of the Declaration of Independence. I still think it is up to us, in the end, but the evidence presented here suggests that there are awfully good reasons, reasons consistent with human nature, for people to form themselves into large, multilayered political communities.

The Naturalistic Fallacy

Although I was surprised to learn that throughout their history as a species, *Homo sapiens* have been organizing themselves into larger and larger groups, the central thesis of this chapter remains untouched: facts about human nature do not settle anything; nature is not our master. As Katharine Hepburn's character in *The African Queen* put it, "nature, Mr. Allnut, is what we are put in this world to rise above."[40] Or T. H. Huxley: "Let us understand, once and for all, that the ethical progress of society depends, not on imitating the cosmic process, still less in running away from it, but in combatting it."[41]

Claims to the effect that human nature requires, in the normative sense, certain forms of social organization commit the naturalistic fallacy, as I've said already. Then, I quoted Peter Singer's formulation of the fallacy, "moving from facts to values," but I actually prefer the following, less intellectual, version: "the belief that what happens in nature is good."[42]

Sometimes, the naturalistic fallacy is hard to spot. The part about whatever is natural being good is usually implied rather than stated explicitly. Anyone who has ever visited a grocery store in the United States will recognize the phenomenon. A staggering number of products are advertised using terms such as natural, non-GMO, organic, and local, the holy quaternity for foodies, millennials, and environmentally conscious consumers in the twenty-first century. If natural, non-GMO, organic, and local did not imply healthy, delicious, sustainable, or something else we associate with goodness, marketers wouldn't use them. (If you're looking for a mildly amusing way to pass the time, go to the supermarket and ask for the genetically modified tomatoes.)

Localism manages to combine two of the four magic words with its claim that local communities are natural. Here's a neat syllogism: If what's natural is good and if local communities are natural, then local communities are good. Now consider a corollary of the naturalistic fallacy, what Steven Pinker calls the moralistic fallacy: "If a trait is moral, it must be found in nature."[43] By a second syllogism, it follows that if what's local is good, what's local is natural.

According to the logic of the moralistic fallacy, we learn that what's local is natural, which then allows us to conclude, according to the logic of naturalistic fallacy, that local communities are good. Similarly, according to the logic of the naturalistic fallacy, we learn that what's natural is good, which then allows us to conclude, according to the logic of the moralistic fallacy, that what is local must be natural. And so on in a never-ending circle.

This is (doubly) fallacious of course, but the pro-attitudes (for example, "approval, admiration, liking, preference, esteem"[44]) produced by calling something local and the pro-attitudes produced by calling something natural reinforce one another and together bridge the unbridgeable chasm between facts and values. Argumentatively, it's a slight of hand; psychologically, it's just common sense. But resist it we must.

For whatever reason, pro-attitudes toward some things sometimes rub off on close associates of those things, a phenomenon I call goodness by association. Goodness by association is like the honor by association effect studied by psychologists, except that it applies to concepts rather than people or objects.[45] Here's a conjectural example of how it works. First, we notice that the part of nature we encounter in national parks is quite spectacular. We then generalize from what we've seen in national parks or on the documentary series *Planet Earth* to the belief that what's natural must be beautiful. And of course what's beautiful is good. We then apply our intuitions about one domain (physical nature) to another (human nature): since what's natural is beautiful and good, if human beings naturally form themselves into small, tight-knit communities, small, tight-knit communities must be beautiful and good.

I'm not claiming that this phenomenon accounts for every instance of the naturalistic fallacy, but it surely helps. It's an explanation, not a justification, of the phenomenon, however. Although we can guess why we associate what's natural with what's good, it certainly does not follow that what's natural is good because it's natural. The vistas of natural parks are beautiful because they are pleasing to the eye, not *because* they are natural features of the world. Great works of art are artificial—unnatural by definition—yet they, too, are pleasing to the eye. Some philosophers have argued that human beings are predisposed to find particular features of nature beautiful, in part because the eye was built by a creator or shaped by natural selection to find particular features of nature beautiful.[46] However, and now I'm repeating myself, just because we are predisposed to find bits of nature beautiful (and therefore good) does not mean we are obliged, normatively, to find them beautiful or good.

Once I've made it abundantly clear what the naturalistic fallacy implies, namely that we cannot move directly from facts about nature, human nature, custom, or tradition to normative conclusions about how we should live, I'll change tack and consider what nature can tell us. But first consider, with the following passage, quoted by Harari, the trouble we can get ourselves into with the naturalistic fallacy: "The person who attempts to fight the iron logic of nature thereby fights the principles he must thank for his life as a human being. To fight against nature is to bring about one's own destruction."[47] The argument for localism from nature is not much different. Human communities set themselves up for failure when they surpass their natural limits, either in terms of size or complexity.

The passage, alas, is from Adolf Hitler's *Mein Kampf.* This is not meant as *argumentum ad Hitlerum*, however. The point is just that nature is normatively neutral; it can be put in service of both good and evil. Most localists are motivated, in fact, by sincere concerns about the negative impact of size on human flourishing. But there's no need to bring nature into it. Instead of saying that we should prioritize the local because doing so is natural, localists, in my view, should just tell us why more local forms of government are advantageous, or why less local forms are disadvantageous. Arguments of this type—those that say local is better because it makes peoples' lives go better—are the subject of part III of this book.

The argument from nature, like the argument from tyranny in chapter 3 and the argument from belonging in chapter 4, appeals to commitments rather than consequences. The argument is that living in supersized communities is unnatural, not that doing so leads to bad outcomes. If negative outcomes are introduced at all, it's to say what inevitably happens when nature is spurned.

One serious problem with arguments for localism that do not appeal to consequences or outcomes, or the lives of flesh-and-blood human beings, is that they are unlikely to convince those of us who don't *already* share localism's underlying worldview. In the case at hand, if you don't already think what's natural is good or that offenses against nature bring divine retribution or tempt fate, you're unlikely to be convinced that we should govern ourselves more locally because doing so is natural. If you don't already think what's natural is good, you need other reasons to accept localism. The argument for localism from nature, unless it is fleshed out by reference to consequences, depends on controversial metaphysical commitments like the intrinsic goodness of nature.

I haven't been completely fair to localists thus far. Most wouldn't endorse the naturalistic fallacy once it had been made plain. In the remainder of this section, therefore, I consider a different, far more challenging, interpretation of the argument from nature.[48]

Let's begin with a similar but slightly different problem discussed by Peter Singer in *The Expanding Circle*. He asks whether our understanding of ethics should change because of what we've learned from evolutionary biology about human nature. For the most part, his answer is *no* and for the same reasons I have resisted the argument from nature thus far. But to get at the sense in which human nature *does* matter, he introduces an important distinction between individual decisions and social codes, between two questions: "What ought I to do?" and "What ought to be the code of our society?"[49]

Facts of human nature do not affect our answer to the first question, Singer argues. From the individual's point of view, the fact that human beings are biological creatures with biases, urges, desires, and drives that motivate us to do things we shouldn't do doesn't mean it's okay to do them. Facts help us understand why we sometimes do what's wrong, but they don't give us license to act wrongly. To blame immoral behavior on our biology is to refuse to take responsibility for our actions.[50]

The second question is more complicated. When we reason about our ethical code, we can take the perspective of society in general rather than an individual whose choices are her own. From the perspective of society in general, we *know* that because of our nature, because of our biases, urges, desires, and drives, we sometimes do what we shouldn't. Usually, we shouldn't do certain things because they are bad for people. The fact that they are bad for people is why we shouldn't do them. The ultimate objective of our moral rules is to keep us from doing bad things to people (and to get us to do good things for people). So we should shape our moral rules so as to get us to do fewer bad things and more good things.

An unforgiving ethical code might be counterproductive. If our society's moral rules are too hard to live by, noncompliance might become socially acceptable. The rogue jury, one that acquits a clearly guilty defendant because the law is too strict or because there are extenuating circumstances, is a familiar example. To be effective, an ethical code must be finely tuned to the biology and psychology of the people it governs. If the ultimate objective of an ethical code is to prevent as much bad stuff from happening as possible, one must consider the facts.

For instance, we *know*, because of facts about our biology, that most young adults really want to have sex. We also know, again because of facts about our biology, that prohibitions on premarital sex will never be perfectly successful, no matter how severe we make the sanctions. This is the rationale for promoting condom use rather than "abstinence only" in the sex education curriculum. Given what we know about our biology, "abstinence only" won't work. So instead of making the ethical rule "don't have sex before marriage," facts about human nature recommend a rule like "don't have unprotected sex before marriage," or "only have unprotected sex in a monogamous relationship." A social stigma against unprotected sex will be far more effective than a social stigma against premarital sex, again because of facts about human nature.

This discussion of human nature and ethical rules is meant to suggest that we can and should make use of facts about nature in deciding how we should organize ourselves socially and politically. That's different than letting the facts decide for us, however.

It's here that the argument for localism from nature is on its firmest footing. Of course it's up to us to organize ourselves however we see fit, but that doesn't mean every form of organization will be equally easy to maintain or equally effective. Localists are especially helpful when they point out the special challenges associated with scaling up. It's just true that if human beings, for most of their history as a species, lived in small, close-knit communities, living in large and fragmented agglomerations will seem strange. One would expect a period of adjustment.

Although I happily endorse this localist insight—that people living in large communities face different, and perhaps more difficult, challenges than people living in small communities—I do not accept the localist conclusion: that we should, therefore, stay local. Some challenges should be met head on, as Huxley might say, rather than avoided altogether. Whether the novel challenges of larger forms of social organization should be taken up or avoided depends, as could be anticipated, on the magnitude of the potential upside. If there is nothing to be gained from new, less local forms of social life, then localism is on the mark. But if the potential gains are considerable, and if we happen to be

the kinds of creatures who are well-suited to tackling unforeseen challenges, I say we should take the plunge.

The Subsidiarity Challenge

Until this point, *nature* in the argument for localism from nature has
meant human nature or physical nature (the environment). Propriety
has fallen out of the discussion. I want to return to it by considering
the principle of subsidiarity in the Catholic natural law tradition. Here
is how Pope Pius XI articulated it in *Quadragesimo Anno*:

> As history abundantly proves, it is true that on account of changed
> conditions many things which were done by small associations
> in former times cannot be done now save by large associations.
> Still, that most weighty principle, which cannot be set aside or
> changed, remains fixed and unshaken in social philosophy: Just
> as it is gravely wrong to take from individuals what they can
> accomplish by their own initiative and industry and give it to
> the community, so also it is an injustice and at the same time a
> grave evil and disturbance of right order to assign to a greater
> and higher association what lesser and subordinate organizations
> can do. For every social activity ought of its very nature to fur-
> nish help to the members of the body social, and never destroy
> and absorb them.[51]

According to the principle of subsidiarity, when social organizations are
successfully performing their proper functions, we shouldn't take those
functions away and give them to larger associations.[52] Each individual
and every association has its own proper social role—the function consistent with its nature. God ordered the universe so that each social body
would have a unique purpose in the pursuit of the common good. When
we take functions that belong, by nature, to one social body and assign
them to another, we disrupt the natural order of things. We also leave

that body adrift—alienated and atrophied—and unable to perform its God-given responsibilities.

Atheists and adherents of other faiths will have trouble with the argument formulated in this way, of course. A secular interpretation is conceivable, however. Since the Second World War, the dominant strands of political and moral theory have embraced the sanctity of the individual, most prominently in the doctrine of human rights.[53] Even those of us who resist the theistic notion of a natural order believe that individual human beings have their own proper sphere—that there is a domain in which the individual is sovereign. We believe it is wrong for the state, or any other social body, to exercise functions that properly belong to individuals. This is what some of us mean by liberty.

This conception of the role of the individual in social life has been called normative individualism. To accept normative individualism is to believe that individual human beings are the ultimate bearers of value. Because individuals are the ultimate bearers of value, organizations and associations are valuable *only* insofar as and *because* they are valuable to individual people. Associations and organizations are not valuable for their own sake.

What does all of this have to do with localism? Well, if individuals are the ultimate bearers of value, and if it is wrong for greater and higher associations to strip individuals of their proper functions, shouldn't we favor smaller associations where "decisions are taken as closely as possible to the citizen"?[54]

The idea, as I understand it, is that because individuals are the ultimate source of value, associations and organizations closer to that source take precedence over associations and organizations further away. Smaller and more local associations are more closely and directly implicated in people's lives. At least according to Catholic social doctrine, the purpose of small and local associations is to provide assistance to individuals in their pursuit of salvation and the common good. Given their special contributions to individuals' ends, small and local associations should, one might think, be protected against interference by higher associations.

There is a kind of argument for localism, then, based on the principle of subsidiarity, according to which we should prioritize the local
because smaller associations and organizations are closer to the loci of
value, individual people. Although I am not entirely sure what work
closeness is doing here, it seems to be that smaller and more local organizations and associations form relationships with individuals that are
less mediated and more natural, and, therefore, proper.

From a purely practical standpoint, and this is a point I return to in
the following chapter, small and local organizations and associations
mean more, and matter more, to most people. People form affective attachments to the small and local, whereas their interactions with large
and distant associations and organizations are cold and transactional.

The argument, then, is that we should favor what's small and local
because those associations and organizations play a special, irreplace-
able role in people's lives. This is the best I can do to make sense of it.

There are two problems with this argument. The first is that subsidiarity's argument for irreplaceability is weak and controversial. It relies
on a kind of essentialism about social organizations. It reasons from how
things have always been to how they must be done. It is doubtful, moreover, that the same kinds of associations and organizations have exercised precisely the same social functions in all human societies throughout history. Simply put, there are lots of ways for people to organize
themselves, many of which work well, and some better than others. I also
find the idea that we've somehow stumbled upon the uniquely best associational order incredible, Burkean objections notwithstanding.

So does Pius XI. He claimed that because "of changed conditions
many things which were done by small associations in former times
cannot be done now save by large associations." In fact, the best interpretation of subsidiarity in Catholic social doctrine does not support
localism. It requires that social functions be exercised by the *appropriate*
associations and organizations.[55] It also permits larger—or smaller—
associations and organizations to step in with assistance.

Secular humanism and Catholic social doctrine part company, however, over the meaning of *appropriate*. Catholic social doctrine has a view

of the social order in which appropriate functions are revealed by reason. My view is much less exciting. I believe the associations and organizations that are the best ones for the job—the ones that make people's lives go better—are appropriate. Whether associations and organizations should be small or big depends on the job, the tools, the personnel—on the facts.

The second problem arises when the phrase "as closely as possible to the citizen" is taken too literally. Or when it is taken to mean that the associational order is organized as a vertical hierarchy in which towns are closer to the citizen than counties, and counties are closer to the citizen than provinces, and so on.

For over two decades now, critical political geographers have been arguing *against* this vertical hierarchy conception of scale. And as I explained in the introduction, scale understood as level is not the same as distance. We shouldn't confuse the schemas and metaphors we impose on the associational order for the order itself. The very idea of a town or county or state being close to or far from citizens makes less and less sense the harder and longer you think about it. Citizens are *members* of their towns, their counties, their provinces; they are *in* them. The bedroom is not closer than the house to the bed.

The phrase "closer to the citizen" is metaphor too. When we use it, we mean that decisions should be made *by* the citizens rather than *for* them. People should control their own destinies. Decisions should be theirs rather than someone else's. Size, distance, scale, and level are peripheral issues that confuse and distract; they don't settle anything.

Compared to the previous two chapters, on the arguments for localism from belonging and from the dangers of tyranny, the argument of this chapter is simple. Some proponents of localism say we should prioritize the local by making decisions, exercising authority, or implementing policy locally or more locally because the local community is the natural or proper form of human social organization. Different versions of the argument appeal to nature in different ways: nature, human nature, Mother Nature, custom, and tradition.

The argument for localism from nature is unsatisfactory for two reasons. First, it's not obvious that it's true that human communities are naturally small. We've seen that some well-respected and well credentialed modern scientists believe that human communities are, by their nature, nested within large, complex social organizations. We've also seen that larger communities have greater evolutionary success.

Second, even if natural human communities are small, that fact does not tell us how we should organize ourselves now. We can use facts about human history to help us organize ourselves even better than before. And it is human nature to exceed itself.

Having considered three arguments for localism from commitments—from tyranny, belonging, and nature—we now turn to three arguments from consequences—from democracy, knowledge, and efficiency. The arguments from consequences we'll see in part III are more promising than the arguments from commitments in part II, but still not promising enough to justify the belief that we should prioritize the local by making decisions, exercising authority, or implementing policy locally or more locally. Turn the page to see why.

PART III

Why Localism? Consequences

SIX

Democracy

Of the arguments for localism considered in this book, the argument grounded in democracy is undoubtedly the most familiar. It is also the most important. Even if the arguments surveyed in part II—from tyranny, belonging, and nature—fail, and even if the arguments considered in the remainder of part III—from knowledge and efficiency—also fail, localism cannot be rejected, not without difficulty, if it promotes democracy.

Democracy is the form of government in which the people, not some favored subset of them, rule. Democracy is also something more abstract—a way of thinking and acting and being. As a form of government, it embodies important moral and political values: democratic values.

We prize democracy as a form of government not out of some fetish for voting or for majorities but because it's the best way, so far as we know, to promote and respect democratic ideals: that some people do not matter more than others; that everyone deserves a voice; that people should have a modicum of control over their lives; that when things affect everyone, we should decide what to do about them together.

Democracy is valuable because, and insofar as, it promotes or embodies these more fundamental moral and political commitments. Democracy is valuable because it makes people's lives go better. As Amartya Sen puts it, democracy is a universal value.[1]

The argument for localism from democracy says that we should prioritize the local by making decisions, exercising authority, or implementing policy locally or more locally either because doing so *just is* democratic or *because* it promotes democracy. Because doing so instantiates or promotes those fundamental moral and political values that embody or justify democracy as a form of government.

There are numerous ways in which our commitment to democracy could recommend or prescribe localism, but we'll focus on three here. They are three strands of the argument for localism from democracy; three independent but overlapping sub-arguments. We'll call them *small is democratic*, *participation*, and *accountability*.

The first strand, *small is democratic*, strikes directly at the heart of the matter. It says that localism is required by democracy because localism *just is* democratic; or that democracy without localism is not democracy at all. We should prioritize the local by making decisions, exercising authority, or implementing policy locally or more locally because to do otherwise is undemocratic, by definition. I borrow the label from the title of Dana Ott's *Small is Democratic*.[2]

The second strand, *participation*, says that localism is recommended by democracy because localism promotes political participation, an indispensable feature of democratic practice and a value in its own right. Prioritizing the local by making decisions, exercising authority, or implementing policy locally or more locally allows and even encourages ordinary citizens to participate in the democratic process in ways they could not if they made decisions less locally. Localism promotes an ideal of citizenship. Some conceptions of the good life and our duties toward others require it.

Finally, according to the third strand, *accountability*, localism is good for democracy because prioritizing the local promotes accountability, another essential democratic value. When people cannot participate in politics themselves, or can do so only occasionally, they appoint representatives to act on their behalf. These representatives, as agents of the people, should be accountable to their masters. Otherwise the people do not rule; their representatives do. When the people inhabit a large territory, their business is conducted by their representatives at a distance. That distance makes shirking and malfeasance inevitable; accountability suffers. When the people divide themselves into smaller territorial units, by contrast, their agents remain nearby, under the watchful eyes of their constituents. Localism keeps representatives honest, or at least more honest than they would be if left to themselves, "distant from the observation of the people" where "men are apt to forget their dependence—lose their sympathy, and contract selfish habits."[3]

Small Is Democratic

Let's begin with the claim that localism is required by democracy *as such*. There are several interesting ways to argue for it. Note, however, that this strand of the argument for localism from democracy could very well have been included in part II of this book on commitments. The thought that democracy *just is* local, or that only local democracy is authentically democratic, or that the quality of democracy has an immutable relationship with size, is better understood as a deep commitment than a claim about consequences. The claim in this first strand is not, principally, that localism promotes welfare, dignity, or other fundamental human values, though it may; it is that localism is required by a particular conception of democracy.

This, I say by way of preview, is the essence of my objection to *small is democratic*. As we shall see, localism is required by democracy only if democracy is understood in a particular, peculiar, and to my mind, needlessly partisan manner. Localism is required by democracy only if localist intuitions are smuggled into the very definition of democracy. This line of argument, however, is question-begging because the argument for localism is supposed to be *from* democracy, not the other way around.

Of course there is a sense in which the argument is perfectly valid. Under certain conceptions of democracy, especially those that seem designed to yield localist conclusions, localism is very much required by democracy. But then we'd want to know why we should accept one of those conceptions of democracy. We'd need good reasons. And they'd have to be reasons independent of localism, at least in principle. If our reason for selecting one conception of democracy rather than another is that it promotes localism, we'll be helping ourselves to our conclusion.

With these prefatory comments in mind, we can now consider two ways in which localism could be required by democracy *as such*. The first is that only direct or participatory democracy is genuinely democratic, and both require localism. If representative democracy is a sham or a farce and if only direct democracy is genuinely democratic, the route to localism is clear. The second appeals to the supposedly necessary relationship between community size and citizens' control.

To address the first, that only direct or participatory democracy is genuinely democratic, consider what Tom Paine said on this topic in *Common Sense*, the pamphlet that got the American Revolution, in some ways the democratic revolution *par excellence*, off the ground:

> Some convenient Tree will afford them a State-House, under the branches of which the whole Colony may assemble to deliberate on public matters. . . . But as the Colony encreases . . . the distance at which the members may be separated, will render it too inconvenient for all of them to meet on every occasion as at first, when their number was small, their habitations near, and the public concerns few and trifling. This will point out the convenience of their consenting to leave the legislative part to be managed by a select number chosen from the whole body.[4]

Here Paine presents a stylized account of the origins of representative government. Democracy began, Paine suggests, with the "whole Colony," all the people, assembled under the branches of "some convenient tree." It was only when it became impossible, or at least terribly inconvenient, for the whole people to assemble there that representatives were contemplated.

Paine implies, at least I read him as implying—and even if he does not, many do or say so explicitly (Rousseau, for instance)—that representative government is an adulteration of democracy.[5] It's a necessary evil at best, oligarchical at worst. One hundred and seventy-three representatives are as despotic—and undemocratic—as one tyrant, to adapt a phrase from Thomas Jefferson's *Notes on the State of Virginia*.[6] That representatives are chosen does not alter the fact that they, and not the people at large, rule.

Notice how easy it is to spot Paine's spatial language. As the colony grew, the *distance* between its members grew also. When its population was small, everyone lived *near* enough to each other and the tree so that all could meet there. Size and distance were responsible for the declension from genuine democracy to representative government.

Even someone who celebrates representative government, John Stuart Mill, argues that "since all cannot, in a community exceeding a single small town, participate personally in any but some very minor portions of the public business, it follows that the ideal type of a perfect government must be representative."[7] For Mill, representative government follows *given* that "all cannot . . . participate personally."

Many thinkers have endorsed representative government because they take the factual premise—that, in general, communities are too large for direct democracy—for granted. Under some conceptions of localism, however, the factual premise is a bugaboo. If representative government is "the ideal type of perfect government" *because* communities are too large for all to meet in person, it could just as well follow that political communities shouldn't be that big. If representation is sufficiently undemocratic, we should organize our political communities so that the need for representation does not arise. We needn't capitulate to the facts, the localist could say.

The question therefore becomes: Is representation sufficiently undemocratic? Should we reject representation on democratic grounds? Is direct democracy democratic in a way representative government is not; or is direct democracy somehow *more* democratic than representative government?

The alternatives being considered here are large communities governed by representatives and small communities governed directly by the people themselves. If representative government and direct democracy are equally democratic, or if both are sufficiently democratic in their own way, we'll lack democratic reasons to favor one over the other. Democracy would not require localism.

I've already hinted that representation could be considered undemocratic if democracy requires that the people rule directly. When the people select agents—representatives—to act on their behalf, they no longer rule, according to this view. They give political power to others that they could and should exercise themselves.[8] They become subjects of their representatives. Representatives would then constitute a favored subset of the people, which means, according to the formulation given earlier, that representative government is undemocratic. It does not matter that the representatives are chosen, either in elections or by lottery, to act on behalf of the people. What matters is who decides. Democracy requires that the people decide.

This conception of democracy is obviously coherent. It might even be compelling on substantive grounds. But it seems to me to be unduly and arbitrarily narrow. Why does democracy require that the people rule directly? This claim is especially dubious if the people have decided that the best way for them to rule is to appoint representatives to administer their business. The people remain principals even as they appoint and empower agents. Agents are not sovereign; they can be dismissed.

Not only is it within the people's rights, there are sound democratic reasons to appoint agents to act on their behalf. Consider expertise. The people want clean drinking water, but they don't know which chemicals in what concentrations will make them sick. So they hire agents (from among themselves, if they wish) who know these sorts of things. The people tell their agents what they want, clean drinking water, and that they expect results. There is nothing at all undemocratic about this. The agents provide clean drinking water; they are granted discretion, but they do not rule. In other words, just because the people appoint agents does not mean they forfeit rule. If democracy is the form of government in which the people rule, representation is consistent with democracy.

Taken from another angle, the argument for direct democracy, and therefore localism, misinterprets the claim that democracy prohibits rule by a favored subset of the people. Rule by a favored subset of the people is aristocracy, plain and simple. Democracy and aristocracy are irreconcilable, on this view.[9]

Is representation aristocratic in the relevant sense? Bernard Manin has argued that elective representation is aristocratic, at least compared to a system in which representatives are selected by lottery. But by "aristocratic," he means that when representatives are elected they are chosen by voters for their distinction on some valued dimension. People typically vote for the better candidate; representation is aristocratic in *that* sense.[10]

In the same vein, there is an important distinction between *rule* by a subset of the people and decisions being made by a subset of the people. Decisionmaking authority does not entail rule. When Jack and Diane want to go for sushi and I want to go for pizza, being outvoted does not make me their subject. The same goes for majorities in general. Strictly speaking, majorities decide; they do not rule.

Now if a particular majority uses its decisionmaking authority to deny decisionmaking authority to a minority in the future, it becomes an aristocracy. The crucial difference is that in democracies under normal conditions, the majority decides while affirming the minority's authority to decide. Minorities rule, together with the majority, even when they lose.

The same reasoning applies to representatives as agents of the people. Representatives decide while affirming the authority of their masters. Their authority to decide comes from the people; their authority is the people's exercised in trust. As long as representatives do not use their decisionmaking authority to deny it to the people, representative government is not rule by a favored subset of the people. Representative government is not undemocratic, at least not for the reasons surveyed thus far.

One further thought is that representative government is not undemocratic by definition, but it *is* more likely to become aristocratic than direct democracy. When you empower representatives, even temporarily and in trust, they are liable to abuse that trust. Representatives amass authority, bit by bit, eventually leaving the people with nothing. The people eventually become subjects of their representatives.

I'm not sure how plausible this story is. I agree that the people should remain vigilant. They should keep their representatives on a short leash, and so on. But another story is at least as plausible. In that story, the people refuse to empower representatives; they make all their decisions themselves. At least for a while. Then they get busy. They begin, innocently enough, by asking their politically savvy friends how to vote. Then they give their friends their proxies. Eventually they call their political savvy friends their representatives and ask them to account for their actions. Then they have representative government, which, as we've seen already, is liable to turn citizens into subjects.

The foregoing is meant to challenge the thought that representative government is necessarily undemocratic and that direct democracy is necessarily more democratic than representative government. If democracy means rule by the people, not some favored subset of them, then direct democracy and representative government are both democratic, because the people rule under both systems. They rule differently, but they still rule.

To repeat, a narrower conception of democracy in which the people must rule directly and actively would count in favor of direct or participatory democracy but not representative government. And if the factual premise from earlier holds—that direct democracy is possible only in a small territory—democracy requires localism. But if representative government is democratic, or not more undemocratic than direct democracy, democracy does not require localism.

The second argument for localism from democracy as such points to a supposedly necessary relationship between community size and the proportion of each citizen's control over collective decisions. When communities contain one and only one member, Henry David Thoreau's dream, citizens retain absolute control over their communities' collective decisions.[11] No one is there to disagree. When each community has ten members, each citizen has a one-tenth share of collective control; in a community of 1 million, each citizen holds a 1/100,000,000 share.

The larger the community, the less influence each citizen has over its decisions. The smaller the community, the more influential each citizen becomes. Probabilistically, citizens are more likely to be decisive and are therefore more efficacious in small than in large communities.[12]

If political systems are more democratic when their citizens exercise a greater share of collective decisionmaking authority, smaller communities are more democratic than larger ones. I readily admit that the conclusion follows *if* the relationship between democracy and citizens' share of collective control is as simple as that.

If we were being charitable, we might say that all else equal, it is better for citizens to have greater control over their collective decisions than less. Some of the reasons for this overlap with what I'll say in the next section. For instance, when citizens exercise a greater share of collective control, they may feel more efficacious; they may even be more effective in getting their way. If democracy is about each citizen getting his or her way as often as possible, localism is democratic. Note, however, that this would be an argument for Thoreau's or Ralph Waldo Emerson's democracy of one—sovereignty of the individual.

If exercising greater control over collective decisions promotes feelings of efficacy, citizens might then take a greater interest in politics, learn more about the issues, and make better decisions. In which case localism could promote better outcomes.

Better outcomes yes, but more democratic outcomes? I'm not so sure. If decisions are more democratic to the extent that they promote welfare, perhaps. This confuses two different goods—democracy and welfare—however. Better substantive outcomes do not automatically make the decisionmaking processes that produce them more democratic.

If we were being less charitable, we could point to the tension between what Robert Dahl and Edward Tufte call the "criterion of *citizen effectiveness*" and the "criterion of *system of capacity*."[13] We're already familiar with the criterion of citizen effectiveness: "in order for citizens fully to control the decisions of the polity, they must participate directly in making those decisions."[14] Citizen effectiveness recommends localism.

According to the criterion of system capacity, however, "if the polity is to have the capacity to respond fully to its citizens, it must be completely autonomous or sovereign."[15] System capacity is a criterion of democracy because the people do not rule if they cannot do anything they want to do. If the scope of decisionmaking, as E. E. Schattschneider argued, is infinitesimally small, democracy is a sham.[16] If the people have authority over the color of their prescribed uniforms and nothing else, they do not, in any genuine sense, rule.

There is a tension between citizen effectiveness and system capacity because small communities promote citizen effectiveness while reducing system capacity. Smaller communities have fewer resources; they govern fewer people and less territory. Smaller communities mean more communities and more borders and more neighbors. And no neighboring community can be made to act against its will. Projects that would have been possible in larger communities are constantly thwarted.

In other words, there is an inverse relationship between citizens' influence over collective decisions and what they can do with it. At one extreme, the community of one, no community can do anything that affects any other unless all agree. At the other, the community of all, the community can do whatever it wants. Of course, there will be disagreement within the latter but not the former. Citizens in large communities are less likely to influence decisions, but those decisions are more consequential and more likely to be translated into outcomes. Citizens in small communities, by contrast, are more likely to influence decisions, but those decisions will be less consequential and more frequently blocked by neighbors.

As you can see, once you consider both criteria, citizen effectiveness and system capacity, there is no clear-cut case for smaller communities. The tension is real. Both criteria, citizen effectiveness and system capacity, have sound democratic credentials. A compelling case for localism would need to show that decreasing the size of communities would promote citizen effectiveness without undermining system capacity. Less stringently, the case for localism would need to show that decreasing the size of communities yields benefits in terms of citizen effectiveness that exceed costs in terms of system capacity. I'm at a loss as to how to demonstrate *that*.

An alternative would be to argue that citizen effectiveness is more important than system capacity. If so, citizen effectiveness could be assigned extra weight in the cost-benefit calculus, perhaps yielding a justification for localism in some cases. This would still depend on the relative magnitude of costs and benefits, however. Unless citizen effectiveness was infinitely important, so that any gains in effectiveness would offset losses in capacity of any magnitude, the case for localism would depend on the facts. The argument for localism would apply in some cases but not others.

Another problem with the argument, not much discussed, is that it assumes that the value to citizens of additional influence is a straightforward function of community size. This is complicated, so let me explain what I mean. Citizens in a community of 100 hold 1/100 of the community's decisionmaking authority. Citizens in a community of 1,000 hold 1/1,000 of the community's decisionmaking authority. Citizens of the former hold ten times as much decisionmaking authority as citizens in the latter. But is ten times as much authority *worth* ten times as much to ordinary people? It's plausible to think that the subjective value of political authority decreases faster than the objective value. That is, people might care much more about increasing their share from 1/100 to 1/10 than from 1/1,000,000 to 1/100,000. I don't know if it's rational, but it isn't completely crazy. With such small chances, why invest time and emotional energy.[17]

If we were being downright hostile, we could insist upon the ecumenical definition of democracy with which we began. Democracy requires that the people rule, not some favored subset of them. It doesn't say anything about each citizen's share in ruling. As Philip Pettit has argued, the "idea of control or power is central to the notion of democracy, since the ideal is one of giving *kratos* to the *demos*: giving maximal or at least significant control over government to the people."[18] It is about giving power to "the people" as a collectivity, not to the people as individuals. As long as the people rule, they do so democratically. Equality matters far more than magnitude.

There may be reasons to bemoan exceedingly small shares of decisionmaking authority; perhaps they make politics too trivial and political influence hopelessly improbable. But I insist these are not democratic reasons; or at least not democratic reasons that would require localism. Democracy as such requires localism only if these peripheral and controversial intuitions rule the day.

Participation

We've just seen why democracy as such does not require localism. It's just not true, under any neutral conception of democracy, that prioritizing the local by making decisions, exercising authority, or implementing policy locally or more locally is democratic by definition or necessarily more democratic than making decisions less locally. We now turn to a more promising idea: that localism *promotes* democracy.

My claim is that localism can be said to promote democracy if prioritizing the local by making decisions, exercising authority, or implementing policy locally or more locally instantiates or advances democratic values. This assumes that polities can be more or less democratic depending on how well they do along certain democratic dimensions. One of which, the subject of this section, is *participation*.

All else equal, democracies are healthier when their citizens participate in politics in the appropriate manner. Different conceptions of democracy celebrate different types of participation, however. Participatory democracy requires active participation by citizens, not just voting.[19] Deliberative democracy requires that citizens discuss policy alternatives in a deliberative forum.[20] The elitist conception of democracy says that citizens should perhaps vote, but little else.[21] Different conceptions of democracy prescribe different kinds of participation, but it's fair to say that some kinds of participation are extremely unlikely to promote democracy according to any conception: hate speech, violence, vote tampering, etc.

From the other end, it's easy to see that democracies are deficient in some way when their citizens fail or refuse to participate in politics in the appropriate manner. Since democracy is rule by the people, democracy requires that they take part in ruling themselves. Abstention from political participation is a symptom of democratic decay, or something far worse.

It can signal malaise or apathy, anomie, mistrust in government, quiescence, fear, or starvation. Active participation in politics separates the sham democracies from the real ones. Falling rates of participation may indicate that institutions have gone astray.

Political participation can also be a source of pride and meaning for communities and their citizens. According to at least one conception of democracy, participation is necessary for true human happiness in the way that pouncing is necessary for genuine feline happiness.[22] Cats who do not pounce, because they cannot, or are afraid to, cannot be happy. Nor are people who do not participate in politics, because they cannot or are afraid to, truly happy. People who say they don't participate because they don't want to are lying or mistaken about what they should want.

For these reasons and more, if prioritizing the local encourages people to participate in politics, localism is good for democracy. Assuming, of course, that any negative side effects produced by localism do not outweigh the benefits of increased participation and that promoting participation through localism does not preclude the acquisition of other, more important goods.

On its face, the argument for localism from political participation is a slam dunk. But to evaluate it properly, we need to address the following questions: Does localism actually promote political participation? Under what conditions? Who participates when decisions are made more locally? With that in mind, is political participation an unalloyed good? Are the kinds of political participation encouraged by localism the kinds we should celebrate? Are there any unique dangers associated with political participation at the local level?

My argument in the remainder of this section will be less sure-footed than elsewhere in the book. I sympathize with the intuition behind the argument for localism from participation. But I'm not sure it will get localism where localists want it to go.

The case for localism from participation borrows a central thesis from participatory democratic theory. According to participatory democrats, citizens "learn to participate by participating."[23] Citizens learn about politics by participating in politics. Carole Pateman called this the "educative" aspect of participatory democracy; C. B. Macpherson called it the "developmental" aspect.[24] Participatory theorists also claim that by participating, citizens acquire "political skills and perceptions of self-competence" which then make "it more likely that individuals will participate in the future,"[25] setting off what Macpherson called "the virtuous circle." In the empirical literature, Alan Gerber, Donald Green, and Ron Shachar have shown that political participation is addictive; those who have participated in the past are more likely to do so in the future.[26]

The persistent challenge for participatory democrats, both in the academy and in the streets (the New Left, for instance), has been to get this positive feedback loop going: to close the loop.[27] Localism is relevant here because if making decisions more locally spurs political participation, as a kind of exogenous shock to the participatory system, it might well settle into a new equilibrium with high levels of participation, knowledge, and competence. A welcome result.

The mechanism thought to drive the participatory feedback loop, Macpherson's virtuous circle, is what researchers call "internal efficacy." In laypersons' terms, it's the feeling that one's own participation matters.[28] In an empirical study, Paul Finkel has shown that feelings of efficacy do indeed make voting more likely, but also that the effect of voting on efficacy is statistically insignificant.[29] People who feel competent are more likely to vote, but those who vote do not, so far as we can tell from the data, thereby feel more competent. Somewhat more encouraging, the effect of campaign participation on internal efficacy is positive and statistically significant (but small). Those who participate in campaigns, then, are somewhat more likely to feel efficacious.

For localism, this means that unless prioritizing the local by making decisions, exercising authority, or implementing policy locally or more locally gets people to participate in campaigns, or other "time-consuming" political activities, the feedback loop remains open.[30] Making decisions more locally might spur participation, but participation won't then strengthen feelings of efficacy. The argument for localism from participation, then, would need to show that prioritizing the local by making decisions, exercising authority, or implementing policy locally or more locally facilitates high-intensity forms of participation rather than low-intensity forms of political participation like voting.[31]

In a more recent study, Nicholas Valentino, Krysha Gregorowicz, and Eric Groenendyk posit that the link between internal efficacy and political participation is mediated by the emotions.[32] Individuals with high internal efficacy tend to feel they have control over their environment. When their control is challenged, they react with *anger* rather than *fear* to unwelcome policy proposals. Anger then spurs political participation; highly efficacious people don't let other people push them around. And if their participation is successful, they tend to feel even more competent, closing the aforementioned feedback loop. Individuals with low internal efficacy, by contrast, feel little control over their environment; they react with fear to policy threats. Fear, unlike anger, is demobilizing. Scared people hunker down, hoping the storm will pass.

This complicates but does not alter our previous conclusion. Even if prioritizing the local by making decisions, exercising authority, or implementing policy locally or more locally encourages political participation, only those citizens who react with anger toward policy threats and are then successful in thwarting them will feel more efficacious in the future. The posited feedback loop closes only for those who already feel efficacious, not for those who feel helpless. The implication, as Anne Phillips has argued, is that "those whose life already offers them some opportunity for influencing decisions are more likely . . . to consider themselves politically competent. The inequities in this are obvious, for those who already have certain decision-making powers will develop in their confidence and claims, while those who have been more marginal may decline into passive acceptance."[33]

From the normative (moral or ethical) point of view, then, the argument for localism from participation faces a serious challenge. Localism benefits some people but not others. Those who miss out need the benefits of participation more than those who already receive them in spades. Boosting participation in this way may even be undemocratic. It skews the distribution of political influence in favor of the politically efficacious, who we know, from one of the most consistent findings in political science, are luckier, richer, and better educated.[34] Democracy recommends, all else equal, interventions that level the playing field. This is another way of saying that rates of participation are an exceedingly rough, and potentially misleading, measure of the health of a democracy.

We've just seen that there is little evidence to support the claim that prioritizing the local by making decisions, exercising authority, or implementing policy locally or more locally would spark the feedback loop supposedly linking participation and efficacy. The argument for localism from participation could be made in another way, however. Both before and since Robert Dahl and Edward Tufte's *Size and Democracy*, scholars have wondered whether the size, in terms of its population, of a jurisdiction affects its democratic credentials, including political participation. If small democracies are better than large democracies, the argument for localism may well succeed.

Unfortunately, the empirical research on this topic does not demonstrate much of anything conclusive. In a wide-ranging recent study, Bas Denters and his colleagues explored the relationship between municipal population size and a series of indicators of the health of local democracy in four European countries: Switzerland, Norway, Denmark, and the Netherlands. They concluded that there "is some weak empirical support for"[35] the argument according to which "size is likely to have *negative effects* on the quality of local democracy."[36] However, this is true for some, but not all, of the indicators the authors considered. They add that "where we find these effects . . . they are typically weak (both in a relative and an absolute sense) and not robust."[37]

The expected relationship was confirmed, in at least three of the four countries, for four of ten indicators—personal political competence, satisfaction with local government, party activity, and local contacting. Municipal size had a negative relationship with two more indicators—

confidence in local politicians and distinctiveness of local voting—in two of the four countries. This is what Denters and others mean when they say that the effects of size on democracy are not robust. Even those relationships between size and democracy that the authors dub "more or less consistent" with expectations hold only in two of the four countries studied.

Notably, there was *no* support for the relationship between size and democracy for the four remaining indicators—political interest, political knowledge, likelihood of voting in local elections, and community activity. Thus, as we saw previously, localism is associated with some kinds of participation but not others, and not the holy grail: voting.

Not only that, the effects of size on democracy supported by the data are quite small. In Norway, for example, satisfaction with local government scored 60.1 in municipalities of 500 people and 50.9 in municipalities of 100,000 people, a difference of 9.2 points. In Switzerland, the difference was only 1.5 points. With respect to local contacting, the largest difference was 23 points (Switzerland); the smallest was 10.4 (the Netherlands). And these are the two indicators—satisfaction and contacting—for which the effect of size on democracy was strongest. The effects of size, then, are quite small, and they are dwarfed by other, more familiar, causal variables.

Denters and others insist that size does indeed affect democratic quality, but note that their results "may come as a bit of a disappointment" to the devotees of the miniature and the gigantic. K. Newton, in an earlier study, concluded that "size is irrelevant to many aspects of functional effectiveness and democracy."[38]

We should also remember that these results are about the relationship between size and democracy at the municipal level. It's unclear whether the findings generalize to the reallocation of political authority from higher-level to lower-level governments. Utilizing Euroborometer surveys from 1983 to 1994 in thirteen European countries, Bonnie Meguid found that "the percentage of respondents who claimed to be interested 'a great deal' or 'to some extent' in politics across these countries is negatively and significantly correlated with the country's level of decentralization."[39] Moreover, among the five European countries "that created regional governments since 1970, none consistently has election turnout rates for the more powerful regional governments that are higher than those for the weaker local governments."[40]

The authors of a recent study in a related but distinct discipline, participatory development, argue that that endeavor has "proceeded, in large part, with little systematic effort to understand the particular challenges entailed in inducing participation or to learn from the failures of past programs." Participatory reform, they add, "is, arguably, still driven more by ideology and optimism than by systematic analysis, either theoretical or empirical."[41]

Furthermore, when scholars contend that development "works better when citizens participate in decisions that shape their lives and allows them to monitor the people whose task it is to govern their destinies," they are talking about how to implement development policy. The contrast is with the ham-handed, top-down interventions of the dark ages. Their claim, so far as I can tell, is that policies, when implemented, should involve the people affected, for all the obvious reasons (obvious in the postcolonial era, at least).

Whether those interventions should consist in making decisions more locally is another question entirely. While the authors of the World Bank report suggest that decentralization of service delivery may improve development outcomes, they insist that decentralization is most likely to be successful when the central state plays an active role in the process. The central state should be "building local capacity, monitoring outcomes, and setting the broad parameters in which management is devolved."[42] This is a far cry from localism as it is sometimes imagined. Local autonomy certainly isn't required; and it may make matters worse.

The development literature, like the literature on size and democracy, raises concerns about equity. One review of the literature "finds that participants in civic activities tend to be wealthier, more educated, of higher social status (by caste and ethnicity), male, and more politically connected than nonparticipants."[43] Moreover, "the poor often benefit less from participatory processes than do the better off, because resource allocation processes typically reflect the preferences of elite groups."[44]

Circling back, recall that the claim under consideration is that we should prioritize the local by making decisions, exercising authority, or implementing policy locally or more locally because doing so gets people to participate. We've already explored one possible mechanism: the efficacy-participation feedback loop. Another can be attributed, without too much distortion, to Joseph Schumpeter. Schumpeter famously argued that in "those regions of national and international affairs that lack a direct and unmistakable link with . . . private concerns," citizens fail to act responsibly or even rationally.[45] Schumpeter added, however, that "in the realm of public affairs there are sectors that are more within the reach of the citizen's mind than others," most notably, "local affairs."[46]

People don't participate much in national politics because they don't see a clear and concrete connection between national issues and their private lives. People are more likely to participate in that which interests them or affects them directly. If decisions were made more locally, the reasoning goes, people would understand what's at stake and get involved. They would come to see far more clearly how public policies shape their daily lives.

However much sense this makes intuitively, it is contradicted by the evidence. People participate less, not more, at the local level. As J. Eric Oliver, Shang Ha, and Zachary Callen observe, in the United States, "turnout in local elections is usually below 35 percent of eligible voters and can be much lower depending on when the election is held and which offices are at stake."[47] Specifically, "when local elections are held on their own," that is, not concurrently with state or national contests, "turnout drops to 18 percent."[48] Very low indeed. And in an interesting attempt to evade the worry about representativeness in low-turnout elections, Oliver, Ha, and Calen argue that although "local elections are dominated by homeowners, the educated, and long-term residents" (they are also whiter and richer), "these voters tend to exemplify all that we expect in a classical notion of the ideal democratic citizen: they are politically engaged, knowledgeable, and have definitive preferences about local policies."[49] Yes, we all know the type. But it is precisely the fact that they are engaged, knowledgeable, and opinionated—more so than those who stay at home on election day—that makes low-turnout local elections so troubling.

Jessica Trounstine, for her part, has shown that in low-turnout local elections incumbents are more likely to run for re-election and more likely to win. Either this means that local officials do a better job, on average, than national politicians, or that the local electorate can't be bothered to throw the bastards out. Elections with low turnout reveal "spending patterns that benefit particular subgroups in the population who have good reason to overcome high participation costs."[50] Worries about accountability and responsiveness are exacerbated when those who vote are an unrepresentative sample of the public.[51]

I don't want to beat a dead horse, so let me just say, to take stock, that there is little evidence to support the claim that prioritizing the local by making decisions, exercising authority, or implementing policy locally or more locally will encourage ordinary people to participate. Localists could argue, and they will, that I'm being unfair, however. The claim was never, they might say, that making decisions more locally would kick-start participation under current conditions.

The claim was always, it could be said, that once significant decision-making authority was transferred from higher-level to lower-level governments, people would come to see that local participation makes a big difference and would then come out in droves. People don't participate in local governments as they are now constituted because there's not much at stake. Localism is supposed to be about making decisions about consequential issues more locally.

I very much agree that people might participate more in local politics if they thought local governments mattered more than they do now. But now the argument is completely muddled. The prospect of increased participation was supposed to be a *reason* for adopting localism. Now we find that to get the promised benefits of participation we must make sweeping changes to the political order—with no guarantee of success.

To my mind, the argument has become a little disingenuous. It requires that we take a leap of faith.

What's more, for localism to have its intended effects, we would need to grant localities significant authority over issues currently handled by higher-level governments. Might doing so diminish citizens' incentives to participate in the affairs of *those* governments? Can we be sure that increased participation at the local level will make up for decreased participation at higher levels?

Moreover, perhaps local governments are less well-equipped to handle certain issues. Paul Peterson has argued that local governments are virtually powerless with respect to redistribution, for example.[52] Because local governments operate in a competitive environment—dissatisfied citizens and firms can move to friendlier jurisdictions—they can't do everything they might like.

Suppose local citizens wish to do something to help the homeless. Local officials comply, enacting a new housing voucher program and raising local property taxes to pay for it. Citizens and firms who do not wish to pay the tax—because they don't care about poor people or, more likely, they'd prefer to help them on someone else's dime—decide to move to a neighboring jurisdiction with lower taxes. The lost revenue must now be made up with higher taxes or cuts to social services. Whatever local officials decide, at least a few residents will be unhappy and may decide to pack up their things. And so on.

When Peterson wrote *City Limits*, so named because cities are limited by their circumstances, it was thought that nation-states were the appropriate site for redistribution. Whereas people can easily move between local jurisdictions if taxes get too high, it is more difficult, and was then considerably more difficult, to cross national borders. A nation-state, especially a wealthy one, can afford to raise taxes for redistribution because the assets located within its borders are difficult to take elsewhere.

We now know that nation-states face the same constraints in muted form. Multinational companies with clever lawyers can hop from country to country just as they do from locality to locality. This makes redistribution difficult, even for nation-states. Countries with high taxes and generous welfare benefits must attract capital in other ways, much as places like New York City have managed to attract capital despite offering relatively generous welfare benefits.

A similar story could be told for any issue liable to fall through the metaphorical cracks between local jurisdictions. As long as we agree that there are some policy areas for which only higher-level jurisdictions can do the job properly or effectively, local governments' authority cannot be plenary.

We take up this issue in earnest in chapter 8 on efficiency, but I'll mention it here because many of the issues people really care about—the issues that spur them to participate—may fall directly into the category just mentioned. If people don't participate in local politics because local issues are less consequential, and all or most consequential policy areas are handled by higher-level jurisdictions for reasons like those above, there may be little that can be done. Localism often assumes, perhaps because it has remained aspirational thus far, that there are uncontroversial policy areas ripe for the picking. It could turn out that most issues belong where they are. If so, it would be a mistake to expect local participation rates to be much different than they are now.

Even if we could get people to participate in politics by prioritizing the local, would that be a good thing? That depends. We've already seen that those who participate tend to be unrepresentative of the population at large. Of course, if everyone participates, they will be representative by definition. But if we assume, not at all unrealistically, that those who participate differ in significant respects from those who abstain, we need to take the bias problem seriously. I've already hinted that inducing participation can make things worse.

If the usual factors that drive participation continue to hold, those with substantial resources, income and education, for instance, are more likely to participate, and benefit from participating, than those with less. Not only will they benefit personally by learning about politics and developing their capacities, they also can be expected to benefit substantively. Let me just call those with substantial resources the rich and those with less the poor. If the rich are already more likely to participate than the poor, and the rich are more likely to respond to new incentives to participate—localism, for instance—the rich will be over-represented among those who participate. Which means they are more likely to get their way. If the policies favored by the rich disproportionately benefit them, the poor will be even worse off, relatively speaking.

These issues are compounded if the goods of participation are positional. According to Harry Brighouse and Adam Swift, positional goods are "goods with the property that one's relative place in the distribution of the good affects one's absolute position with respect to its value."[53] Cars are positional goods if the value of having one more car than your next-door neighbor is more than the car. Education is the paradigmatic positional good. In 1940, when fewer than 5 percent of Americans had completed four years of college, a university degree was worth a great deal more than it was in 2020, when 38 percent had one.[54] Many jobs for which one once needed a high school diploma now require a four-year degree.

Political efficacy, especially in the mundane sense, is undoubtedly positional. The sycophant who can decipher the ravings of a lunatic king may not have much political influence, but he certainly has more than most. His influence is probably worth as much as that of the prime minister of a "patriot king."[55]

If prioritizing the local by making decisions, exercising authority, or implementing policy locally or more locally is more likely to induce participation—and therefore efficacy—for the rich than for the poor, and if efficacy is a positional good, localism will add insult to injury for the poor.

Speaking flippantly for a moment: the sorts of people who now participate in local politics are busybodies who frequently get their way. They know and use the adage to good effect: the squeaky wheel gets the grease. The problem with localism is not the busybodies, who in all seriousness provide an important public service; it is that those who are induced to participate by prioritizing the local by making decisions, exercising authority, or implementing policy locally or more locally are more likely to ally themselves with the busybodies than the little guy. Or it seems reasonable to assume. Unless, that is, special effort is made to induce participation by the down-and-outs. And if that is something worth doing, I see no compelling reason to believe that localism will do the trick. To repeat, if the goal is to get poor people to participate, tactics other than localism may be more promising.

Last but not least, I worry a bit about what people might do with their newfound power at the local level. When lots of people participate, might that lend legitimacy to otherwise suspect behavior? What if the people decide to do something unjust?

This worry may fall outside the purview of the narrow conception of democracy we've been using in this chapter. A different worry does not. Democracy requires that the people rule. Do the people rule when a subset of them—in this case, a geographical subset—gets to decide without having consulted outsiders? The question here is a big one: does localism create new peoples? Localists do not ordinarily contend that every decision should be made locally, so we are not talking about plenary sovereignty. At most, localism would grant final authority (that is, sovereignty, autonomy) over a set of issues to a new people—a subset of the old people—constituted for that purpose. If localism creates new peoples, and those peoples rule, localism is democratic.

Or is it? If localism instead grants authority—but not final authority— over a set of issues to a group of people residing in a particular place, I contend that localism does *not* create new peoples. In these cases, "the people" authorize some of their number to make decisions about certain issues, subject to conditions. If there were no conditions, the people would be granting plenary authority to a new people, thereby reconstituting itself.

By attaching conditions to grants of authority, the people maintain their final authority. They remain whole. And as the people, they, not some favored (perhaps geographical) subset of them, must rule. The conditions the people attach to grants of authority could include respect for rights or duties of justice. The conditions could be substantive, that is. Or they could be democratic. We could think, reasonably enough, that when the people grant authority to some of them, they could require that the authority granted be exercised democratically; in effect, preserving the people's authority to rule.

The people could even require that local decisions respect the public good—the good of the people, the whole people. Why, after all, would the people authorize some of them to harm the rest? This turns out to be a serious constraint on what local people may do. Some of the things a newly mobilized local electorate might want to do will be off limits. And some of those things may have been their reason for participating in the first place.

This leads us to a final—somewhat deeper—point about the argument for localism from democratic participation. Scholars and citizens alike are quick to note the potentialities of political participation in terms of empowerment, social justice, and human rights. They are slower to admit and may not even recognize the awful responsibility participation engenders. The difference between participation and democratic participation is wide and profound. Participation in politics with others, while it is empowering in some respects, is disempowering in others. By acting with others, we limit how we may act.

Accountability

The basic intuition behind the accountability argument for localism is simple. It's easier to keep local officials accountable because they are closer. It's harder to keep track of what distant officials are up to. Proximity is the crucial mechanism.

Citizens are better equipped to evaluate conditions in their locality than in their region or country. To hold officials to account, we need to know what we are holding them accountable *for*. It's easier to tell if things are going poorly around here than over there. To evaluate local conditions, people don't need to do anything special or onerous. Are the streets lit? Are potholes repaired forthwith? Are the shops downtown shuttered?

Evaluating conditions in larger jurisdictions is more complicated. We might need to rely on official statistics like economic growth, inflation, the unemployment rate, crime rates, and so on. Those sorts of things are abstract and boring. And who's to say that national conditions matter to us here? According to a popular narrative of the 2016 presidential election in the United States, voters in depressed local communities turned out for Donald Trump because he recognized, unlike his opponent, that moderately encouraging national conditions obscure genuine pain in people's actual lives. Even if the country as a whole is doing well, shouldn't we hold officials accountable for how we're doing here? The nation is a cold abstraction.

At the local level, it's also easier to see the link between policies and outcomes. For accountability to work, we need to be able to hold the appropriate officials accountable. We shouldn't punish our mayors for the boondoggle in Iraq; nor should we punish the president for the sorry state of our city's streets. If we can't establish this causal link, we'll end up throwing out good leaders and reelecting bad ones.

At the national level, the link between policies and outcomes is obscure. When the economy is doing well, for instance, it's hard to tell with certainty who is responsible, or if anyone is responsible. Maybe it was President Trump's tax cut, in which case we might have been justified (on economic grounds) for voting for his reelection; maybe it's just the business cycle, and the tax cut just adds to the deficit. In polls leading up to the 2008 election, John McCain and Barack Obama were neck-and-neck, but when the economic crisis peaked in September 2008, voters blamed John McCain for what may or may not have been President Bush's fault.[56]

In contrast, when the mayor says she'll have the new aquatic complex open for visitors by Memorial Day, voters won't have trouble deciding what to do on election day in November. It helps, as Schumpeter argued, that people are more attentive to issues that affect their daily lives.

So voters at the local level are more likely to have the kind of information they need to hold their officials accountable. Local officials are also easier to monitor because it's easier to monitor what's near than what's distant. People can easily go down to city hall to see what's up. Doing likewise for national officials is onerous and expensive. In most cases, people rely on secondhand information when they evaluate the performance of national or even regional officials. Secondhand reports may leave out crucial information or misrepresent the facts. It's safer to go and see for yourself.

Presumably, then, local officials know they are being watched, and act accordingly. They know they can't get away with anything when they're under a microscope. National officials, by contrast, know that their constituents don't have the money or the time to keep watch. It's only natural to expect that, absent careful monitoring, national officials will do things they would not otherwise have done. They'll shirk their duties and betray their constituents.

The same holds from the other direction. It's easier for local officials to go out and feel the pulse of their constituents. They can update their sense of their constituents' wishes in real time, even on the way to work. In contrast, national-level officials, members of Congress or Parliament, for instance, spend a great deal of their time in the nation's capital. Whenever they are there, they are not at home among their constituents.[57] They, too, can obtain information secondhand, but it's not entirely reliable for the same reasons as before. Officials who aren't always in touch with their constituents won't be able to serve them well.

At the local level, then, it's easier for citizens to assign blame and monitor officials for malfeasance. It's also easier for local officials to satisfy their constituents' preferences, a point we'll revisit in chapter 8. As Dahl and Tufte explain, smaller communities "are likely to be more nearly homogenous with respect to beliefs, values, and goals."[58] Greater homogeneity within a jurisdiction—less disagreement—means that more preferences can be satisfied with the same policy.

To see why, pretend there's a country with two localities, equally populated. In one locality, 70 percent favor regulating emissions and 30 percent oppose regulation. In the other locality, 40 percent favor regulation, whereas 60 percent are opposed. Do some arithmetic and you'll find that in the country as a whole 55 percent favor regulation and 45 percent oppose it. A uniform national policy requiring regulation would satisfy 55 percent of the population. Making this decision at the local level, by contrast, would satisfy 65 percent of the population. The first locality would regulate emissions, satisfying 70 percent of its citizens and 35 percent of the country, and the second would leave things be, satisfying 60 percent of its citizens, and 30 percent of the country.

This means that, in one sense, lower-level governments are more accountable to their citizens than higher-level governments. If accountability means giving more of the people more of what they want, and if lower-level governments are more homogenous than higher-level governments, lower-level governments can be more accountable. It's just easier for officials to give the people what they want when they all want the same thing. Making policy for a relatively homogenous constituency means fewer angry voters.

Taken together, then, there are three reasons to suppose that making decisions more locally promotes democratic accountability. First, people are more likely to have the information they need to hold officials accountable at the local level. Second, local officials are physically closer and therefore easier to monitor. Third, local governments are more accountable because they satisfy more of their constituents' preferences. The question now is whether these are good reasons.

Consider, first, the suggestion that people are more likely to have the information they need to hold officials accountable at the local level. I want to concede, at least for the moment (but see chapter 7), that citizens have special access to certain kinds of information. People pick up all kinds of potentially useful information in their day-to-day lives. New Yorkers, for example, get a pretty good sense of how well the Metropolitan Transit Authority is doing when they try to squeeze one more body onto the A-train at rush hour. Or when suburbanites encounter reduced hours at the local library.

But it's not obvious, at least to me, that the attribution problem is any easier at the local level. Maybe the library is an easy case. Libraries are run by cities, right? So citizens who are unhappy about library hours should hold their city officials accountable: perhaps the mayor and the city council. In my hometown of Fremont, California, however, libraries are organized at the county level. The Alameda County Board of Supervisors has the authority from the state of California to establish and maintain a county free library.[59] To complicate matters further, the Alameda County Library Advisory Commission (the purpose of which I cannot discern) is composed of one council member from each participating city, four members appointed by the county Board of Supervisors and six at-large members.[60] Who, exactly, are we supposed to blame? Likewise, disgruntled New Yorkers are mistaken if they believe subway crowding is the mayor's fault. The subway system is run by the Metropolitan Transit Authority, itself under the purview of the governor in Albany.[61]

Returning, again, to libraries: even if people can figure out who actually runs their libraries, there is no guarantee that those officials are responsible for the problem. Perhaps library hours were slashed because of budget cuts imposed by higher-level governments. Well here, one might say, is a good argument for localism. If lower-level governments had more control, they wouldn't be subject to the whims of outsiders.

Suppose, instead, a library system with its own elected board and an independent source of tax revenue. Here the lines of responsibility are as clear as they can get. Nevertheless, as Larry Bartels and Chris Achen have shown, voters are sometimes willing to punish their elected officials for shark attacks and the like.[62] If library hours are cut because of a recession, is voting the library's board out of office really *accountability*?

Or suppose local citizens are unhappy with the vulgar graffiti on the library's facade and the shady characters loitering nearby. Would punishing the library's board at the polls count as accountability if such matters are the responsibility of the local police department?

Even if people are especially likely to obtain relevant information about local conditions, vicariously perhaps, it's not clear they would know what to do with it. This line of argument assumes it's easier to correctly attribute responsibility at the local level. That assumption is questionable, to say the least.

Besides direct experience, the other way voters obtain information about their elected officials is through the news media. To rest on firm ground, then, the accountability argument should show that the news media provide enough local information for voters to make informed decisions. Even though local governments are closer, it may be easier to hold national officials accountable if we have better information about them.

Whatever may have been true in the past, in the present we know that local news is in decline. In an analysis of local news coverage in the 2010 and 2014 midterm elections, Danny Hayes and Jennifer L. Lawless show "that, even during this relatively brief period, newspapers published less, and less substantive, local political news."[63] They also show that "citizens exposed to a lower volume of coverage are less able to evaluate their member of Congress, less likely to express opinions about the House candidates in their districts, and less likely to vote."[64]

In a related study, James M. Snyder and David Strömberg demonstrate that voters whose newspaper markets are "congruent" with their congressional districts (and are therefore exposed to more relevant local news) are more likely to "report reading about their House representative in a newspaper or magazine" and are "better informed about their House representative."[65] Members of Congress "from highly congruent districts are more disciplined by their constituencies: their voting conforms less to the party line, they are more likely to stand witness before congressional hearings, and they are, perhaps, more likely to serve on constituency-oriented committees and also less likely to serve on broad policy-oriented committees."[66] More simply, voters who are exposed to more local news read more and know more; representatives whose constituents read more local news are more accountable.

These results would be encouraging if the local news were not in such sorry shape. In 2017, per capita weekday newspaper circulation was 30 percent of its postwar peak in 1946. Newspaper circulation has dropped 50 percent since 2000.[67] Although newspapers' emphasis on local issues has increased somewhat relative to national news in the last several decades, national news still dominates local news, with roughly twice as many nationally oriented news articles.[68] Americans prefer to read stories about the president than their governor or their mayor.[69] Moreover, Americans' attention has shifted, relatively speaking, from news sources that emphasize local news (print newspapers, local television) to those that emphasize national news (cable news, online news).[70] Younger people are more likely to get their news from nationally oriented outlets, indicating that interest in local news, in the aggregate, is likely to decrease even more in the future. All told, the American media market is more nationalized than ever before, and can be expected to become even more so in the future.

In one of the few studies of retrospective voting—the idea that voters use their officials' past performance to inform their vote choice—at the local level, Christopher Berry and William Howell find little evidence that voters evaluate their representatives according to objective measures of performance. In school board elections in South Carolina, for example, vote choice was a function of student test scores in only one election, in 2000, of the three elections studied.[71]

The evidence assembled thus far is not encouraging for the accountability argument for localism. People are losing interest in the media outlets that provide the kinds of information they need to hold local officials accountable. And those outlets are disappearing because of market pressures. Contrary to expectations, citizens receive more information about national officials than their representatives close to home. What's more, they care more about national issues than local ones.

Another way to put the point is that technology and market forces are making it easier and easier for citizens to learn about national-level officials, especially relative to their local officials. The facts, in this case, do not support the claim that localism promotes accountability.

That said, committed localists could argue that the trends described only reinforce their argument for localism. Look what happens, they could say, when we refuse to prioritize the local by making decisions, exercising authority, or implementing policy locally or more locally. Localism envisions a radical restructuring of political, social, and economic life, not minor reforms, so the fact that localism would not improve accountability in the short term is not a mark against it.

Maybe so, but then localism needs to show how we'll get from here to there. Earlier the argument was that prioritizing the local by making decisions, exercising authority, or implementing policy locally or more locally would improve accountability; now it's that prioritizing the local by making decisions, exercising authority, or implementing policy locally or more locally will improve accountability under certain conditions, conditions that do not presently exist. Localism has moved from the actual to the hypothetical.

What about the claim that officials are easier to monitor when they are close by? Presumably this is an empirical question. Perhaps because politics occurs in physical space, there are built-in constraints that favor the local. But are those constraints immutable?

This is as good a place as any to suggest that many of our political intuitions can be traced back to a time when physical space meant much more than it does now. Prior to the first telegraph message, sent on May 24, 1844, information could travel no faster than a human being. Horses and ships let people travel faster than they could run, but not much faster. The speed of information transfer was then a function of physical distance. Politicians really could use distance as a shield. Ordinary citizens had to wait days or even weeks for news, time in which representatives might sell their liberty for a pittance. Distance was dangerous.

Samuel Morse and his telegraph changed everything.[72] The speed of information transfer became a function of distance to the nearest telegraph, something subject to human control. Citizens could now read about what happened yesterday in the national capitol in the morning newspaper. Of course citizens could not, and still cannot, directly observe what goes on in Washington. But now it is no more difficult to obtain mediated information about national than local politics.

Technology has progressed considerably since the telegraph. In some cases, it is now easier to monitor officials of higher-level governments. Those officials are further away, but they have more people watching them. Adapting a point from Thomas Schwartz and Matthew McCubbins, it only takes one citizen to raise the alarm.[73] Social media has made it that much easier to keep tabs on government officials. Some of them even expose their own malfeasance. In 2015, Congressman Aaron Schock was forced to resign his seat after posting pictures of his Downton Abbey themed office decor. His "lavish lifestyle . . . was well documented on his Instagram feed . . . but not always as well chronicled on his financial disclosure forms."[74]

National-level officials are easier to monitor in this way, simply because they usually have more followers on social media. Rep. Ro

Khanna, the congressman representing my childhood home, has, at the time of writing, more than 112.6K followers on Twitter (@RepRoKhanna), whereas the mayor of Fremont (@LilyMei4Fremont) has only 2,360 followers. Twitter, to be clear, is just an example. Each citizen is, on average, further away from national officials, but national officials have more eyes upon them, on average. It's not clear which is better in terms of accountability.

The discussion thus far has assumed that citizens are directly responsible for holding their representatives accountable. But in the real world, citizens benefit from the work of a variety of nongovernmental and quasi-governmental organizations, some of which are dedicated to keeping government accountable. Organizations that monitor higher-level government officials have more resources, all else equal, because higher-level governments represent more people and, more importantly, more donors. Watchdog and advocacy groups at higher levels benefit from economies of scale. All else equal, lower-level jurisdictions have fewer organized interest groups with fewer resources. For these reasons, it could be that it's harder to keep local officials accountable. At the local level, citizens are far less likely to benefit from professionalized advocacy groups.

The intuition with which we began—that lower-level officials are easier to monitor because they are closer—is therefore questionable at best, mistaken at worst. The one benefit available exclusively at the local level, direct experience, must be weighed against the benefits available at higher levels: more watchmen and specialized organizations. And technology is rapidly eroding the local level's built-in accountability advantage.

We said earlier that there is a sense in which lower-level governments are more accountable because they are more homogenous and therefore can satisfy more of their citizens' preferences. I now want to push back against the accountability aspects of this idea. The question is whether making decisions more locally improves government accountability overall.

It's certainly true—I've conceded as much—that making decisions more locally makes local governments more accountable to *their* citizens.

It's just not clear, however, that this is what matters most. Consider two compelling principles: the all affected and the all subjected principles. According to the all affected principle, everyone who is affected by a government's policies should have a say in what that government does. Similarly, according to the all subjected principle, everyone who is subjected to a government—forced to obey its laws—should play a role in making them. In terms of accountability, government should be accountable to those whom its policies affect, according to the all affected principle, and to those subjected to its rule, according to the all subjected principle.

Localism is interesting in this regard because it narrows each citizen's sphere of authority. When decisions about regulating emissions, for instance, are made by a higher-level government like the nation-state, everyone within the nation-state has some, however small, influence over the outcome. When decisionmaking authority over this issue is transferred from higher- to lower-level governments, however, citizens have greater influence over those decisions in their jurisdiction, but *no* influence over those decisions in any other jurisdiction.

If decisions in one jurisdiction affect people in other jurisdictions, the people in those jurisdictions now have no say in decisions that affect them. I chose regulation of emissions as my example for a reason. Emissions in one jurisdiction are likely to affect the air in neighboring jurisdictions. When Fremont decides to regulate emissions, and Newark chooses not to, the citizens of Fremont are affected by decisions in Newark. (Fremont and Newark are real cities; Newark happens to be surrounded on all sides by Fremont.)

Suppose the regulation in question requires that vehicle owners install an expensive tailpipe filter. Anyone in Fremont caught without a filter has to pay a hefty fine. Yet whenever residents of Newark want to drive anywhere other than Newark, they have to drive through Fremont, which requires tailpipe filters. Newark residents had no part in making that law, however. They are subjected to laws they had no say in.

Fremont is more accountable to residents of Fremont and Newark is more accountable to residents of Newark, but Fremont is not at all accountable to residents of Newark and Newark is not at all accountable to residents of Fremont. Localism generates what I'll call accountability externalities. When we prioritize the local by making decisions, exercising authority, or implementing policy locally or more locally, citizens of neighboring jurisdictions are denied democratic accountability. Accountability is undersupplied in the marketplace.

The way to internalize accountability externalities, as E. E. Schattschneider recognized long ago, though not in those terms, is to expand the scope of the decisionmaking process.[75] Make decisions accountable to everyone affected by them or subjected to them. Localism does precisely the opposite; it makes decisions more accountable to some people while denying accountability to others.

To be clear, it's conceivable that some kinds of decisions do not generate accountability externalities when they are made more locally. These are easy to identify, at least in principle. Decisions made locally that do not affect outsiders, or make outsiders subjects, do not generate accountability externalities. Making these decisions locally improves accountability for insiders without diminishing accountability for outsiders. Outsiders shouldn't care about what does not affect or subject them.

To round out our discussion, I want to suggest that democratic accountability should be assessed from a systemic point of view. In another context, Cass Sunstein has warned of the dangers of *system neglect*: the failure "to see the complex, system-wide effects" of policy interventions.[76] We need to ask ourselves whether increasing accountability in one respect decreases it in another. We shouldn't discount the possibility that prioritizing the local by making decisions, exercising authority, or implementing policy locally or more locally increases local accountability while decreasing accountability overall.

We've covered a lot of ground in this chapter. We've considered whether localism is democratic as such, whether localism promotes political participation, and whether localism facilitates accountability. Surely some of the counterarguments I've developed in this chapter are more convincing than others. At the very least, I hope to have cast serious doubt on the claim that we should prioritize the local by making decisions, exercising authority, or implementing policy locally or more locally because doing so is democratic or promotes democracy. Localism may be defensible on other grounds, but the case from democracy is far from obvious. I hope to have shown that there is nothing especially democratic about politics at the local level. There is no predicable or consistent relationship between the value we care about—democracy—and facts about the world such as size, scale, or distance.

Consider, before turning to the argument for localism from knowledge, that making decisions more locally promotes democracy only if local decisions are made democratically. If decisions are made democratically at higher levels and oligarchically at lower levels, for instance, localism will promote oligarchy rather than democracy. At its simplest, the argument for localism from democracy is conditional on local democracy.

SEVEN

Knowledge

According to a 2018 report from the American Enterprise Institute, *Localism in America: Why We Should Tackle Our Big Challenges at the Local Level*, "local governments are in a unique position to harness data to better self-assess through evidence, as they have access to data and the ability to integrate it more seamlessly."[1]

The idea that local governments are uniquely or especially capable of gathering and using certain kinds of knowledge is not new. Two figures, the economist F. A. Hayek and the anthropologist James Scott, will stand in as representatives of that tradition in what follows.

The kind of knowledge Hayek had in mind was "knowledge of the particular circumstances of time and place . . . of people, of local conditions, and special circumstances."[2] Patsy Healy refers to it as "experiential and craft knowledge of the many different people who 'inhabit' the place in question in one way or another."[3] Hayek believed this was a kind of knowledge "which by its nature cannot enter into statistics."[4]

Knowledge of particulars and of local conditions is necessarily *dispersed*; different people have access to different bits of it. Hayek argued further that no central planner, no matter how sophisticated, could acquire and utilize all of the various pieces of dispersed local knowledge. Only the price system could do that, that "marvel."[5]

Hayek did not explicitly endorse localism in his famous article about the "use of knowledge in society." He did, however, insist upon "some form of decentralization."[6] He claimed, moreover, that because "the economic problem of society is mainly one of rapid adaptation to changes in the particular circumstances of time and place, it would seem to follow that the ultimate decisions must be left to the people who are familiar with these circumstances, who know directly of the relevant changes and of the resources immediately available to meet them."[7]

According to Hayek's localism, then, decisions should be made by those with access to local knowledge rather than by distant bureaucrats. Hayek is of course talking about *economic* decisions, but we can extrapolate a bit and say that *political* decisions should be made by lower-level governments because they are more familiar with the circumstances that matter most in politics: local conditions. As former Speaker of the House of Representatives Tip O'Neill put it, "all politics is local."[8]

Let's pry the argument apart into two pieces. The first is that people have access to different kinds of information depending on their circumstances, specifically their location in physical space. The second is that decisions should be made by those with knowledge of the "particulars of time and place."

Hayek argues that people have access to different kinds of information depending on their circumstances, but also that certain kinds of information are only accessible to people in specific places. One has to be there to know, Hayek would say. This is a strong claim. It drives his critique of central planning. If *only* the "man on the spot" can know things the central planner needs to know, central planning is a fool's errand.

Not only that, Hayek implies that certain kinds of information cannot even be transmitted from the "man on the spot" to others. When he says that local knowledge "by its nature cannot enter into statistics," he means there is simply no way for those who possess knowledge of particulars to pass that information along. I think this is because when Hayek says "particulars," he means it in a philosophical sense. Something is a particular if it cannot be described as an instance of something else. A cat is not a particular because it is an instance of the universal "domesticated feline." *That cat* is a particular because it cannot be fully described by a set of abstract properties. Hayek's thought, then, is that knowledge of particulars cannot be transmitted because abstract properties do not exhaust what's true about particulars. Even a thorough report to the central planning board on the local cat population would leave out the fact that Whiskers goes bonkers for chicken.

If we need knowledge of particulars to decide what's best to do, it follows that decisions should be made by those with special access to them. This is how Hayek gets from the observation about distributed knowledge to localism. Decisions should be made locally whenever the necessary information is accessible only locally.

Note, however, that Hayek's argument for localism relies on two controversial moves. First, he argues that certain kinds of knowledge are only accessible to people in particular places. A weaker but more plausible claim is that certain kinds of information are easier for people to obtain in particular circumstances. The idea that local knowledge is easier to obtain locally is practically a truism. But Hayek's claim is that local knowledge can *only* be obtained locally. Hayek's second controversial claim is that local knowledge is knowledge of particulars. Surely *some* local knowledge concerns particulars, but all of it? If some local knowledge pertains to abstract properties, that knowledge can be transmitted, at least in principle.

Whereas Hayek's point is about the nature of local knowledge and its accessibility, James Scott's in *Seeing Like a State* is about what happens when local knowledge is neglected. In essence, Scott's book is a critique of what he calls "authoritarian high modernism."[9] We have seen something akin to high modernism before; think back to Adam Smith's man of system. According to Scott, high modernism is "a strong (one might even say muscle-bound) version of the beliefs in scientific and technical progress that were associated with industrialization in Western Europe and in North America from roughly 1830 until World War I."[10] It is "a particularly sweeping vision of how the benefits of technical and scientific progress might be applied—usually through the state—in every field of human activity."[11]

High modernist states, in their efforts to render their people and territory "legible," abstract away from what Hayek called the particulars of time and place. In the 1980s, for example, Ethiopia attempted to resettle its population according to high modernist principles. In the Arsi region of Ethiopia, Scott writes, "there was a strict template which local surveyors and administrators were ordered to follow. The plan was carefully replicated in each location, inasmuch as this was not a regime inclined to tolerate local improvisation."[12] The template "would make it that much easier for the authorities to send out general directives, to monitor crop production, and to control the harvest."[13]

The problem was that "massive resettlement nullified a precious legacy of local agricultural and pastoral knowledge."[14] Before they were forced to move, farmers knew what to plant, when to plant it, how to care for their crops, and so on; they had all the place-specific knowledge they needed to feed themselves and their families. Following resettlement, much of their place-specific knowledge became useless. Even with the latest techniques and equipment, it would have taken years for farmers to learn what they already knew back in their old villages. In the meantime, Ethiopians starved to death. Alexander de Waal of Human Rights Watch estimates that "a minimum of about 50,000 people were killed by the resettlement program" alone, implemented, as is the high modernist's custom, in the midst of a famine.[15]

The hubris of it all is paradigmatic high modernism. Ethiopia's planners believed everything would go according to plan, and they did not even consider that something would be lost—lost forever—in the transition. It's not just that they forgot to ask the people what they thought; they didn't even think to ask.

We don't need to go all the way to Africa in the 1980s to find examples of government neglect of local knowledge. We've probably all encountered it in our own lives.

From Scott, then, we learn that governments ignore local knowledge at their own peril. Note, however, that Scott does not argue for local control or localism in our sense: prioritizing the local by making deci-

sions, exercising authority, or implementing policy locally or more locally. Scott, like Adam Smith before him, does not even object to planning as such. He says he is "emphatically not making a blanket case
against either bureaucratic planning or high-modernist ideology."[16]
Rather his argument is "against an imperial or hegemonic planning
mentality that excludes the necessary role of local knowledge and
know-how."[17]

What, then, is the argument for localism *from knowledge*? It is that we
should prioritize the local by making decisions, exercising authority, or
implementing policy locally or more locally because to do otherwise
neglects local knowledge, with potentially disastrous results.

My objection to the argument for localism from knowledge is
simple—and rather benign. My claim is that the conclusion, localism,
does not follow. Critics of localism can, and should, recognize the value
of local knowledge. Nevertheless, taking local knowledge seriously does
not require prioritizing the local by making decisions, exercising authority, or implementing policy locally or more locally.

Before getting to the ways in which higher-level governments can
gather and use local knowledge, I want to respond to Hayek's controversial moves, introduced above. First, that certain kinds of knowledge
are only accessible to people in certain circumstances. Hayek's intuition
here isn't crazy; my objection is to its categorical nature. Is it really true
that some kinds of information are *impossible* to acquire remotely?

Temperature, humidity, air pressure—these are all place-specific
facts. The people in a given place have direct, experiential access to the
approximate temperature, humidity, air pressure, and so on. With some
scientific instruments, they can even get exact readings. But then there's
no reason this information cannot be transmitted to distant officials.
Sometimes central government officials can gather data of this kind even
when no one is there to gather it experientially. Weather conditions in
remote places, for example. Here's a case, then, in which distant officials have special access to "local knowledge."

Presumably, however, there are kinds of information for which the
techniques mentioned will not work. Not everything is like the weather.

Utilitarians, for example, have long dreamed of having direct access to people's feelings. If we could somehow measure how happy people are, or how satisfied they are, or how fulfilled they are, we could design policies to maximize utility, or whatever. This sometimes makes people squeamish because they imagine compulsory brain implants and the attending invasion of privacy. George Orwell's *1984* and Aldous Huxley's *Brave New World* do surreptitious work in this regard.

Even the best brain implants Big Brother can buy won't measure everything, however. They might be able to detect general happiness, but probably not disgust, malaise, despondency, and a range of other fine-grained emotions. In that case, whoever is pulling the strings won't be able to pull all of them.

The real question here is whether the obstacles are technological, ethical, or metaphysical. Hayek's argument goes through if they are metaphysical. If it's metaphysically impossible for people at a distance to obtain necessary local information, central planning founders and flounders. If the obstacles are ethical, we are talking about a completely different argument. And if the obstacles are technological, they can be overcome, in principle. As Richard Epstein writes, local knowledge "can become ineffective in at least some walks of life relative to more systematic, number-crunching attacks on certain problems."[18] Or as Cass Sunstein puts it, "Hayek meant to state a logical truth, but he was really speaking about the epistemological limits of the available tools in his time."[19]

I happen to believe that the relevant obstacles are in large part technological. I don't endorse brain implants, but there are other, more indirect, techniques. There is a vibrant scientific literature dedicated to these kinds of problems, and some progress has been made.

What's more, this line of argument ignores the fact that distant officials can ask people questions. If there are bits of information that only local people can gather, there is nothing stopping them from passing that information along. Unless, of course, transmission is metaphysically impossible.

Even if there are some kinds of information that are metaphysically impossible to acquire at a distance, either directly or by asking people, it could be the case that those kinds of information are irrelevant. It's incredible to believe that all of the local information a government might need is metaphysically impossible to acquire. If I'm right, we'd then want to know how much local knowledge is inaccessible at a distance and how important it is. These are empirical questions.

Hayek's second move, that local knowledge is knowledge of particulars, is controversial because of the contention that transmitting knowledge of particulars is metaphysically impossible. I don't know enough about particulars in Hayek's sense to know whether they are metaphysically impossible to transmit. My guess, however, is that the work is being done by definition. According to this view, particulars are the kinds of things the knowledge of which is impossible to transmit. If that's true, it's impossible to transmit knowledge of particulars. Hayek would still need to show, however, that all local knowledge is knowledge of particulars, or that knowledge of local particulars is sufficiently important and necessary.

To put the point simply: Hayek could be right that some kinds of information are irreducibly local, but it's not obvious that those kinds of information matter. We need to see an argument to the effect that those kinds of information are ubiquitous and essential. Otherwise, distant officials, properly motivated, will be able to get a great deal of the information they need.

I hope I've shown that Hayek's view, as I've interpreted it, is rather strange. He took a reasonable intuition, that certain kinds of information are easier to acquire on the spot, a step too far. I agree that people close to the problem at hand, and affected by it, are likely to notice things that people further away will not. Hayek's observation that knowledge is distributed is unimpeachable.

Scott is also right that governments that ignore local knowledge do so foolishly. Why not just say, then, that governments should take local knowledge into account? Instead of riding roughshod over local peoples, why not consult them?

Consultation should be about ends as well as means. Had Mengistu, former president of Ethiopia, consulted ordinary Ethiopians before proceeding with forced villagization, he would have learned that the people didn't want it. Ethiopians could have told him it wouldn't work or, at the very least, how it could be done with less pain and suffering.

We're drifting toward a point we've encountered several times before. If the problem with high modernism and the spirit of system is that they don't take local knowledge into account, the solution is to take local knowledge into account, not adopt localism. It does not follow that because central governments sometimes do stupid things that central government is necessarily stupid. I'd like to think we've learned something from people like Adam Smith and James Scott. The fact that we've done something poorly in the past does not mean we will do so in the future.

Unless, of course, the disease is chronic. Liberals of a certain disposition are wont to argue that centralized government, by its nature, can't help but ignore local knowledge. The thesis here is that governments, and the officials who run them, never learn. There is just something about government that compels its officials to do stupid things. Being in government distorts incentives; it gives people a false sense of their own powers and delusions of control. Government officials are wont to treat people as means rather than ends, as statistics rather than persons. No matter what the likes of Smith and Scott say, governments will always ignore local knowledge.

This doesn't seem right to me. We can concede some of the pathologies of central government without being fatalistic about them. Identifying pathologies is where work must begin. Is it impossible, in principle, to develop practices that mitigate failures of government?

Less abstractly, are there not ways to *make* government officials attend to local knowledge? I believe there are mechanisms with which we can counteract or mitigate many of governments' dangerous tendencies. This is the very idea behind institutional design, the brainchild of liberalism. We can make government less stupid if we try.

Before jumping to the conclusion that we should prioritize the local by making decisions, exercising authority, or implementing policy locally or more locally because higher-level governments are bad at gathering and using local knowledge, we'd want to know whether local governments are any better. It may be easier for local people to access certain kinds of knowledge, but their local governments aren't necessarily better at collecting it or using it well. Local governments are governments too.

It's a mistake to think local governments acquire local knowledge from their citizens vicariously. Local governments are "closer," but that does not make information transmission automatic. More concerning is the fact that local governments might use local knowledge in ways that harm outsiders. Think resource management. Instead of ensuring that natural resources are used sustainably, local governments might use their special access to local knowledge to plunder the environment more effectively. Local governments may even lack the capacity to use the information they have gathered.

Thus far we've been considering what follows from local government's privileged position with respect to local knowledge. Now we need to ask whether higher-level governments have special privileges of their own. I think they do. Higher-level governments may be at a disadvantage when it comes to gathering local knowledge, but they have the advantage when it comes to collecting, organizing, analyzing, and distributing information from several localities at once.

On this point, it's interesting that Justice Louis Brandeis's suggestion that states operate as laboratories of democracy gets used as an argument for localism.[20] Federalism and localism let individual states and localities experiment with new policies. No one contests that. But we should keep in mind that the argument depends on cross-jurisdictional institutions of some kind. If an experiment works in one place, we need some way of transmitting that fact to other places. The system as a whole only benefits from place-specific experiments if information is shared. It seems, then, that states or localities are only laboratories of democracy if they cooperate with higher-level, integrative institutions.

Experimentation, we might add, requires variation on the independent variable. To be sure that a policy worked in one jurisdiction, we need to be able to compare it to a jurisdiction that did not implement the same policy. We need experimental controls. And it's hard to see how one jurisdiction, operating in isolation, will have the perspective required for causal inference.

That said, localism does not require autarky. Multiple jurisdictions can work together to experiment with new policies. Institutionalized intergovernmental cooperation is ubiquitous, and does not necessarily require participation by higher-level governments. Nevertheless, when intergovernmental cooperation becomes institutionalized, it takes on some of the features of government. And when local governments participate in intergovernmental institutions, they necessarily lose some of their decisionmaking authority. Decisions are made, at least in part, by what amount to "higher-level" institutions. Cooperation requires that decisions be made *less* locally.

Beyond experimentation, higher-level governments perform underappreciated integrative functions. Higher-level bureaucratic agencies serve as depositories of place-specific information. They also, to the extent that they draw on the pooled resources of lower-level governments, have advantages in terms of expertise. Instead of having to keep an army of experts on the payroll, lower-level governments can call upon higher-level government agents when the need arises. Lower-level governments can cut costs by operating within a multilayered political system.

The price of cooperation, however, is a modicum of decisionmaking authority, a point we have seen before. Higher-level governments simply cannot perform their integrative functions with respect to knowledge if lower-level governments have too much power. To collect, organize, and disseminate information, higher-level governments need the authority to make rules and set guidelines. They may require that lower-level governments submit data in a particular format, by a particular time, and in a particular place. These requirements are not necessarily onerous; they do, however, require that some decisions be made less locally.

Just as there is an argument *for* localism from knowledge, there is a corresponding argument *against* localism from knowledge. Different levels of government have distinct advantages with respect to knowledge. Where decisions should be made—locally or at a distance—depends on the balance of advantages and disadvantages.

It's worth repeating that rejecting localism does not require support for central planning or authoritarian high modernism. The insights we've pulled from Hayek and Scott instead recommend cooperation between higher- and lower-level institutions. If localism means only that—that local governments and local people have an indispensable role to play in policy development and implementation—then localism is just plain common sense. But then localism is hardly controversial and there's nothing especially local about it.

We can go one step further. Because local knowledge is important, and because local people have distinct advantages in accessing it, we should think hard about how to institutionalize the collection and implementation of local knowledge. If it's the case, as some liberals argue, that higher-level governments are disposed to ignore local knowledge, we the people should do something about it. We should ask our governments to develop procedures for collecting local knowledge, and we should do our best to make those procedures compatible with incentives—using sticks as well as carrots.[21]

This chapter is shorter than the others because I don't really contest the insights of scholars like F. A. Hayek and James Scott. It's the inferences some people draw that I take issue with.

There really was a time—an entire era before my time—in which people thought they could arrange everything like "the different pieces upon a chess-board." But that time has long passed, in part thanks to the likes of Hayek and Scott.

Do people still say that we can ignore local knowledge? Our error, for the time being, is in the opposite direction—overemphasizing local knowledge and underemphasizing the role higher-level governments play in allowing us to use local knowledge to its utmost.

The local knowledge argument is a victim of its own success. Hayek and Scott have won the game they were playing: to get us to care about local knowledge. Caring about local knowledge does not require localism, however.

EIGHT

Efficiency

We've made it to our final cluster of arguments for localism: arguments grounded in efficiency. Unlike the arguments considered in previous chapters, the argument from efficiency is largely drawn from a single discipline: economics. And like the last chapter, on knowledge, two figures will stand in as representatives of a larger debate, this time Charles Tiebout and Wallace Oates.

In essence, the argument for localism from efficiency says that we should prioritize the local by making decisions, exercising authority, or implementing policy locally or more locally because doing so is more efficient—either in the technical sense meant by economists or the colloquial sense in which "more efficient" means "more effective." Government in general does a better job, the argument goes, when as many tasks and functions as possible are exercised by lower-level governments. Put differently, "the greater the degree of autonomy, the stronger the scope for enhanced efficiency and for efficiency in public spending to be growth enhancing."[1]

You'll notice that the argument from efficiency has a great deal in common with the principle of subsidiarity in the European Union, which we've seen twice already: "In areas which do not fall within its exclusive competence, the Union shall act only if and in so far as the objectives of the proposed action cannot be sufficiently achieved by the Member States, either at [the] central level or at [the] regional and local level, but can rather, by reason of the scale or effects of the proposed action, be better achieved at [the] Union level."[2]

When we discussed subsidiarity in chapter 5, on nature, we were concerned with its interpretation in Catholic social doctrine, according to which tasks and functions should be exercised by lower-level units because it is *proper* for them to do so. In the European Union, by contrast, subsidiarity is all about efficiency and effectiveness.[3] Tasks and functions should be exercised by higher-level units only when they would do so more efficiently. Taken from the other end, subsidiarity in Europe says that tasks and functions should be executed by lower-level units when they can be expected to perform those tasks and functions more efficiently than higher-level governments: the European Union and its member states.

This chapter won't be about subsidiarity, but I mention it because what I have to say about the efficiency argument in general applies to subsidiarity specifically. Subsidiarity is a well-known, institutionalized variant of the argument from efficiency considered here.

Before getting to the argument proper, let's consider in some detail what we mean by efficiency. On the technical side, we first need to distinguish between allocative and productive efficiency. Allocative efficiency refers to the allocation of existing resources. If Jack likes bananas and Diane likes oranges, and Jack has an orange and Diane has a banana, fruit is being allocated inefficiently. It would be better—both Jack and Diane would be happier—if Jack had the banana and Diane had the orange. More preferences would be satisfied if Jack and Diane made a trade. With respect to allocative efficiency, then, the argument for localism says that prioritizing the local by making decisions, exercising authority, or implementing policy locally or more locally makes people better off by allocating resources more efficiently, thereby satisfying more of their preferences.

Productive efficiency, by contrast, refers to the relationship between inputs and outputs in the production of goods and services. Lower-level governments, more so than their higher-level counterparts, are in the service delivery business: sewers, water, streets, libraries, festivals, and so on. Producers, including governments, who make more or better stuff with the same materials are more efficient than their competitors. So are those who make the same stuff, of equal quality, at a lower cost. Here the argument for localism says that in some cases lower-level governments can offer the same or better services at a lower cost than higher-level governments.

With respect to allocative efficiency, we need some way of determining whether one state of affairs is more or less efficient than another. Vilfredo Pareto's famous criterion, according to which an arrangement is efficient if no one can be made better off without making someone else worse off, is attractive but won't do for reasons that will become obvious in a moment.

For the argument for localism from efficiency to have any bite, it will need a weaker criterion such as Kaldor-Hicks efficiency.[4] Most of the time, even good public policies make some people better off and other people worse off. This is why Pareto efficiency is too strict for our purposes; it paralyzes rather than facilitates public policy.

According to the Kaldor-Hicks criterion, by contrast, if under some policy the gains to winners exceed the losses to losers, that policy is more efficient than the status quo. An arrangement is more efficient than another if it produces greater total welfare, regardless of how it is distributed. The argument for localism from allocative efficiency says, therefore, that making decisions more locally will increase aggregate welfare.

Efficiency in the colloquial sense, in which more efficient means more effective, requires no elaboration. Here the argument is that we should make decisions more locally because local governments are better at doing certain things. Typically, the contention is that local governments will do a better job because they are "closer" to the people, whatever that means (we return to this baffling proposition in chapter 9).

Fit

According to Wallace Oates's decentralization theorem, "In the absence of cost-savings from the centralized provision of a [local public] good and of interjurisdictional externalities, the level of welfare will always be at least as high (and typically higher) if Pareto-efficient levels of consumption are provided in each jurisdiction than if any single, uniform level of consumption is maintained across all jurisdictions."[5]

We've been through the logic once before, but it bears repeating. Suppose there's a jurisdiction, let's call it the Twin Cities, composed of St. Paul and Minneapolis, in which 52 percent of the population wants high-quality schools and is willing to pay higher property taxes to get them. The remaining 48 percent would prefer to keep property taxes low.[6] If decisions about education policy are made by the Twin Cities together, as one jurisdiction, maximizing welfare would make 52 percent of its population happy, leaving 48 percent disgruntled.

For the remainder of this example, assume that Minneapolis and St. Paul are geographically distinct and equally populated and make decisions separately, that is, locally. If 60 percent of the population in Minneapolis and 44 percent of the population in St. Paul want high-quality schools, Minneapolis could satisfy the most people by paying for high-quality schools (60 percent) and St. Paul could make the most people happy by keeping taxes low (56 percent). In this case, localism could satisfy 58 percent of the population, whereas centralized decision-making could have satisfied only 52 percent. A miracle!

This is usually what people mean when they say that local governments can tailor their policies to the preferences of their constituents. One size may fit all, but nearly everyone prefers, all else equal, a visit to the tailor. A community of retirees doesn't need to pay for excellent schools; Orthodox Jewish communities don't need or want Sunday closing laws; and rural Montanans don't care much for designated bike lanes. Uniform policies imposed from on high neglect variation in local preferences.

Let's not forget about the decentralization theorem's caveats, however. If in the Twin Cities there are significant economies of scale in the provision of education, centralized provision can work out better than localism. If the consolidated city can eliminate redundancies or reduce overhead, it may be able to provide the high-quality education preferred by 60 percent in Minneapolis and 44 percent in St. Paul, all while keeping costs low, as preferred by 40 percent in Minneapolis and 56 percent in St. Paul.

Things never work out quite that well in the real world, of course, but the thought is that by working together, the Twin Cities may get more bang for their buck. *Any* economies of scale will alter the cost-benefit calculus at the margin, so if the welfare gains from tailoring are small, economies of scale could tip the balance in favor of centralized provision.[7]

Interjurisdictional externalities—when the actions of one jurisdiction affect the welfare of the residents of another—threaten to swamp the gains from local tailoring in another way. Suppose, for instance, that education policy decisions are made locally and that the Minneapolis economy is driven by technology and innovation. Now if Minneapolis and St. Paul share a labor market—if firms in Minneapolis hire workers from St. Paul and vice versa—the labor pool available to companies in Minneapolis will be comparatively less well-educated (remember that St. Paul skimps on education funding). Minneapolis's economy will suffer because of decisions made in St. Paul. And if the welfare losses in Minneapolis (and in St. Paul, since their economies are intertwined) exceed the gains from local tailoring, localism would again be less efficient than centralized provision.

The decentralization theorem's caveats—economies of scale and interjurisdictional externalities—cannot be brushed aside. The meat of the theorem, that decentralized provision is superior to uniform provision, is undoubtedly more interesting than its caveats—indeed, some of its popularity can be traced to its counterintuitive elegance; nevertheless, the caveats limit the scope of efficient decentralization. Note that even if the theorem is true, it's possible that centralized provision is always more efficient than localism.

The decentralization theorem can be challenged in another way. Making decisions more locally increases total welfare *only* when preferences vary geographically. Let me explain: If the proportion of the population that wants high-quality schools in Minneapolis is exactly equal to the proportion in St. Paul, making decisions more locally won't make *anyone* better off. Each local jurisdiction acting separately, as well as the consolidated city, would adopt the exact same policy. Since there are no welfare gains from tailoring in these cases, if there are *any* economies of scale or *any* interjurisdictional externalities, localism will reduce total welfare.

This limits the scope of beneficial decentralization yet again. If everyone living within a higher-level jurisdiction agrees about some policy, localism does nothing. Even if people disagree, if each jurisdiction is a microcosm of the larger unit, localism does nothing.

Beyond geographical variation, economies of scale, and interjurisdictional externalities, we also need to consider the substantive domain—the kinds of policies to which the allocative efficiency argument applies. The argument makes the most sense in policy areas for which implementation is feasible at the local level. Most of the literature on this subject is concerned with public service delivery, which is part but certainly not all of what governments do. When policies do not fit neatly into the public service delivery mold, the argument becomes considerably less tractable.

Anything a government does can be interpreted as a service it delivers to its citizens. The tailoring argument is typically applied to consumption goods, however, because they are more likely to pass muster with respect to the three conditions discussed so far: no economies of scale, no interjurisdictional externalities, and geographical variation.

Authority over something like defense (we almost always say *national* defense—and for a good reason) *could* be transferred to lower-level governments, but it's hard to imagine that doing so would satisfy the three conditions. The economies of scale are obvious. And the positive externalities of providing protection in one jurisdiction would, almost certainly, encourage neighboring jurisdictions to take a free ride. In public goods provision, positive externalities generate shortages of the good in question. Under reasonable assumptions, therefore, protection services would be undersupplied if they were devolved to the local level.

We can tell a similar story about justice and police. Local autonomy in these areas would generate ample opportunities for criminals to get away with their dastardly deeds. If Minneapolis decides to ban marijuana, but St. Paul does not, the Minneapolis police department will have to spend scarce resources policing the cross-jurisdictional marijuana trade. Furthermore, variation in legal regimes imposes cognitive costs on citizens who cross jurisdictional borders. Residents of Fort Lee, New Jersey, who cross the George Washington Bridge into New York City had better remember that turning right on red is always illegal in the Big Apple, unlike everywhere else in the United States.[8]

The point here is that it's entirely possible that tasks and functions are already efficiently allocated in most cases. Goods and services that can be provided efficiently at the local level are typically provided locally, and goods and services that are subject to economies of scale and interjurisdictional externalities are typically provided by higher-level jurisdictions. Welfare gains from reallocating responsibility within an institutional hierarchy (for example, nation, state, county, municipality) are low-hanging fruit, and most low-hanging fruit has already been picked. It would be surprising to find higher-level governments providing services that could be provided more efficiently (and obviously so) at the local level. Good politicians are entrepreneurs, always looking for opportunities to claim credit, as David Mayhew has argued.[9]

If local governments really are more efficient in some policy areas, there will be incentives built in, so to speak, to reallocate decision-making authority accordingly. We don't need to stack the deck in favor of the local, as localism suggests. Unless, of course, there is some ideology distorting our calculations. If we are in the throes of high modernism (see chapter 7), for instance, we may believe, falsely, that higher-level governments are always better. Assuming ideological distortion, then, localism might help rebalance the scales.

Localism can operate ideologically too, however. If localism is taken too far—beyond what the decentralization theorem and its caveats recommend—we'll end up giving local governments authority that would be more efficiently exercised elsewhere. If both ideologies, localism and high-modernist centralization, are debunked (an endeavor I wholeheartedly endorse), there are reasons to believe everything will end up where it should. I'm not normally a booster for markets but here it seems that if there are efficiency gains to be had, the invisible hand will point the way.

I don't want to deny that there is room to maneuver at the margins. Surely in a few cases it would be more efficient to let localities handle policy areas currently under the remit of central governments. The same can be said in the other direction, however. In cases of the latter, we may have underestimated the benefits of economies of scale or the costs of interjurisdictional externalities, in which case centralized provision could be more efficient. Oates's decentralization theorem is also a centralization theorem.

Not only that, the efficiency case for local government "applies to individual service outputs," as Stephen Bailey puts it.[10] The efficient site of local public service delivery is different for different goods, which may not line up with existing jurisdictions. Really, the argument recommends devolving decisionmaking authority over issues one by one, to a different geographical jurisdiction for each. It imagines a proliferation of "special purpose districts," which is problematic because, as Christopher Berry has shown, "an overspending bias emerges when authority over fiscal policy is shared by multiple officials or jurisdictions serving different constituencies."[11]

Finally, the decentralization theorem "only justifies decentralization of choices rather than government *per se*."[12] Efficiency gains come from tailoring, and strictly speaking, it does not matter who does it. The issue here is that many proponents of localism and the decentralization theorem assume that higher-level governments impose policies uniformly. But higher-level governments can provide a unique bundle of local goods and services to each administrative subunit. Doing so has costs, but if they are less than those from diseconomies of scale and interjurisdictional externalities, centrally directed tailoring could work out well in the end.

Until this point, we've been considering whether the decentralization theorem, on its own terms, counts in favor of localism. I now want to consider the argument from a normative (moral or ethical) point of view. Localism is efficient, according to the theorem, because it increases total welfare in the society in question. What is welfare, though? Welfare is utility or well-being. And for economists, welfare is subjective. To avoid technicalities, let's just say that people are better off if they are happier or if more of their preferences are satisfied. People are happier, all else equal, when more things go their way—when good things happen to and for them.

The problem is that some people's preferences are morally objectionable. Some people are happy when other people suffer: psychopaths, for instance. When welfare is subjective, however, all preferences count, and all count equally. Let's return to the Twin Cities. If 36 percent of the people in Minneapolis and 62 percent in St. Paul want *de jure* racial segregation, the consolidated city would ban segregation by a slim margin (49 percent to 51 percent). Under localism, however, segregation would be legalized in St. Paul and banned in Minneapolis.

Alternatively, suppose all Black people and 40 percent of white people oppose segregation. Minneapolis is 10 percent Black and 90 percent white (in this example), so only 46 percent oppose segregation. St. Paul is 30 percent Black and 70 percent white, so 58 percent oppose segregation there. In the consolidated city, segregation lacks majority support (48 percent), but if decisions about segregation and integration are made locally, segregation would be legal in Minneapolis and illegal in St. Paul.

The latter example isn't farfetched. Prior to the Civil War, majorities in the U.S. House of Representatives routinely voted to limit the spread of slavery (the Wilmot Proviso in 1846, for example), but were stopped by the counter-majoritarian Senate. Localism caters to local rather than national majorities.[13] Or as Alexis de Tocqueville put it, "a minority of the nation, dominating the Senate, can completely paralyze the will of the majority, represented by the other house; this is contrary to the spirit of constitutional government."[14]

The decentralization theorem says that localism in these examples increases efficiency. The winners (the racists) gain more than the losers (including Blacks) lose. The fact that more racist preferences are satisfied counts *in favor* of localism, assuming the subjective conception of welfare.

It's not that localism is racist. It's that localism, in its allocative efficiency variant, treats racism as a legitimate preference. All preferences are legitimate because people have them and they are happy when they get what they want.

The foregoing is admittedly a bit crude. We've known about these criticisms of welfare economics for a very long time. People still find the enterprise attractive. Its advantage is that it lets us compare states of affairs according to a single metric: welfare.

Sophisticated forms of consequentialism also allow comparisons, however. It's possible to place constraints on the kinds of utility or preferences that count toward total welfare. We can decide which preferences should count according to our favorite moral theory.

My worry with this argument is that if we add a normative filter to the efficiency argument for localism, it will end up doing unexpected work, work that could count *against* localism. Let's see why, using discrimination as our example. Scholars disagree about what exactly makes racial discrimination wrong, but let's just say that it's wrong to discriminate on the basis of race because race is morally irrelevant. There is nothing about skin color that justifies differential treatment on that basis. It's okay for NASA to discriminate on the basis of mathematical ability, by contrast, because people who work at NASA need to know math. NASA's refusal to hire the innumerate is not arbitrary at all.

If discrimination is treating people according to a morally arbitrary characteristic, race, why isn't localism treating people according to a different morally arbitrary characteristic, location?[15] We addressed this question in chapter 5, on belonging. There I argued that it's harder than you might think to justify place-based discrimination. Perhaps we are permitted to favor those around us because they are implicated in our plans and projects. The fact that particular people are implicated in our plans and projects is not morally arbitrary, after all. They are *our* plans and *our* projects; they are part of who we are.

Nevertheless, we could choose to involve different people in our plans and projects, in which case we would be morally permitted to favor *them*. That is, to some extent, who we choose to associate with is morally arbitrary; treating our associates differently given our association is not.

Surprisingly, perhaps something similar can be said about discrimination on the basis of race. It's wrong to treat people differently on the basis of race because race is morally arbitrary, right? However, racism perpetrated by white people toward Black people over the past 500 years has, unfortunately, made race morally relevant. White people's decision to discriminate on the basis of skin color was morally arbitrary; treating Black people differently—affirmative action, for instance—given the history of racism, is not arbitrary (this is controversial, but that's okay because we're just using discrimination as an example).

But here the history of racism demands a different kind of differential treatment toward Black people. That race is morally relevant for historical reasons does not justify *negative* treatment toward people of color. Rather it demands compensatory or rectificatory treatment.

We might say, abstractly, that morally arbitrary differential treatment in the past generates claims to specific kinds of morally nonarbitrary differential treatment—tailored to past wrongs—in the present. Extending the argument from race to place, morally arbitrary treatment in the past—for example, choosing to associate with people in one place rather than another—generates claims to specific kinds of morally nonarbitrary differential treatment in the present. It may well be that people in places other than our own are morally entitled to special consideration.

That is the problem, I think, with relying on moral side-constraints in an argument premised on aggregate welfare. Once we've admitted moral considerations, we can't arbitrarily exclude some of them, for example, place-based moral entitlements. More generally, the efficiency case for localism "ignores the legitimacy of values other than allocative efficiency."[16] It ignores the legitimacy of values that aren't captured by subjective welfare.

All told, "Oates' theorem cannot be used to justify a particular level of decentralization."[17] Although there are cases at the margin in which prioritizing the local by making decisions, exercising authority, or implementing policy locally or more locally could improve allocative efficiency, I doubt there is all that much low-hanging fruit. Reaching for higher fruit brings costs and risks that may doom the enterprise altogether. Whatever the decentralization theorem shows, it does not generate a strong argument for localism. Rather than an argument for localism, the decentralization theorem draws attention to one relevant consideration: allocative efficiency.

Sorting

Wallace Oates's decentralization theorem is all about allocative efficiency or, more colloquially, fit. Charles Tiebout's theory is about sorting, by contrast. Fit and sorting are sometimes jumbled together, but each relies on a separate mechanism. For Oates, the mechanism is, unsurprisingly, decentralization. For Tiebout, it is what Albert O. Hirschman called exit.[18]

Tiebout argued, convincingly, that when the residents of one jurisdiction can pack up their things and move elsewhere, local governments take note. In the market for private goods and services, when people don't like a particular product, they buy something else. In the market for local public goods and services, when people don't like what they're getting, they move someplace else. At the local level, people "vote with their feet."

With respect to public goods, consumers are required to "buy," with their tax dollars, the bundle of goods and services offered by the relevant jurisdiction; if they want to buy a different bundle, they need to move. In economic theory, Tiebout's contribution was to show that the possibility of exit reveals consumers' preferences and allows them to be satisfied, "in the same sense that a private goods market does," that is, efficiently.[19]

Two things are supposed to happen when people pick their governments. First, local governments will operate as efficiently as possible, so as not to lose residents and their tax dollars. They will strive for productive efficiency. If schools in Minneapolis and St. Paul are equally good but Minneapolis charges less in taxes, residents of St. Paul have a good reason to move across the river.

Second, the threat of exit is thought to keep local governments accountable to their taxpaying residents. In the previous section, we saw that tailoring policy to local residents' preferences *can* increase total welfare, not that local governments *will* take their residents' preferences into account. Foot voting gives local government officials an incentive to tailor. If a local government doesn't do what its residents want, they and their money will leave, with detrimental effects on the local economy and the local budget. Without sufficient tax revenue, local officials will be out of work. Note that this mechanism works to keep local officials accountable even if they are unelected or no one votes; this is why this kind of accountability is considered here rather than in chapter 6 on democracy.

The threat of exit does more. It encourages local officials to determine what their constituents want, but it also fights corruption, graft, waste, and slack. It promotes thrift, transparency, accessibility, efficiency, and more; it promotes good government. Some might even argue that foot voting works better than ordinary voting. Hirschman's voice—voting—only works to keep government accountable when the voters understand the issues, pay attention, and go to the polls. With local turnout rates as low as they are, at least in the United States, voice alone would give officials too many opportunities to cut corners or skim off the top. Foot voting is so effective, the argument goes, because the threat of exit does the work that voting sometimes fails to do. Money is louder than voice, one might say.

Foot voting also lets those residents who don't like what their government is doing, even if it's doing it effectively, move somewhere that better fits their tastes. If retirees don't like paying high taxes for excellent schools, they can move somewhere less invested in education. If people in Salt Lake City want to smoke marijuana legally, they can move to Denver or Las Vegas; residents of Colorado Springs who don't like that smell can move north to Wyoming (for now).

The phenomenon is usually known as sorting, most famously described in Bill Bishop's *The Big Sort*.[20] People sort themselves into jurisdictions that offer bundles of services that fit their tastes. More jurisdictions mean the potential for a tighter fit between residents' preferences and services offered. At the upper limit, the number of jurisdictions equal to the number of distinct preference profiles, everyone gets exactly what they want (à la Thoreau and Emerson). The lower limit, a single jurisdiction, is equivalent to centralized provision, which is inefficient for the reasons discussed in the previous section.

Fit and sorting end up working in tandem, at least in theory. As people move from jurisdiction to jurisdiction, looking for the best bundle of taxes and services (for them), they end up living among people like them. Sorting makes jurisdictions more homogenous, internally. It also generates variation between jurisdictions. I like Gregory Weiher's term, eccentricity, because it "indicates not that the population is uniform, but that it is distinguishable from others in terms of the distribution of some characteristic," in this case preferences.[21] Sorting makes jurisdictions more eccentric and more homogenous.

Imagine, in our first Twin Cities example, that everyone in St. Paul who wants high-quality schools moves to Minneapolis, and everyone in Minneapolis who likes low taxes moves to St. Paul. Now when Minneapolis invests in education and St. Paul keeps taxes low, everyone is happy. Without tailoring or sorting, only 52 percent of the Twin Cities get what they want. With tailoring, that number rises to 58 percent; with tailoring *and* sorting, it rises to 100 percent.

It bears repeating that it is highly unlikely that sorting will be perfect in this way for every public good or service. We'd have to assume that jurisdictional boundaries line up perfectly with geographical concentrations of identical preferences. It might require an odd degree of central planning to get jurisdictional boundaries exactly right. Perhaps boundaries would shift over time in response to market pressures; inefficiencies in the short term would be unavoidable though.

Tiebout's theory is now quite old—his original paper appeared in 1956—and has been attacked on many fronts, so not everything I have to say here is new. I do, however, want to flesh out the theory's implications (or lack thereof) for localism. It's important to recognize, moreover, that the theory is an exemplar of armchair economics. It's a clever theoretical solution to a theoretical problem: competitive equilibrium in the market for public goods. Tiebout himself calls the theory a "conceptual solution."[22] My sense is that Tiebout's followers have granted the theory more significance than its creator ever would have. (Tiebout died in 1968.) The theory has taken on a life of its own, much like Frankenstein's monster.

As before, let's consider theoretical issues first, normative issues second. All theories in economics make theoretical assumptions, of course, but Tiebout's "requires a series of demanding assumptions, many of which are unlikely ever to hold."[23] The following is a nonrandom sample of Tiebout's assumptions, reproduced from Daniel Treisman's *The Architecture of Government.*[24]

1. Individuals can move costlessly between communities.
2. In deciding where to live, individuals care only about differences in local public policies.
   2.1 There is no land and no housing (so tax differentials across localities are not capitalized into real estate prices.)
   2.2 Individuals do not care who their neighbors are.
   2.3 They have no historical, cultural, or aesthetic attachments to particular localities.
3. Individuals have perfect information about the public policies of all localities.
4. There are no public policy externalities across communities.

We'll consider assumptions 2 and 4 in detail here and assumptions 1 and 3 a bit later.[25] Under assumption 2, people decide where to live based on the bundles of local goods, services, and taxes offered in each jurisdiction. Assumption 2.2, then, says that differences in the quality and price of bundles of local goods and services are not captured by (capitalized into) real estate prices.

Imagine, returning to our Twin Cities example, that Minneapolis and St. Paul offer schools of equal quality but Minneapolis charges only half (in property taxes) what St. Paul charges. If differences between the two bundles are not captured by real estate prices, residents of St. Paul have a clear incentive to move to Minneapolis, and St. Paul has an incentive to cut costs to retain taxpaying residents.

There are, however, good reasons to believe that the quality and price of bundles of local goods and services affect real estate prices.[26] The fact that Minneapolis can provide schools as good as those in St. Paul, at a fraction of the cost, makes real estate more desirable and therefore more valuable in Minneapolis. All else equal, people would be willing to pay a bit more (up to the present value of the difference in property taxes) to live in Minneapolis.

Alternatively, note that if residents of St. Paul see that they can get a better deal in Minneapolis and decide to move there, real estate prices in Minneapolis will rise because of increased demand. Real estate prices will rise until people are indifferent between living in Minneapolis, with its superior bundle of local public goods and higher real estate prices, and St. Paul, with its inferior bundle of local public goods and lower real estate prices.

Only relative real estate values matter here. If the public school system in St. Paul is headed in the wrong direction, real estate prices in St. Paul will fall relative to neighboring jurisdictions. Residents of St. Paul will then find that their homes are worth less than before, meaning that they can get less house for their money should they wish to move elsewhere. There's no such thing as a free lunch.

If we assume that real estate prices are sensitive to the quality and price of local public goods and responsive to changes in quality or price, real estate prices will reflect any differences between policy bundles offered by each jurisdiction. In this case, most people—except those with idiosyncratic preferences—will be indifferent between staying and going.[27] That is, if public policy differentials are capitalized into real estate prices, Tiebout's theory founders.[28] Threats to move would be empty except in rare cases, and public officials would know it. Only those residents whose preferences for idiosyncratic features of jurisdictions were particularly strong would move, and such moves would not provide much useful information for local officials.

Wallace Oates, a pioneer of fiscal federalism and our advocate for the tailoring argument, has presented empirical evidence suggesting that policy differentials *are* capitalized into property prices in the real world. In a sample of New Jersey municipalities, Oates found that "local property values bear a significant negative relationship to the effective tax rate and a significant positive correlation with expenditure per pupil in the public schools."[29] In other words, lower taxes and better schools translate into higher property values: capitalization. So much for accountability through exit.

Now consider assumption 4, that there are no public policy externalities across communities. Assumption 4 is critical for Tiebout's argument, though less so than assumption 2.2. Without assumption 2.2, the whole edifice comes crashing down. Without assumption 4, it stays upright but doesn't inspire awe.

For sorting to work perfectly, people must decide where to live based on the quality of bundles of services and taxes offered in each jurisdiction (assumption 2). However, if there are cross-jurisdictional externalities, some of what residents observe about their communities will be attributable to policy choices in *other* jurisdictions. If Minneapolis builds a fancy new light rail system, fueling economic growth, St. Paul will reap some of the benefits. A company like Google might decide to build a new office complex in Minneapolis, offering thousands of new high paying jobs, some of which would be filled by residents of St. Paul. But now St. Paul will be a more desirable place to live for reasons unrelated to the bundle of taxes and services it offers. Externalities make signals of quality in the market for local public goods noisy.

This example involves a positive externality. Suppose, in an example of a negative externality, that Minneapolis decides to build a cheap water treatment facility that does a great job for Minneapolis residents, but dumps its waste into St. Paul's water supply. St. Paul will now need to upgrade its own facilities, at a substantial cost, which will be passed on to local residents in higher property taxes. (This is just an example; it's not how water treatment is typically financed.[30])

When St. Paul residents see their property taxes jump, they could decide to punish their officials for mismanagement. Residents of St. Paul could even move to Minneapolis, even though it's Minneapolis that's the problem. Minneapolis officials are rewarded, and St. Paul's officials are chastised, for Minneapolis's bad behavior. Externalities generate inefficiencies in the market for local public goods. If efficiency losses from externalities exceed efficiency gains from sorting, there will be an efficiency-based argument for implementing policy *less* locally.

The scholarly literature on interjurisdictional externalities tends to focus on fiscal externalities, especially the spillover effects of tax competition. Fiscal externalities arise when "each government independently (or 'non cooperatively') chooses its tax or subsidy policies to maximize the welfare of residents within the region, and its choice affects the size of the tax bases available to other governments."[31] The paradigmatic example is when governments lure capital to their jurisdictions by slashing taxes; neighboring jurisdictions lose tax revenue when their residents or businesses relocate. Neighboring jurisdictions must then lower their tax rates to compete. The proverbial "race to the bottom" generates inefficiently low tax rates throughout the region. And inefficiently low tax rates translate into public goods shortages. John Wilson, in an extensive review of the tax competition literature, concludes that "the original insight that tax competition can lead to inefficiently low taxes and public goods levels has been shown to hold in more general settings than originally investigated."[32]

Externalities are not a serious problem for Tiebout's sorting argument if they are rare or small. Unfortunately, the empirical literature addressing these issues is sparse. It's extremely difficult to calculate the magnitude of spillover effects, even with the best data.[33] And we know even less about the *frequency* of interjurisdictional externalities; intuitively, they appear to be ubiquitous.

The problem may be worse than it looks. Most studies of externalities are concerned with what Christopher Berry calls horizontal externalities, which arise as a result of "competition among multiple nonoverlapping governments for a mobile tax base."[34] Vertical externalities, by contrast, arise "from the vertical layering of jurisdictions on top of one another rather than the horizontal partitioning of territory into competing units."[35] Berry uses the proliferation of special purpose governments in the United States to study vertical externalities. Special purpose governments are usually single purpose governments handling schools, drainage, mosquito abatement, parks, fire protection, and so on. General purpose governments, by contrast, provide a range of services for everyone residing within their borders.

As we've seen already, competition between general purpose governments generates economically inefficient spillover effects. Consider, further, that when multiple, overlapping special purpose governments draw on the same tax base, they have an incentive to charge too much. To see why, consider an example: overfishing. Fish are scarce, and if you catch too many at any given time, there won't be enough to reproduce the next generation. Ideally, fisherfolk would agree among themselves to catch a limited number—enough to keep the fish population stable. But if fisherfolk act independently (in jargon, noncooperatively), each has an incentive to catch more than their fair share. If one fisherfolk catches a few more fish, she makes more money and has only a marginal effect on the population of fish. Problems arise only when enough fisherfolk adopt the same logic. Overfishing is rational individually, but irrational collectively.

Fish are a "common pool resource." So is local tax revenue. Each special purpose government, acting independently, has an incentive to take a bit more than its efficient share. When enough overlapping special purpose districts adopt the same logic, cumulative taxes are inefficiently high. Berry corroborates the logic with data, concluding that "increasing the extent of jurisdictional overlap in a county from the 25th to the 75th percentile—that is, increasing from two to five overlapping jurisdictions per municipality—results in a $130 increase in own-source revenue per capita."[36]

What does this mean for localism, which, as we know, recommends that public policy should be implemented more locally? If it means devolving tasks and functions to independent general purpose governments, we'll run into horizontal externalities. If it means reassigning tasks to a series of hyperlocal special purpose governments, we'll run into vertical externalities. Transferring decisionmaking authority from a large, centralized jurisdiction to a multitude of smaller, local jurisdictions multiplies potential externalities.

We return to evidence at the end of the chapter, but here it's sufficient to say that the jury is definitely still out on externalities. Even if
the capitalization problem were magically resolved, we'd still want to
know whether spillover effects—horizontal and vertical—negate the potential benefits of interjurisdictional competition.

For the remainder of this section, let's assume, in sympathy with Tiebout,
that public policy differentials are *not* capitalized into real estate prices
and that interjurisdictional externalities are rare or small or both. Let's
also weaken assumption 1, that individuals can move costlessly between
communities, and assumption 3, that individuals have perfect information about the public policies of all localities. Both are wildly implausible, but since I want to move on to normative issues, let's just say that
moving costs aren't always prohibitive and that the information needed
to make informed decisions is at least available.

My normative concerns are primarily distributive in nature. *Cui bono?*
The discussion of capitalization and real estate prices should have sent
up a red flag. As of the first quarter of 2021, 65.6 percent of families in
the United States owned their homes; the remaining 34.4 percent were
renters or homeless.[37] Since it is property owners who pay property taxes,
only they pay for local public goods directly. Of course, owners of rental
units take property taxes into account when they decide how much to
charge in rent. It would be difficult to argue, however, that owners and
renters evaluate the market for public goods and services in precisely the
same way. If we assume that homeowners own their homes outright or
make fixed mortgage payments, changes in their housing costs will be
attributable to changes in their home's assessed value or property tax
rates, both of which are directly observable by homeowners. For renters, by contrast, rent increases could be the result of any number of
factors: property tax hikes, increased demand, supply shocks, and so on.
Renters, in short, will have a harder time knowing when to hold their
local officials accountable.

The Tiebout mechanism depends on the actions of homeowners: a
pugnacious and unruly lot. And hardly representative. Again, as of the
first quarter of 2021, 73.8 percent of non-Hispanic whites, 45.1 percent

of Blacks, and 49.3 percent of Hispanics owned their homes.[38] In families with an income above the median, 79.4 percent of households were owner-occupied, whereas only 51.7 percent of those below the median were.[39] Finally, 38.1 percent of those younger than thirty-five years of age were homeowners as compared to 79.3 percent of those over sixty-five.[40] Typical homeowners are old, white, and comparatively well off.

Homeowners are like the busybodies we met in the democracy chapter: they are good at getting what they want—what's best for *them*. If we think localism is a good idea because it keeps local governments accountable, it has to matter that the Tiebout mechanism makes local governments accountable to homeowners. William Fischel thinks this counts in favor of Tiebout, but he claims, drawing on work by Denise DiPasquale and Edward Glaser, that homeowners are "more conscientious citizens."[41] Maybe so, but unless homeowners faithfully represent the interests of renters, which seems doubtful, local governments can be expected to advance the interests of some, but not all, of their constituents.

It's possible, however, that homeowners will do a decent job; perhaps when it comes to local government, the interests of homeowners and renters are pretty much the same. But that's preposterous. To see why, consider another example of the "race to the bottom" phenomenon: redistribution to the poor. As Paul Peterson tells it, communities that raise property taxes to fight poverty are inevitably subjected to capital flight. Some property owners don't like paying more in taxes to benefit people other than themselves, and if some of them (it doesn't have to be everyone) move to jurisdictions that better match their preferences (pocketbooks), their former jurisdictions will need to raise taxes again (engendering more capital flight) or cut spending to balance their books.[42]

With respect to redistribution, then, the interests of homeowners, who are more likely to be rich, and the interests of renters, who are more likely to be poor, are diametrically opposed. According to standard economic theory, however, if demand for rental housing is perfectly inelastic—if the price of housing has no effect whatsoever on the quantity of housing demanded (a standard example of an inelastic good is insulin)—renters bear the entire burden of property taxes on owners. That is, given perfectly inelastic demand, increases in property taxes are fully passed on to tenants. Renters would then feel the effects of property taxes just like homeowners.

In practice, however, demand for rental housing is not perfectly inelastic. If it were, we'd never see people living on the streets. When demand is elastic, at least some of the burden of property taxes falls on owners. If we then assume that the additional tax revenue is used to pay for direct transfers to renters (redistribution), renters will end up better off. In this extremely simple model, some of what property owners pay in additional taxes lines the pockets of renters, the beneficiaries of redistribution. Presumably, renters would favor, and owners would oppose, a scheme of this kind. Then it really matters that local governments are responsive to owners rather than renters.

Note, furthermore, that when people can move from jurisdiction to jurisdiction, as in Tiebout's model, demand for housing will *not* be perfectly inelastic. If a property tax hike increases the price of rental housing in one community, its residents can move someplace cheaper (in jargon, housing in the two communities are substitutes). According to Richard W. England, citing work by Robert J. Carroll and John Yinger, in a recent review of the property tax incidence literature, "if tenants are perfectly mobile and if the price elasticity of demand for rental housing is infinite, then landlords alone bear the burden of any tax hike."[43] And if landlords bear *any* of the burden of a tax hike, and tax hikes are used to pay for services that benefit renters, landlords will favor low taxes and meager benefits while renters will prefer higher taxes and generous benefits. If local governments cater to wealthy landlords rather than poor renters, the poor lose: a normative quandary.

Assumption 1, that individuals can move costlessly between communities, raises similar distributive concerns. The simplest is that while moving is relatively easy for rich people, moving costs can be downright prohibitive for poorer people. Poor people are therefore less likely to be able to take advantage of welfare-enhancing sorting. If taxes go up, or if the quality of social services declines, rich people can "vote with their feet," but the poor are stuck.

According to the American Moving & Storage Association, it costs an average of $2,300 to move in-state and $5,630 between states.[44] In 2019, the median value of transaction accounts (checking, savings, money market, call accounts, and prepaid debit cards) for all families with holdings in the United States was $5,300, according to Federal Reserve data.[45] Families with income in the bottom (fifth) quintile had an average of $810 in their transaction accounts; families in the fourth quintile had $2,050 on average; and families in the third quintile had $4,320.[46] Among renters, the median family's transaction accounts contained $1,640.[47] This means that two in five families in the United States cannot afford to move in-state and at least three of five cannot afford to move between states. The median renter can barely afford an in-state move.

There is, therefore, every reason to believe that adding moving costs to Tiebout's model would generate income stratification. Richer people can afford to move, with their taxable assets, to jurisdictions offering superior bundles of local public goods and services. Poorer people, who cannot afford to move, are left behind in jurisdictions with fewer valuable assets to tax. The original jurisdiction (from where the rich moved), now with a smaller property tax base (the value of land and buildings), must raise tax rates or cut social services. Instead of saying that "Tiebout sorting" lets people move to jurisdictions that better match their preferences, we might as well say that it lets rich people abandon the unwashed masses.[48]

In a formal model, the economist Stephen Durlauf has shown that when a community's income distribution influences "individual occupational attainment," and therefore income for future generations, and when "families choose which neighborhoods in which to live, ... uniformly poor and prosperous communities can emerge among a population of initially nonpoor families."[49] Durlauf calls it a "theory of persistent income inequality," in which Tiebout sorting plays a starring role.

The Pew Research Center's residential income segregation index (RISI), which is calculated by "adding together the share of lower-income households living in a majority lower-income tract and the share of upper-income households living in a majority upper-income tract," increased from 32 in 1980 to 46 in 2010.[50] In other words, more poor people were living with other poor people and more rich people were living with other rich people in 2010 than in 1980.

Interestingly, geographical income segregation has increased during a period in which geographical mobility has been decreasing (since the late 1980s).[51] One might have thought that decreasing mobility would lead to less sorting and therefore less income stratification. However, as Timothy Noah suggests, people are moving less *because* they cannot afford to: real incomes have stagnated while home values have risen.[52] According to Charlynn Burd, "the decrease in the overall mover rate was partially driven by declining mover rates for renters."[53] From 2017 to 2018, families living below the poverty line were more likely to move (16.1 percent versus 9.3 percent), but families above the poverty line made up 80.3 percent of movers.[54] Arguably, then, trends in mobility and residential income segregation corroborate my point: that Tiebout sorting is a rich man's game. So let's call a spade a spade. Tiebout sorting and, by extension, localism can be bad (at least relatively) for poor people.

Last but not least, assumption 3: that individuals have perfect information about the public policies of all localities. We've already weakened the assumption to allow imperfect information. We said that the information needed to make informed decisions is at least available. The question, just as before, is available to whom?

Tiebout sorting relies on *choice*. Residents choose the communities that best match their preferences; they choose by staying or going. Sorting doesn't happen unless people sort themselves.

Choice is a shot in the dark unless the chooser is informed. Economic theory, at least the kind motivating Tiebout and his followers, requires that consumers make informed decisions. When Volkswagen installed "defeat devices" (a way of circumventing emissions regulations) in 11 million of their diesel fueled cars, consumers had no idea they were emitting up to forty times the acceptable level of nitrogen oxide.[55] Some of them would have bought Toyotas or Fiats, or regular gasoline VWs, had they known. At the very least, the cars and the company were overvalued. After the news finally broke in 2015, Volkswagen "reported its first quarterly loss in at least 15 years" and is now being forced to buy back its faulty cars.[56]

In some ways, communities are like cars; it's hard to know when you have a nitrogen oxide-spewing lemon. Even when everyone follows the rules, it's hard to know whether to buy a Pontiac Aztek or a Honda CR-V, both crossover sport utility vehicles released around the turn of the century. *Car and Driver* called the latter "a gold mine on wheels" and the former (deliberately misspelled, apparently) "an irredeemable shit heap."[57]

Some people know a thing or two about cars, however. Regular readers of *Car and Driver* or *Road and Track* (like my father) would have known to pick the Honda. The car buying neophyte would have been more likely to get themselves stuck with the Pontiac (it was the prize awarded to Richard Hatch on the first season of *Survivor*). To make a long story short, some people have access to more and better information than others.

While some people know a lot about the market for cars, others know a lot about the market for communities. In the latter, differential access to information "creates an asymmetry in the sorting process."[58] "High resource settlers," as Gregory Weiher calls them, "undertake a different strategy of housing search than low resource settlers. Their wealth permits them to indulge different preferences than those less advantaged, and they are likely to seek different information."[59] Weiher adds, moreover, that geographically based income segregation is the product of "not only the segregation of the least advantaged, but the aggregation of the most advantaged."[60] The most advantaged are advantaged in terms of wealth and education, of course, but also free time,[61] social networks,[62] and access to little known sources of useful information. They know what kinds of information they are looking for and where to find it. To add insult to injury, once concentrations of poor people become identifiable as such, viz. ghettoes, they effectively *become* information that some can use, others will exploit, and still others must endure.[63]

Tiebout-style sorting is about choosing communities, but it is also, at the same time, about choosing schools and school systems. In the United States, for public schools at least, children usually go to schools near their homes, in their neighborhoods. In fact, many people choose their communities because of their schools.

Because of the similarities and overlap between school choice and jurisdiction choice, it's worth looking at what scholars of the former have to say. Gary Orfield, the preeminent scholar of school segregation, and his colleague Erica Frankenberg, recently edited a book titled *Educational Delusions: Why Choice Can Deepen Inequality and How to Make Schools Fair*, which one reviewer argued "ought to be required reading for anyone who cares about our children and the public schools that serve them."[64]

According to Orfield and Frankenberg, "the market theory of choice," which, I add, also motivates Tiebout sorting, "presupposes that there are good choices, that information is rich and fairly distributed, and that the most disadvantaged families and those with far more resources and contacts will equally understand and have access to the best choices."[65] Orfield and Frankenberg add that "research shows that this set of assumptions has no basis in fact."[66] Indeed, "more-privileged families clearly make better use of choice opportunities and have much better information about them."[67] According to survey data gathered in Louisville, Kentucky, which instituted a new school choice plan in 2009, "black and poor residents were more likely to not know about their options, to use fewer information sources, and to submit choice applications late."[68]

What does this all mean? Richer people are more likely to have the capital they need to buy homes in desirable jurisdictions, more likely to have funds on hand to finance a move, and more likely to obtain the information they need to decide where to move. Poorer people, by contrast, are often left behind in decaying communities. Homes in undesirable jurisdictions are worth less, so even if poorer people own their homes, they are less likely to be able to afford housing somewhere more desirable. They are less likely to have cash on hand to hire movers, or even to rent a truck. Last but not least, they are less likely to know where to move.

We should add that good information is even more essential for poorer families. Those on a tight budget would really want to know where homes in "up and coming" neighborhoods are undervalued. But as we know from the phenomenon of gentrification, it is the young, well-educated, and well-informed who are most likely to take advantage of these opportunities.

Take Harlem brownstones as an example. In 2016, the *New York Times* ran a story with the headline, "The End of Black Harlem." The author of the piece, Michael Henry Adams, tells a heart-wrenching story. He was, as he says, "picketing a fund-raiser for a politician who was pushing for denser mixed-use zoning along 125th Street," when a few boys from the neighborhood rode up on their bikes and asked, "Why are y'all yelling that?" When the protestors told the boys that New York City was encouraging new housing and taller buildings in the area, one of the boys turned to his friends and said, "You see, I told you they didn't plant those trees for us."[69] When that little boy grows up, beats the odds, goes to college, and decides to major in economics, he may end up repeating himself: "Tiebout sorting is not for us."

Even if Tiebout sorting works the way its boosters say it should, we're faced with a difficult trade-off: efficiency versus equity. For a mechanism like Tiebout sorting to improve efficiency, according to the Kaldor-Hicks criterion, gains to winners must exceed losses to losers. But Kaldor-Hicks improvements are only *Pareto* improvements—that is, make someone better off without making anyone worse off—if the winners compensate the losers. That hardly ever happens. If it did, somehow, we can guess who would compensate whom; we can guess who would be no better off than before.

Experimentation

According to the efficiency argument for localism, we should empower local governments by granting them more authority or assigning them additional tasks because doing so increases aggregate welfare. The argument thus far has been that local governments are more efficient because they can tailor their policies to their constituents' preferences (fit) and because people are free to move to the jurisdictions they like best (sorting).

A further thought is that independent, relatively autonomous local governments are free to experiment with new policies in ways that large, centralized governments cannot. We briefly touched on the logic of the experimentation argument in the previous chapter, where we saw that distributing the lessons learned from experimentation requires inter-jurisdictional cooperation. Here, however, I want to interrogate the intuitions behind the experimentation argument directly.

Experimentation belongs with efficiency because when local governments are free to experiment, they may stumble upon new, more efficient ways of doing things, which they can then share with their neighbors. I consider experimentation separately from fit and sorting because experimentation can improve efficiency even if people can't move or governments can't tailor policy to local preference. Welfare gains from experimentation are separable from gains from fit or sorting.

One way to think about experimentation at the local level is to return to Alexis de Tocqueville's distinction between administrative and governmental centralization.[70] Under administrative centralization, local government officials are agents of the central state. Their job is to administer, as directed, policies decided upon by higher-level governments. Local governments are therefore not free to experiment under administrative centralization.

They are, however, free to experiment under administrative *decentralization*. Administrative decentralization is compatible with governmental centralization, as Tocqueville observed in the antebellum United States. Centralized governments can set objectives and guidelines while also granting local governments discretion in implementation. As Tocqueville put it in his discussion of the town: "To be sure, the town's actions are strictly circumscribed, but within limits its movements are free."[71]

Discretion opens the door to experimentation. It is in the interest of local communities to implement policy efficiently; if local officials think they know a better way, they are free to try it. Adding fit and sorting, local governments that implement successful experiments gain an advantage against their competitors; they can gain residents and expand their tax base.

Administrative decentralization is also compatible with governmental decentralization, as in a federal system. When government and administration are both decentralized, local governments can decide what to do and how to do it. They are not subjected to objectives or guidelines from higher-level governments. Arguably, this means that local governments have even more freedom to experiment. Without higher-level governments looking over their shoulders, local governments are free to try anything they want.

It matters that experimentation is possible under both governmental decentralization and governmental centralization. If the argument for localism is that it grants local governments the freedom to experiment, both do the job localists want done.

We've been led into a conceptual quandary, however. Does localism *require* governmental decentralization? According to our definition, I think not. Localism, for our purposes in this book, is prioritizing the local by making decisions, exercising authority, or implementing policy locally or more locally. Administrative decentralization, even without governmental decentralization, allows local governments to make more decisions, exercise more authority, and play a larger role in implementing policy than under administrative centralization.

Of course, administrative decentralization combined with governmental decentralization would let local governments make even more decisions, exercise even more authority, and implement policies even more to their liking. But now we're talking about matters of degree, not a categorical difference. Conceptually, localism requires only administrative decentralization. Note, furthermore, that complete administrative decentralization combined with complete governmental decentralization would amount to sovereignty, not localism. Complete decentralization makes Westphalian states.

The argument for localism from experimentation, as we've seen, counts in favor of administrative decentralization but not necessarily governmental decentralization. To get the efficiency benefits of experimentation, local governments need the discretion to experiment. It's not yet clear what kind of discretion they need, or how much.

Gregory Clark has developed a useful fourfold typology—he calls it a theory of local autonomy—that supplements Tocqueville's. Instead of distinguishing between government and administration, centralization and decentralization, Clark specifies two distinct facets of autonomy: initiative and immunity. Initiative is the power—and I mean power, not authority—of localities to decide upon and implement policies; immunity is the "power of localities to act without fear of the oversight authority of higher tiers of the state."[72]

To experiment, local governments need the power of initiative in the relevant policy domain. That much is clear. What's less clear is whether local governments need immunity. Presumably, some experiments would go through without a hitch even without it. Others would trigger oversight by higher levels of government. We can also imagine experiments being completed before higher-level governments have a chance to intercede, or cases in which higher-level governments choose not to intercede.

Recreational marijuana legalization in Colorado is a perfect example. Colorado had the power of initiative: it could direct its law enforcement officials to allow people to use the drug. It did not have the power of immunity. Marijuana is still illegal under federal law, causing headaches for buyers and sellers alike. And it is still an open question, at least in the legal literature, whether the national government can "commandeer" state officials; that is, make them enforce federal law.[73]

Marijuana legalization was so successful in Colorado that as of 2021, seventeen states and the District of Columbia have followed suit.[74] The online magazine *Thrillist* suggests there are "26 countries where weed is, if not legal, at least super chill and legal-ish."[75] It's reasonable to conclude—unavoidable, I think—that policy experimentation requires initiative but not immunity.

There are, moreover, very good reasons to deny local governments the power of immunity. Americans, especially southerners and African-Americans, know full well what local "experimentation" can look like. All state governments had the power of initiative to conduct the experiments to which I refer; the "strange career of Jim Crow"[76] began in the late 1870s, when federal troops withdrew from the South, along with their oversight authority. The Southern states held their immunity from federal oversight for at least another seventy-five years. In 1954, the Supreme Court declared school segregation unconstitutional in *Brown v. Board of Education*, beginning years of halting and arduous oversight by federal courts.

Oversight by higher-level governments is clearly beneficial in some cases, as Reconstruction (1865–1877) and court directed desegregation (1954–2007) demonstrate.[77] To claim, therefore, that local governments need immunity in addition to initiative, it would have to be the case that the costs of higher-level government oversight exceed the benefits. That would be a hard circle to square.

One cost of oversight is the chance that higher-level governments will make mistakes. Higher-level governments could quash local government policies that would have done a lot of good. Another cost is the chilling effect on experimentation. Local governments could choose to forego experiments they believe might trigger higher-level government oversight. Consider, however, that some chilling is a good thing; local governments should be wary of violating the Fourteenth Amendment to the U.S. Constitution (equal protection of the laws), for example.

This problem calls for cost-benefit analysis of some kind. Do the costs of mistaken oversight exceed the benefits of successful oversight? Does the opportunity for oversight significantly mitigate the costs of experimentation? Are there benefits associated with uniform policy implementation? These are difficult questions. That they are difficult counts against the case for localism. Instead of concluding that we should prioritize the local by making decisions, exercising authority, or implementing policy locally or more locally because doing so encourages beneficial experimentation, it would be wiser, I think, to attempt to answer the questions just posed.

In the chapter on tyranny, we talked a lot about separation of powers, checks, and balances. There we were concerned with checks among co-equal branches of the central government (legislative, executive, judicial) and checks on the central state from lower-level governments. We didn't say much, because they are not much discussed, about checks on lower-level governments from higher-level governments. If we are really concerned about tyranny, however, and if we think that dividing power works to prevent despotism, why not encourage checks on lower-level governments by higher-level governments, what I have been calling oversight? Clint Bolick documents the problem of local despotism in *Grassroots Tyranny: The Limits of Federalism*, so I needn't say anything more here.[78]

Let me review the experimentation argument thus far. We've seen that conceptually, localism does not require governmental decentralization in addition to administrative decentralization. The argument for localism from experimentation requires discretion, for which administrative decentralization is sufficient. Nor is immunity from higher-level government oversight necessary for local experimentation. Immunity can be pernicious, too.

Now let's consider the claim that administrative decentralization does not facilitate *enough* experimentation, and by adding governmental decentralism, localism closes the gap. The claim can be spun out in a couple different ways. Perhaps administrative decentralization doesn't give local governments enough room to maneuver. Administrative decentralization permits experimentation within the bounds set by higher-level government officials. If the most promising experiments fall outside those bounds, administrative decentralization may not do the trick.

The proposal to reform the Medicaid program (low-income health insurance) in the United States by replacing categorical grants to states with block grants is a potential example. It's a bit tricky, however, because of complexities in U.S. Constitutional law. Categorical grants to the states specify guidelines as to how the money granted should be used. States are required to cover everyone in what are called "mandatory eligibility groups." States may choose, if they wish, "to cover other groups, such as individuals receiving home and community-based services and children in foster care who are not otherwise eligible."[79] Block grants, by contrast, provide a lump sum to be used as the states see fit.

Strictly speaking, healthcare is under the remit of the states, not the national government. On paper, healthcare is an example of governmental decentralization—the states get to decide what to do. The national government wiggles around the problem by offering money to the states on condition that they cover the mandatory eligibility groups. Because the money is too good to pass up—state officials would be crazy not to take it—the national government has essentially usurped governmental authority. In practice, then, the current program is an example of governmental centralization combined with a degree of administrative decentralization. Under the categorical grant scheme, the national government sets policy, and states may choose whether to do more than required.

Replacing categorical grants with block grants would effectively restore governmental authority to the states. States could then choose what to do and how to do it, with fiscal support from the national government. A well-rehearsed argument for Medicaid block grants is that they would encourage the states to experiment. If states receive a lump sum with no strings attached, they have an incentive to cut costs. States might use some of the money to fight poverty, reducing the number of sick poor people. This would accomplish the broad goals of the policy, to keep people from suffering because they are poor, by reducing the number of poor people rather than treating poor people who become sick. Block grants would allow the states to experiment with policies of this kind; categorical grants do not. We'd have to run the numbers, but if a dollar spent fighting poverty would save two dollars treating poor people, the experiment would be a resounding success.

The thought behind the example is that the current policy—governmental centralization combined with administrative decentralization—does not provide *enough* freedom for the states to experiment. Instituting block grants, effectively restoring governmental decentralization, would provide the requisite freedom, or so the argument goes.

Whether governmental decentralization in healthcare, block grants in this case, would increase aggregate welfare is an open question. It really depends on the facts. Are the experiments requiring governmental decentralization really that promising? It's the low-hanging fruit problem all over again. If a policy were really that great, why wouldn't the national government try it?

This is a good place to mention that higher-level governments can experiment too. The national government is fully capable of developing pilot programs on its own or with the cooperation of lower-level governments. The argument for localism assumes, it seems, that only local governments have good ideas—or that they refuse to share them.

To make a long story short, local governments need discretion, but not localism, to experiment. If there are extremely promising policy ideas out there that require greater discretion, or even a degree of autonomy, national government officials have an incentive to grant it. National governments succeed when their constituent parts succeed. I worry that the argument for localism assumes ineptitude or malevolence on the part of national government officials and ingenuity and benevolence on the part of local government officials.

The localist has one more bullet in the chamber. Perhaps I have the argument for localism from experimentation all wrong. All localism requires, according to this maneuver, is administrative decentralization. It could be said that my attempt to pin ambitions for governmental decentralization on localism is disingenuous.

But if all localism requires is a degree of administrative decentralization, I'm a localist, and so is almost everyone else. We've seen this point before. It would be downright stupid to deny administrative decentralization altogether. The question, as with anything else important, is: How much? It's a hard question that localism—according to some interpretations—makes too easy. Answering it requires detailed study. In what policy areas would greater discretion encourage beneficial experimentation? In what areas would greater discretion open the doors to inefficiency and injustice? Can the experiment be conducted with extensive higher-level government oversight? Can the national government conduct the experiment more efficiently itself?

Normatively, I think we'd all agree that there are some policy areas for which experimentation is wholly inappropriate. Rights protection is one example. In the United States, the Fourteenth Amendment exists to prohibit experimentation with people's freedom and dignity. The International Declaration of Human Rights exists to discourage certain kinds of experimentation as well. We've tried racism, sexism, homophobia, and genocide before; no one should be allowed to try them again.

Experimentation is appropriate in some areas but not others, and I don't think efficiency can settle the matter. This is a political question. We must decide *together* what we should be allowed to do separately, in our own communities. Of course, we think communities should be able to do exactly as they wish sometimes, but not all the time. The status of a group of people as a community does not supersede what we owe to each other.

Evidence

Evidence for the supposed positive relationship between decentralization and efficiency is mixed at best; at worst, the relationship goes the other direction. As Andrés Rodríguez-Pose and Adala Bwire summarize the literature: "in general, empirical analyses of the link between devolution and efficiency and economic growth emphasize that it varies from country to country, and is contingent upon underlying national characteristics such as income levels, the quality of institutions and the institutional structure, and country size."[80]

Rodríguez-Pose and Bwire, looking at decentralization in Germany, India, Italy, Mexico, Spain, and the United States, were led to "reject the hypothesis of a positive link between devolution and greater economic performance in all cases."[81] Roberto Ezcurra and Rodríguez-Pose found that in OECD countries, "the connection between fiscal decentralization and economic performance is negative, significant and robust to the inclusion of measurements of political and administrative decentralization and of a number of control variables."[82] The connection between administrative decentralization and growth was also negative, but "weaker and less robust than that of fiscal decentralization."[83] Yolanda Ubago Martínez, Pedro Pascual Arzoz, and Belén Iráizoz Apezteguía, also studying OECD countries, "show that fiscal decentralization of expenditure and revenue has a negative impact on technical efficiency; that is, countries that are more decentralized show lower levels of technical efficiency."[84]

Admittedly these are studies of the relationship between decentralization and economic growth, not efficiency. But efficiency is hard to measure, in part because it is concerned with welfare, which is notoriously difficult to measure. That said, you'd expect efficiency to improve economic performance. Technical efficiency is about using resources more efficiently; when fewer inputs are used to produce the same output, the unused inputs can be used to make or do something else, with positive effects on the economy.

Allocative efficiency from jurisdictional sorting means that people are getting the bundles of local goods and services they want, at the right price. They are no longer paying for things they don't want, and they're getting what they're willing to pay for. Surplus generated by efficiency can be used to produce additional private goods and services.

It's not really a problem, then, that studies of decentralization use economic growth rather than efficiency. If decentralization were more efficient than centralization, you'd expect places with decentralization to grow faster than places with centralization, all else equal. Of course, all else is never equal, but these studies are heroic in their attempt to control for confounding variables. The results of a quasi-natural experiment in China suggest that "fiscal decentralization does not necessarily make local governments more responsive to the long-term benefits of local residents."[85]

I have not attempted a comprehensive review of the massive and sprawling literatures on decentralization, economic performance, and efficiency. The fact that serious scholars employing sophisticated techniques, some friendly to the theoretical argument, find mixed results is sufficient to cast doubt on the argument for localism from efficiency.

Nevertheless, it's possible that decentralization has been implemented under suboptimal conditions. New, more sophisticated techniques may demonstrate a link between efficiency and localism in the future. For now, we just don't know. My view, however, is that until we have moderately consistent evidence to support the link between decentralization and efficiency, the argument for localism from efficiency should be kept on ice.

Theoretical work by Susan Rose-Ackerman, Daniel Treisman, and Hongbin Cai suggests that the relationship between localism and experimentation is hardly straightforward. Rose-Ackerman's model "predicts that few useful experiments will be carried out" by state and local governments.[86] One reason is that politicians need to get reelected, so prefer not to take the risks that experimentation—especially long-term experiments—require. Another is that "in a multiple government system the overall incentive to take risks is reduced if the politician hopes to free ride on the activities of other governments."[87] Politicians want the benefits of experimentation but without paying the costs (in money and risk). Experimentation is undersupplied, an economist might say.

In the model developed by Treisman and Cai, "candidates compete for office by credibly promising to enact policies, which can be either experimental or those of the *status quo*."[88] Under decentralization, elections are held in each subnational jurisdiction, whereas under centralization, "candidates compete for votes nationwide by proposing a set of local policies, one for each district."[89] The model shows that "compared to the social optimum, centralization tends to produce too much experimentation, while decentralization generally leads to too little."[90]

Decentralization leads to too little experimentation, echoing Rose-Ackerman, because local governments want to learn from their neighbors without experimenting themselves. Centralization leads to *too much* experimentation because national-level politicians can try risky experiments in a few districts without paying an electoral cost. National-level politicians don't need to win everywhere to win nationally, so they can experiment where they are weakest electorally. The model also suggests that under decentralization local governments may "duplicate each other's efforts, choosing the same, most-promising experiment," whereas "the central government picks a variety of experiments to increase the chance of useful discoveries."[91]

The evidence for the argument for localism from experimentation is therefore just as sketchy as that for the arguments from fit (Oates) and sorting (Tiebout). Decentralization permits experimentation, sure, but it does not guarantee that local governments will conduct useful experiments. Central governments can experiment and, as I suggested in the previous chapter, they have advantages with respect to case selection, coordination, analysis, and dissemination.

All told, the argument for localism from efficiency is a promising dead end. But it's really not all that surprising. Why should we expect the factors that promote economic efficiency to line up, so to speak, with localism? Decentralization promotes efficiency, if it ever does, under an extremely demanding set of conditions. It seems to me a better bet to try to satisfy the conditions that promote efficiency directly, rather than working through an unreliable proxy. And that's setting normative concerns aside. Add those, and the case for localism from efficiency looks pretty grim.

PART IV

Against Localism and Beyond

NINE

Against Localism

In the previous six chapters, we've considered arguments for localism—from tyranny, belonging, nature, democracy, knowledge, and efficiency—in isolation, one at a time. Chapter 2 argued that this was the best way to proceed, given the nature of our subject. Localism is too big and too complicated to approach all at once. Now we need to consider whether localism makes sense, all things considered.

I should stress that nothing I've said against localism amounts to proof. I've had to use my judgment. In many cases, I've introduced countervailing considerations that muddy the waters rather than challenging localism directly.

When philosophers say that something is good or justified "all things considered," they mean good or justified on balance, given all the relevant considerations, which may point in opposite directions. The considerations themselves, in isolation, are called *pro tanto* considerations. As Maria Alvarez explains, "if a reason favours my doing something, then I have a 'pro-tanto' reason to do it: it is pro tanto (i.e., to that extent) right for me to do it."[1] As Alvarez suggests, the fact that a joke is funny is a *pro tanto* reason to tell it—a consideration in favor of telling it.

Localism introduces a lot of *pro tanto* considerations in favor of prioritizing the local. For example, if it's true that making decisions more locally "affords citizens an opportunity to participate in decisionmaking," we have a *pro tanto* reason to do so.[2]

Localism seems more persuasive than it deserves to be because its proponents emphasize the considerations *in favor* of localism while deemphasizing, ignoring, or belittling the considerations *against* localism. Much of this book shines a bright light on the considerations against localism. As Alvarez adds, the fact that a joke will embarrass someone is a *pro tanto* reason not to tell it.

Should I tell the joke? The joke is funny, which gives me a reason to tell it. But the joke will embarrass someone, which gives me a reason to shut my mouth. Whether I should tell the joke depends on which reason is stronger. Most of us would say I shouldn't tell it.

Whether we should accept localism, or any of the arguments in its favor, depends on whether the considerations in favor of localism reliably outweigh or defeat the considerations against it. When the considerations against localism are ignored, the case for localism stands unopposed. Introducing countervailing considerations makes everything a whole lot harder but far more realistic. Balancing reasons is not an exact science.[3]

I don't think we actually need to demonstrate conclusively that the considerations against localism defeat the considerations in its favor. That would be really hard. Rather, I think it's enough for us to show that the case for localism has *not* demonstrated that the considerations in its favor reliably defeat or outweigh the considerations against it.

It's proponents of localism who have claimed that we should prioritize the local by making decisions, exercising authority, or implementing policy locally or more locally. The onus should be on them to show that prioritizing the local by making decisions, exercising authority, or implementing policy locally or more locally is justified.

If my position in this book were the obverse of localism, that we should make decisions, exercise authority, or implement policy *less* locally, the onus would be on *me* to show that making decisions, exercising authority, or implementing policy less locally is justified. I would need to show that the considerations against localism reliably outweigh the considerations in its favor.

But that is not my position. My claim is not, and never has been, that we should never make decisions locally. It's that we don't have strong reasons to adopt localism as a presumption in favor of the local. If we had strong reasons to believe that the considerations in favor of making decisions locally or more locally reliably outweigh the considerations against making decisions locally or more locally, localism would be justified, by my own admission. But our reasons don't come out reliably in either direction.

The examples I gave in the preface—that localism has exasperated school segregation in the United States and the availability of affordable housing in the United Kingdom—were meant to raise the stakes for localism. If the stakes are trivial, say I'm deciding whether to go on vacation to Arizona or Florida, it's okay to choose Arizona even though reasons don't balance out reliably in favor of Arizona over Florida. In fact, when the stakes are trivial, hunches are fine. Hunches are not fine when the stakes include rights, welfare, and the public good.

With stakes such as these, the victims of localism are entitled to hear the reasons for these assumptions and hunches. To be clear, localism does not need to show that the considerations in favor of prioritizing the local by making decisions, exercising authority, or implementing policy locally or more locally *always* outweigh the considerations against prioritizing the local. That would be a ridiculously high standard.

To endorse localism, I think we need good reasons to believe that the considerations in favor of prioritizing the local by making decisions, exercising authority, or implementing policy locally or more locally outweigh the considerations against prioritizing the local *consistently, reliably, or predictably enough* to justify the risk that we are wrong or will do wrong. Our presumption in favor of the local must be reliable. We need to have good reason to believe that prioritizing the local by making decisions, exercising authority, or implementing policy locally or more locally does enough good overall to justify the harm it does when it does harm. The greater the risks, the stronger the case for localism needs to be.

I am not recommending a strict cost-benefit calculus. If I were, it would be a matter of comparing the expected benefits of localism against its expected costs. The problem with the cost-benefit approach is that it's mind-bogglingly difficult to ascertain the expected costs and benefits of something as complicated and abstract as localism. Proponents of localism argue as if the expected benefits were clear and large. Typically, they do not say much about expected costs. I've argued that the expected benefits of localism are hardly obvious, and that, if they exist, they are not as large as many proponents of localism insist.

One way to put the problem is that with what we now know, localism is a shot in the dark. We have a lot of reasons to think localism *could* do good for people, but we know very little about the conditions under which localism *will* do good for people. This book makes a plea for epistemic humility. Until we know more, let's hold off on localism or proceed with caution.

I don't want to give the impression that all I've done in this book is introduce countervailing considerations. I've also pointed out where and when the various arguments for localism go astray on their own terms.

Since I've already introduced *pro tanto* reasons, we may as well avail ourselves of another bit of philosophical jargon: *prima facie* reasons. As Shelley Kagan explains in *The Limits of Morality*, "a prima facie reason *appears* to be a reason, but may actually not be a reason at all, or may not have weight in all cases it appears to."[4] *Pro tanto* reasons are real reasons. Some *prima facie* reasons are real reasons, too; other *prima facie* reasons are fake reasons—not actually reasons at all.

Some philosophers use these terms differently, and that's fine; all that matters is that we distinguish between genuine reasons that count in favor of something and reasons that seem to count in favor of something but don't. Many of the arguments we've seen in this book make use of the latter, what Kagan and I call *prima facie* reasons.

Believing the joke is funny is a *prima facie* reason to tell it. But if the joke is not funny, there is no reason to tell it, no reason at all. Telling the joke may have seemed like a good idea because you thought, erroneously, that it was funny. Bad reasons are not reasons because they are not considerations in favor of doing the thing you thought you had reason to do. Since what you thought were reasons to tell the joke aren't actually reasons, once you introduce the *pro tanto* reasons against telling the joke—that it would embarrass someone—it's obvious that you shouldn't tell it.

Consider an example from the efficiency chapter. Say you've been led to believe that prioritizing the local by making decisions, exercising authority, or implementing policy locally or more locally in relatively autonomous local jurisdictions is a good idea because doing so is more efficient than centralized decisionmaking. Little did you know, though, that the decisions you want to make locally would have sizable positive spillover effects on neighboring communities. Perhaps you want the authority to decide locally because you want to require that factories install state-of-the-art pollution reduction technology. But then a neighboring jurisdiction, which also has the authority to decide locally, decides to free-ride on your jurisdiction's efforts. The neighboring community scraps its own pollution reduction plans because your community's fancy technology will do a good enough job on its own. Now your jurisdiction has spent a great deal of money for not much pollution reduction. You were mistaken to believe that making decisions about pollution more locally would be more efficient. You thought you had a reason, but you didn't.

Consider another example, from the democracy chapter. You think it would be a good idea to make decisions more locally because those decisions would be more democratic—more democratic insofar as they would give ordinary people greater control over their lives. However, it turns out that your local government is controlled by a party machine, a warlord and his cronies, a military junto, or the Chamber of Commerce. Under these conditions, you would have preferred "the master far away to the exploitation and cruelty of the smaller master near at hand," to quote Franklin Roosevelt once again.[5] You thought you had a reason to make decisions more locally, but on reflection, you realize you didn't.

Sometimes matters aren't so simple. In the belonging chapter, we encountered the claim that we should prioritize the local by buying local products. Under certain conditions, I think you really do have reasons to "buy local." If by buying local you increase overall economic output—by spurring new economic activity, for example—you have a genuine reason to buy local products.

The reason would be a *pro tanto* reason, however. The fact that buying locally would increase economic output would be a genuine consideration in favor of doing so; that does not mean there aren't countervailing reasons against buying locally. Maybe buying locally generates a bunch of new, high-value products that cater to upper-middle-class millennials (a far-fetched example, I know). That may lead to the collapse of the market for comparable low-value products, once the lifeblood of less well-off neighboring communities. Buying locally will have increased overall economic output while distributing it unequally and perhaps unjustly.

Under different conditions, which seem to me to cover the vast majority of cases, buying locally just means not buying somewhere else. If buying locally means local producers get the business that would have gone to producers in other communities—remember that every community is a local community for the people who live there—one community benefits while others suffer. If buying locally does not increase overall economic output, the question is whether the fact that it's your own community that stands to benefit counts as a reason to buy local.

Perhaps. Some people go further; they say that if buying locally makes your community better off, even if it harms other communities more than it helps yours, you have a reason to buy locally. I have difficulty sympathizing with this view. It's not even putting yourself first in a zero-sum game; it's putting yourself first in world that's worse off, overall, because you're better off.

If my actions don't make the world worse off, overall, what's wrong with doing the best I can for myself and my community? If you agree with this line of reasoning, you'll have a reason, a *pro tanto* reason, to buy locally. You'll of course have an additional *pro tanto* reason against buying locally: because doing so will harm a seller somewhere else. You'll then have to decide which reason is stronger. I happen to think the reasons are equally weighty and, therefore, that you don't have an "all things considered" reason to buy locally. But others disagree.

Some arguments for localism, as we've seen, rely on *pro tanto* reasons. *Pro tanto* reasons to prioritize the local by making decisions, exercising authority, or implementing policy locally or more locally are genuine considerations in favor of doing so. However, to repeat what I said earlier, whether we should prioritize the local depends on whether the *pro tanto* reasons in favor of making decisions locally or more locally are stronger than the *pro tanto* reasons in favor of doing otherwise.

Other arguments for localism rely on reasons that turn out not to be reasons at all. In these cases, we can say that we were wrong, epistemically speaking, to think our stated reasons were considerations in favor of prioritizing the local. *Prima facie* reasons to make decisions more locally that turn out not be reasons at all don't count in favor of making decisions more locally. Fake reasons in favor of making decisions more locally are always defeated by real reasons.

Still other arguments for localism depend on reasons that are good epistemically but bad normatively (morally or ethically). If I'm a racist, the fact that making decisions more locally allows me and my friends to discriminate against members of other races counts as a consideration in favor of making decisions more locally (for me).[6] Nevertheless, we want to be able to say that my racist reasons don't count, morally, as considerations in favor of making decisions more locally. I might have other reasons, but the racist reasons shouldn't count.[7]

If the reasons we have to make decisions more locally are normatively bad, they don't count as considerations in favor of making decisions more locally. In the previous chapters, we've seen when and where the case for localism relies on normatively objectionable reasons.

My case against localism, then, is built on three considerations. First, the reasons we have to prioritize the local by making decisions, exercising authority, or implementing policy locally or more locally are genuine reasons, but those reasons don't reliably outweigh other genuine reasons, countervailing reasons, against making decisions more locally. Second, the reasons we have to prioritize the local by making decisions, exercising authority, or implementing policy locally or more locally aren't genuine reasons; they seem like real reasons, but they aren't. Third, the reasons we have to prioritize the local by making decisions, exercising authority, or implementing policy locally or more locally are objectionable, normatively; they are reasons that could count but shouldn't.

Now it's time to step back and consider whether localism is justified, considering all six arguments at once. I've attempted to make the strongest possible case against each argument: from tyranny, belonging, nature, democracy, knowledge, and efficiency. I believe each argument is weak and should be rejected. Nevertheless, I want to grant, for the sake of argument, that I've missed something. Perhaps I've been too critical in places.

Specifically, I want to grant that one or several of the arguments considered in this book really do count in favor of prioritizing the local by making decisions, exercising authority, or implementing policy locally or more locally. I hope I'm not wrong about all of them. If I'm right about some, but not all, we'll need some way to determine whether we should endorse localism, given that one or some of the arguments genuinely count in its favor.

We can start by asking whether the arguments that count in favor of localism outweigh those that do not, on balance. Here we need to establish and then compare the weight of each argument, for or against localism. In my view, some arguments are weightier than others. The arguments from democracy, belonging, and tyranny seem especially important. If I'm right about the arguments from nature, efficiency, and knowledge but wrong about the arguments from democracy, belonging, and despotism, it wouldn't be crazy to endorse localism.

It would be a mistake, however, to conclude that localism is an unalloyed good in this scenario. Localism would be good for democracy and belonging, and for preventing tyranny, but bad for efficiency and knowledge. We'd do well to recognize localism's drawbacks.

In other scenarios, in which the arguments that support localism are less weighty than those that do not, we could reasonably conclude that localism—as a presumption in favor of the local—should be rejected. If the arguments that support localism and those that oppose it are equally weighty, we'll be in a tough spot.

So far, we've been assuming that the six arguments for localism operate independently. It seems quite likely, however, that some of the arguments work against each other. For instance, it's possible that when the argument from democracy counts in favor of localism, the argument from efficiency won't, and vice versa. Or when the argument from nature counts in favor of localism, the argument from knowledge will not, and so on.

Recall that one of our strategies in chapters 3 through 8 was to specify some of the conditions under which the argument counts in favor of localism, and then to argue that they are extremely demanding. It would be an incredibly unlikely coincidence if the conditions were the same for each and every argument. If the conditions are different for different arguments, as it seems reasonable to assume, satisfying the conditions for one argument could *preclude* satisfying them for another.

We touched on an example of the preclusion problem in the democracy chapter. There we decided that for localism to promote political participation by ordinary citizens, the decisions being made locally would have to be consequential. People aren't likely to get involved in politics if the decisions they would make are trivial. Now consider the argument for localism from efficiency. Making decisions more locally is more efficient, absent economies of scale and interjurisdictional externalities. But if the issues that matter most to people—the ones that make them want to get involved in politics—are more likely to be subject to economies of scale or interjurisdictional externalities, localism can't promote both values, democracy and efficiency, at the same time.

This is a long way of saying that even if each argument for localism is plausible, independent of the others, it would be surprising if they worked together harmoniously. Adding an additional argument for localism doesn't necessarily strengthen the case for localism overall. Here our challenge is not to compare the strength of the arguments in favor of localism with the strength of the arguments against it, but to choose which arguments to use. If the conditions for all six arguments cannot be satisfied simultaneously, we need to decide which ones to count, and jettison the others. Claiming them all at once would be disingenuous.

Once again, we'll be forced to admit that localism is not an unalloyed good. We'll want to recognize that localism promotes certain values while undermining others. Then, whether we should endorse localism depends on which values we want to promote. Even so, something is lost; localism isn't a free lunch.

For eight and a half chapters, I've been skirting around a formidable objection to my position in this book. We've been operating under the assumption that localism is intended as a general presumption in favor of prioritizing the local by making decisions, exercising authority, or implementing policy locally or more locally.

The objection is that I'm wrong to characterize localism in this way. Someone could say that localism is *not* intended as general presumption. Localism, according to this view, simply introduces a number of considerations in favor—*pro tanto* considerations—of doing things locally or more locally. It doesn't say that localism is justified, or even that there is a presumption in its favor. Not only that, the objection claims that localism recognizes that the benefits of localism accrue under certain conditions and that some of these conditions are quite demanding. Localism, in short, is much more modest than I've presented it.

If this is localism, I'm wrong to have criticized it as I have. I've been going on and on about an extreme version of localism that no one actually supports. However, if what I've just described is localism, I don't understand what all the fuss is about. If that's localism, there's a massive disconnect between the principle and its discourse. Proponents of localism certainly write and talk *as if* it were a generally applicable principle. It's even strange to use a word like localism, with its revealing suffix, to refer to a set of considerations or guidelines.

My response to the objection helps round out our discussion of how the six arguments for localism fit together. In the chapter thus far, we've assumed that the arguments ultimately point in one direction or the other, for or against localism. Perhaps they don't, however. If I'm wrong about one or a few of the arguments, there are some respects in which we should prioritize the local by making decisions, exercising authority, or implementing policy locally or more locally and some respects in which we shouldn't. Whether we should, in particular cases, make decisions more locally then depends on how the arguments apply in particular circumstances.

But now we're not talking about localism, if localism is what we've said it is. We're talking about a set of practical principles, guidelines, or rules of thumb that help us decide what to do in particular cases. The principles say that if we care about certain values, and if certain conditions obtain, making decisions more locally could help. The principles also say that if we care about other values, and if particular conditions don't obtain, we shouldn't make decisions locally or more locally. Localism becomes a decision algorithm of sorts rather than a presumption favoring the local.

I have absolutely no objection to practical principles, guidelines, or rules of thumb. I believe, nevertheless, that my objections in chapters 3 through 8 demonstrate that some of these principles are mistaken. I've shown that even as practical principles many arguments for localism don't make sense.

If localism amounts to a set of practical principles—a set of guidelines—for determining when decisions should be made more locally, less locally, or neither, the enthusiasm for localism we're seeing is misplaced. Why get excited about a set of guidelines that don't actually favor the local? Why call a set of guidelines that specify some conditions under which making decisions more locally could make people's lives go better *localism*? Why does localism announce itself as a presumption favoring the local when it really does no such thing?

Skeptics of my position in this book who have made it this far may think I've made a mountain out of a mole hill—that my objection is to *dogmatic* localism rather than *sensible* localism. It isn't. Even so, ideas have minds of their own. Dogmatic localism crowds public discourse, leaving little room for its more sensible variants. Sensible localism isn't particularly exciting, so its murmurs have trouble being heard over the shouts of its dogmatic cousin.

Ordinary people—those who don't read academic periodicals—are far more likely to encounter localism in its dogmatic forms. They see bumper stickers, t-shirts, and labels at supermarkets lauding the local. Can we blame them for thinking localism is as good as it says it is? Won't they believe dogmatic localism is localism? That's reason enough to concern ourselves with what people actually say rather than what they could or should have said.

Some of my friends and colleagues have told me that I'm going after a straw man. They say that the kind of localism I critique in this book doesn't exist. They say that there are better arguments out there. I don't agree. As you've noticed, I've done a lot of hard work to make localism look as sensible as possible. I've had to fill in what my colleagues say are the "real" arguments.

It would be a serious mistake to assume that the best arguments are the ones people use and the ones that matter politically. We shouldn't let localism off the hook because its proponents *could* have made better arguments, especially because the good arguments support something quite different than localism as it is often understood.

Academic philosophers in the analytic tradition adhere to what they call the principle of charity. According to the *Oxford Dictionary of Philosophy*, the principle of charity "constrains the interpreter to maximize the truth or rationality in the subject's sayings."[8] It's a good principle for philosophy, and has its place in works of applied ethics, political theory, or political philosophy like this one. It can be taken too far though. If charity bars us from examining the arguments people actually use—the ones that affect people's decisions and judgments—it can prop up what should be torn down.

Even if this book fails to do what I most want it to do—convince scholars, pundits, commentators, practitioners, and people in general that localism is misleading at best and mistaken at worst—I'll consider it a success if it encourages proponents of localism to revisit their arguments to strengthen them. In fact, I think what I've done to reconstruct the various arguments for localism in chapters 3 through 8 could help its proponents do just that.

If localism is to remain on the political agenda, and I think it will, it should do so with its best foot forward. Localism deserves a hard-nosed, analytically rigorous, and empirically sophisticated defense. In the next chapter, the conclusion, I offer suggestions for localism from the perspective of a skeptic. I'm not going to refashion the arguments for localism out of whole cloth, but I will indicate some pitfalls localism should do its best to avoid. I think localism is mistaken, but also that it can make fewer mistakes than it currently does. It can do better.

TEN

Beyond Localism

Back in chapter 1, I promised to speculate a bit about why localism is so popular. I think it's because we tend to like what's near more than what's far away. Surely that affects our attitude toward localism. If localism is prioritizing the local by making decisions, exercising authority, or implementing policy locally or more locally, perhaps we believe it because we are drawn, psychologically, to what's local.

What I am about to say really is speculative. In the *Treatise of Human Nature*, David Hume argued that even if we are convinced that a distant "object excels" an object nearby, "we are not able to regulate our actions by this judgment; but yield to the sollicitations of our passions, which always plead in favour of whatever is near and contiguous."[1] Our preference for the local is a passion; our reason sometimes yields to it.

David A. O'Connor and his colleagues at the University of Melbourne have since corroborated Hume's contention using contemporary experimental techniques. They have shown "that behavioral responses to rewarding objects are influenced by their position in near or far space."[2] In one of their experiments, "participants made faster and more accurate decisions for objects associated with high reward; however, this improvement was diminished when the same objects were presented in far space."[3] In other words, people react better to rewards that are nearby.

According to construal level theory in social psychology, "psychologically distant events are represented more by their essential, general, and prototypical features (high-level construals) and psychologically near events are represented in terms of their incidental, specific, and unique features (low-level construals)."[4] This corroborates what I have said on multiple occasions: the local is more familiar and more concrete. People also "expect events in distant locations to more strongly resemble prototypical events, which are relatively schematic and abstract."[5]

In another fascinating experiment, conducted by Lawrence E. Williams and John A. Bargh, participants were asked to plot two sets of coordinates on a Cartesian grid. For the first treatment, the points were close to each other (the closeness prime); for the second, they were far apart (the distance prime); and for the third, they were "halfway between those used for the closeness and distance primes" (the intermediate prime).[6] Participants then read an excerpt from a book depicting embarrassment. Subjects who plotted points that were close together (the closeness prime) liked the excerpt less than those who plotted points that were far apart (the distance prime). Not only that, participants exposed to the intermediate prime liked the excerpt more than those exposed to the closeness prime. Incredibly, the distance between two points marked on a piece of paper affected participants' evaluation of the excerpt. Keeping embarrassment at a distance, even in the abstract, makes it less uncomfortable.

In a second experiment, Williams and Bargh found that "people primed with a sense of spatial distance report less negative affect" in response to a violent film "than people primed with a sense of spatial closeness."[7] More important for our purposes in this book, Williams and Bargh discovered, in a third experiment, that "when people are primed with a sense of spatial distance, rather than closeness, they report weaker bonds to their siblings, parents, and hometown."[8] Williams and Bargh therefore demonstrate experimentally that in our minds physical proximity is associated with strong attachments to siblings, parents, and hometown.

Psychologists have long believed that "people adopt interpretations of the world that lead them to think well of themselves, their prospects, and their environments."[9] Building on this insight, Adam Alter and Emily Balcetis have shown that "people overestimate their proximity to appealing destinations."[10]

In one experiment, subjects were asked to walk from one place to another on a college campus. They were stopped en route and asked how far they had travelled. Participants *overestimated* how far they had travelled when their destination was more desirable than their starting point. Participants *underestimated* how far they had travelled when their origin was more desirable.

In another experiment, participants in Washington Square Park (Greenwich Village, Lower Manhattan) were asked how far they were from Coney Island (southern Brooklyn), 10.4 miles away. Participants who read a positive description of Coney Island thought it was closer than participants who read a negative description. Alter and Balcetis refer to this relationship between evaluation and distance as the "positivity-closeness" hypothesis, which "predicts that the more pleasant the location, the closer it should be experienced."[11] As they suggest in the title of their article, "fondness makes the distance grow shorter."

These findings were replicated and extended by Jerry Han and Andrew Gershoff. They found that "participants felt positive targets were physically closer than equidistant negative targets when they had higher control over movement in physical space. However, when control was decreased, people felt that the positive target was further away and the negative target was closer."[12] When people feel they can approach a positive target or obtain a desirable object (achieve their goals), they perceive it as closer. When people feel they cannot approach a positive target or obtain a desirable object, they perceive it as farther away. Control matters, for our purposes, because people usually feel they have more control over what's near than what's far.

We also know, from the work of Daniel Kahneman and Amos Tversky, winners of the Nobel Memorial Prize in Economic Sciences, that salient events are more "easily retrieved from memory."[13] In their work on proximity and framing in the news media, Joshua DeLung, Robert G. Magee, Rachel DeLauder, and Roxana Maiorescu report "that proximity to the event covered adds salience to a story because of its personal relevance."[14]

The question, then, is whether salient distant events are more likely to be negative or positive. Kirby Goidel, Stephen Procopio, Dek Terrell, and H. Denis Wu have argued that "there is a qualitative difference between national and local media outlets: Local news tends to be 'fluffier' and less likely to 'stir up' problems, while local reporters often engage in 'boosterism' for the local communities."[15] According to Phyllis Kaniss, author of *Making Local News*, "the typical weekly community newspaper, whether in a city or suburb, tries to balance its hard news with upbeat stories, on its front page as well as throughout its issue."[16]

If national news coverage is more negative than local news coverage, people are more likely to recall positive events happening nearby than at a distance. Even if news is negative generally, my guess is that it's less negative locally. When we conjure images in our minds of the various spatial scales—local, state, national—positive and negative memories compete at the local level. However, for higher levels, negative memories dominate, simply because we have fewer positive memories about what happens far away.

Intuitively, this seems right to me; but remember that I'm just speculating. Local newspapers report high school sports scores, acts of charity and heroism, and updates on local projects; national newspapers tell us the world is going to hell in a hand basket. I could be wrong about this objectively, but it's subjective perceptions that matter. It's truthiness, not truth, that matters, to borrow from Stephen Colbert.

Fundamental attribution error is the "tendency to underestimate the importance of external situational pressures and to overestimate the importance of internal motives and dispositions in interpreting the behaviour of others."[17] We are tough on others but make excuses for ourselves. Now to the extent that people identify with where they live, they will see themselves *in* those places; they will interpret negative events in distant places as characteristic of those places and negative events in near places as exceptions. They will be tough on other places but make excuses for *their* places.

Tocqueville said something along these lines in *Democracy in America*: "The New Englander is attached to his town not so much because he is born there as because he sees the town as a free and powerful corporation of which he is a part and which it is worth his trouble to seek to direct."[18] His amusing comment about patriotism in America applies just as well as to its towns as to the country: "Nothing inhibits ordinary social intercourse more than the irritable patriotism of the American. A foreigner may be prepared to praise a great deal in the United States, but some things he would like to criticize, and this the American absolutely refuses to allow."[19] People defend their localities like they defend themselves; they make excuses they would never allow in their judgments of others.

In the chapter thus far I've suggested that localism has a psychological basis. It makes sense intuitively. Psychological biases like our bias toward the local make sense evolutionarily, but they also lead us astray, as the literature in psychology has shown and continues to show. Thinking things matter more, or are more valuable, merely because they are near is, I believe, a mistake. It's a mistake of the same caliber as thinking things matter more, or are more valuable, merely because they are mine: "there is no magic in the pronoun 'my' which gives greater intrinsic importance to my interests, or those of my father, relatives, friends, or neighbors."[20]

Just as there are plenty of reasons, good moral reasons, to favor the self, there are plenty of good moral reasons to favor what's near and local; but those reasons do not include the mere fact that they are mine or local. To know whether it's okay, morally speaking, to prioritize the self over others, or what's near over what's far, we need reasons that aren't reducible to egoism—personal or geographical.

We naturally favor ourselves and what's local because the psychological distance between ourselves and others and what's near and what's far makes other people and what's far away seem foreign or fuzzy. We have trouble understanding what's psychologically distant; and we don't like what we don't understand.

Psychologists say we "traverse" psychological distance through abstraction.[21] Children learn that objects continue to exist even after being covered when they form "a belief about the substitutability for a specific purpose of two or more subjectively distinct objects."[22] Abstractions allow us to focus on what's essential about something for our purposes while ignoring what's irrelevant for our purposes. When I use a pen to point to something, the fact that it has ink, or is shiny, is irrelevant.

Abstractions allow us to traverse psychological distance because they are "more invariant than their elements."[23] Factoring out what's variable or irrelevant about an object allows you to keep it in your mind's eye even as it recedes.

Even though it's easier, psychologically, to grasp what's near than what's far, it's not as if we don't know how to grasp what's further away. Maybe the idea of abstraction makes you uncomfortable, though. That's precisely why we need localism, you could think. There is danger in abstraction; some of what you thought was irrelevant could be, in fact, essential. By keeping things close, by keeping things local, we can keep track of potentially critical details. That's why governing at a distance is problematic; distant officials rely on misleading abstractions.

I'm not entirely comfortable with the idea that we traverse psychological distance with abstraction either. Abstraction seems to me too cold and imprecise. Abstraction allows us to traverse psychological distance, but at a cost. Let's turn to imagination instead.

Abstraction and imagination are not actually all that different. We abstract away irrelevant features of an object, any object, by imagining the object without those features. When I think of a pen as a pointer, I imagine the pen without its ink—as a pointy thing.

There are other ways to imagine, however. We can imagine by *adding* relevant features to an otherwise abstract object. In *The Theory of Moral Sentiments*, Adam Smith explained that "because we have no immediate experience of what other men feel, we can form no idea of the manner in which they are affected, but by conceiving what we ourselves should feel in the like situation."[24] It is "by the imagination," he said, that "we place ourselves in his situation . . . we enter as it were into his own body, and become in some measure the same person with him, and thence form some idea of his sensations, and even feel something which, though weaker in degree, is not altogether unlike them."[25] Smith later insisted that a person who wishes to understand another person "must adopt the whole case of his companion with all its minutest incidents; and strive to render as perfect as possible" his situation.[26]

This was known as sympathy in the eighteenth century. We don't use the same word anymore; the closest we have is empathy. But empathy is less cognitive than sympathy in Smith's sense. Like empathy, sympathy is something we do naturally (or not), but it is also something we can do intentionally. We can make an effort to sympathize by imagining ourselves in the situation of another. It is no coincidence that scholars of Adam Smith call sympathy "imaginative projection."[27] We project ourselves into others by filling in features about them based on our own experiences and what we know about their situation and circumstances.

I think sympathy is how we should traverse psychological distance, especially the psychological distance physical distance engenders. People far away feel abstract; because they feel abstract, they feel less salient, less important, less worthy of our love and regard. People close to us feel concrete; because they feel concrete and because their lives intersect with ours, we think they matter more than others. Sympathizing is a way to make what is abstract less so. If abstraction is taking relevant features away, sympathy is adding them back in: "imagination carries the distant back to us, and ultimately elicits the very sentiments that physical proximity would have produced."[28]

Of course sympathy is never perfect. When we sympathize, we add attributes we think belong to the object. Sympathizing is hard because when the psychological distance is vast, we may have never encountered, experientially, the features that properly belong to the other, the object of our sympathy. Attributes must be conceivable for us to be able to project them onto others.

When cultural distance is added to physical distance (they were once more closely correlated) sympathy can seem impossible. I am picturing the moment in 1532 when a Spanish priest traveling with Francisco Pizarro handed the Sapa Inca Atahualpa a rectangular object, a bit bigger than a human hand, and told him, through an inexperienced translator, that the object "represented the word of God."[29] Atahualpa, who was himself a god, threw the object onto the ground in disgust. The priest, disgusted by Atahualpa's desecration of what was, for him, the Holy Bible, "shouted to Pizarro to commence the attack."[30]

How could Atahualpa have known that the rectangular object was a book, and that that book contained what the strange men before him considered to be the word of God? How could the priest have known that the strange men behind the man he was talking to believed that the man he was talking to was a god? Atahualpa didn't have the concept "book," let alone "holy book." The priest didn't acknowledge the concept "living god," or at least the concept of "living god other than Jesus Christ." How is sympathy possible in cases like these?

It's hard, possibly heroic. Atahualpa could have imagined himself as the priest, carrying a strange object in a dignified manner toward a person of importance. Imagining himself in this way, Atahualpa could have realized that the object was not something to be thrown to the ground. The priest could have imagined himself as Atahualpa, a man who other men carried around like a king. He could have imagined what it was like to be a king being approached by a funny looking, impertinent man carrying a strange object and muttering threats in an incomprehensible language. The priest—his name was Valverde—could have realized that Atahualpa was to be treated with great respect.

Adam Smith thought that increasing the distance between two people made it harder for them to sympathize with each other. He was right about that. He also thought that a moral duty to sympathize with distant others was contrary to nature:

Whatever interest we take in the fortune of those . . . who are placed altogether out of the sphere of our activity, can produce only anxiety to ourselves, without any manner of advantage to them. To what purpose should we trouble ourselves about the world in the moon? All men, even those at the greatest distance, are no doubt entitled to our good wishes, and our good wishes we naturally give them. But if, notwithstanding, they should be unfortunate, to give ourselves any anxiety upon that account seems to be no part of our duty. That we should be but little interested, therefore, in the fortune of those whom we can neither serve nor hurt, and who are in every respect so very remote from us, seems wisely ordered by Nature; and if it were possible to alter in this respect the original constitution of our frame, we could yet gain nothing by the change.[31]

Sympathizing with people far away is "no part of our duty," according to Smith, because it would be distressing for us and would do no good for them.

Maybe we don't have an affirmative duty to sympathize with people far away. Smith could be right that such a duty is contrary to nature. Nevertheless, Smith never quite denies that sympathizing with people far away would be good, morally speaking. This is where I part company with the leading scholar of Smith's spatial thought, Fonna Forman-Barzilai.[32] Smith argues that favoring what's near is morally permissible, but he never, as I read him, argues that favoring what's near is morally praiseworthy.[33] His theory is about what can be expected of us, not what would be best to do.

Smith's argument is morally dangerous. By stressing that it's *permissible* to favor what's near over what's far, he invites his readers to conclude, erroneously, that it's *praiseworthy* to do so, something he never actually says. I think we have an affirmative duty to *attempt* to sympathize with distant others, but that's not part of my argument in this book. My claim is that just because sympathizing with distant others is difficult does not mean that it's *good* not to try. We have a duty to try to do what's not actually a duty of ours.

There is a kind of radicalism in sympathy, as David Bromwich observes, though he calls it moral imagination: "the power that compels us to grant the highest possible reality and the largest conceivable claim to a thought, action, or person that is not our own, and not close to us in any obvious way."[34] Moral imagination urges us to "grant the highest possible reality and the largest conceivable claim" to what isn't local.[35] Moral imagination is imagination because it asks us to imagine thoughts, actions, and people not as they appear to us but as they could be—as though they were near. It is a "going out of our nature."[36] Moral imagination recommends that we do what we cannot be expected to do.

As Bromwich explains, "moral imagination is not to be found in the reliable sentiment anyone may be supposed to have on such an occasion."[37] Our natural affinity for what's local is a "reliable sentiment." Moral imagination requires that we conjure *unusual* sentiments, sentiments we are not disposed to have. Bromwich agrees that following our natural sentiments is permissible but not praiseworthy: "the more unlikely or remote the path of sympathy, the surer the proof of moral imagination. Thus, to sympathize with someone like myself is commendable, perhaps, but it shows nothing much."[38] Sympathizing with what's near as opposed to what's far, just like sympathizing with someone like myself, is an "extension of the future-regarding aspect of ordinary egoism."[39] To quote the Gospel of Matthew: "For if you love them that love you, what reward have ye?"[40]

I hope you can see why we've turned to moral imagination at the end of a book about localism. Localism is natural and even praiseworthy in certain cases, but it is not praiseworthy generally. Capitulating to our ordinary sentiments may be inevitable, but it is not, thereby, something to celebrate. There are occasionally good reasons to favor what's local, as I've said many times, but the fact that we are disposed to favor the local is not one of them. There are, moreover, good reasons to try to set our reliable sentiments aside—to try to imagine distant people and places as if they were here and not there.

I don't want to end the book on a somber note, so let me say something useful on behalf of localism—some lessons for localism from a skeptic. In this book, I've tried to show that the case for localism is misguided at best, mistaken at worst; nevertheless, I believe localism can work out better than it would otherwise if its practitioners attend to the following observations.

1. *Don't assume the local is good because it's local.* Try not to assume that there is anything inherent about the local, or any spatial scale, for that matter.[41] Bringing decisionmaking, authority, or policy implementation to the local level empowers the actors there. If those actors have dispositions or motives that aren't conducive to democracy, efficiency, or whatever we care about, doing what localism recommends can make things worse.

2. *Higher-level governments can check the excesses of local governments.* Higher-level governments have what could be called the benefit of distance. When local governments try to impose costs on each other, higher-level governments can act as neutral arbiters. That is not to say that higher-level governments are neutral, just that they can help adjudicate conflicts from another point of view.

3. *Don't confuse locality with community.* The local is spatial; community is relational. The people living in a particular place are related to one another insofar as they live there together, but that does not make those relationships those of community. We could say that the relationships between people living in the same place are formal whereas the relationships between people in community with one another are substantive. We can belong to communities that transcend space and time.

4. *Remember that every place is local for someone.* The local is relative. Something is local with respect to something else. What's local for me might not be local for you. When we prioritize what's local for us, we are prioritizing what isn't local for others.

5. *Scrutinize the claim that "these are purely local matters."* Whether a matter is "purely local" depends on the frame of reference. Everything affects everything else, so whether the issue in question is "purely local" depends on what effects we care about.

Matters can seem like they are "purely local" from the inside—
or because we think other people shouldn't have a say in them—
but others may disagree. What counts as "purely local" is an
irreducible political question.[42]

6. *Consider costs alongside benefits.* This one's easy. Of course
   localism sounds like a good idea when you don't count the costs.
   Localism has upsides and downsides; my argument in this book
   is that when you consider both, localism loses its luster.

7. *Don't forget about externalities.* This is related to what I just said
   about "purely local" matters. If what a particular locality decides
   to do affects other localities, the matter isn't "purely local."
   Unless, of course, we've decided that those effects don't count.
   Even if externalities are small, they are abundant.

8. *Notice when "the local" acts as a proxy for what actually matters.*
   This is crucial. Sometimes good outcomes are associated or
   correlated with particular spatial scales. That does not mean,
   however, that the scale itself is what's good. If we care about
   political participation and we notice that people participate
   more at the local level, local participation does not become
   valuable in itself as a result. Don't confuse means with ends.
   Proxies are just proxies.

9. *Avoid place-based discrimination.* Place on its own is morally
   arbitrary.[43] Until we have reasons to think otherwise, favoring a
   place because it's mine is no different than favoring someone's
   interests because that person is me. Localism without reasons is
   egoism scaled up.

10. *Proponents of centralization aren't always foolish or evil.* A corollary:
    just because centralization has gone poorly in certain cases
    doesn't mean it will go poorly in all cases. Centralization can
    seem terrible because we remember only the disasters, never the
    successes. Centralization can liberate those who are oppressed
    locally. Note, furthermore, that proponents of centralization in
    certain policy areas do not necessarily support centralization in
    every policy area. Contemporary proponents of centralization
    happily accept the insights of Adam Smith, James Scott, and

F. A. Hayek. They think centralization can be done better and smarter than before.

11. *People find meaning in different ways.* Some people do not identify with their localities, especially those who have been ill-treated at home. Be kind to "rootless cosmopolitans." They're people with hopes and dreams like everyone else. When I pass the Stonewall Inn in New York City or walk through the Castro District in San Francisco, I think of how liberating cosmopolitan anonymity must have been and may still be. Meaning is meaning, wherever one finds it.

12. *Gather evidence; avoid "weasely modal auxiliaries."*[44] Although I have not conducted original empirical research for this book, I've tried to consult the evidence. Much of localism is driven by unsubstantiated hypotheses. Just because a mechanism makes sense theoretically does not mean it works in the real world. "Weasely modal auxiliaries" are words like *can, could, may,* and *might.* It's true that prioritizing the local by making decisions, exercising authority, or implementing policy locally or more locally *could* improve efficiency; but will it? Making decisions, exercising authority, implementing authority *less* locally could improve efficiency too. Can, could, may, and might express possibility, not probability; it's the latter that matters.

13. *States are not points.* States aren't located where their legislatures meet or their heads of state sleep. A state governs its territory— all of it. Writing this paragraph in Lebanon, New Hampshire, I was 412 miles (as the crow flies) from Washington, D.C., the capital of the United States, but I was *in* the United States. I was one mile (as the crow flies) from Lebanon City Hall, but I was *in* Lebanon. If states are located where their governments meet, how far are citizens of South Africa living in Pretoria from their national government, whose legislature meets in Cape Town and whose highest court meets in Bloemfontein?

14. *Sympathize with distant others.* Even though it's natural to care more about what's near than what's far, we owe it to distant

others to try to imagine what it's like to be them. Conjuring an image in our minds of how our actions affect those at a distance helps to check our geographically partial instincts.

In 1973, E. F. Schumacher complained that "we suffer from an almost universal idolatry of gigantism. It is therefore necessary," he said, "to insist on the virtues of smallness—where this applies."[45] He added parenthetically that "if there were a prevailing idolatry of smallness, irrespective of subject or purpose, one would have to try and exercise influence in the opposite direction."[46] Here and now in 2022, we have reached the point Schumacher barely imagined: an idolatry of localism. This book is my effort "to try and exercise influence in the opposite direction,"[47] with words, the only way I know how.

Notes

PREFACE

1. Sam Sturgis, "2014's Dumbest Local Ordinances," Bloomberg City-Lab, December 30, 2014, www.bloomberg.com/news/articles/2014-12-30/2014-s-dumbest-local-ordinances.

2. The latter three examples are from Caroline Simon, "Weirdest Laws Passed in Every State," *USA Today*, October 29, 2018, www.usatoday.com/list/news/nation-now/weirdest-laws-every-state/53ad0541-3518-4432-adc4-0fec193d389e/.

3. *Milliken v. Bradley*, 418 U.S. 717 (1974), 741.

4. See, especially, the work of Erika Frankenberg and her colleagues.

5. Alvin Chang, "School Segregation Didn't Go Away. It Just Evolved," Vox, Jul 27, 2017, www.vox.com/policy-and-politics/2017/7/27/16004084/school-segregation-evolution.

6. Ibid.

7. Department for Communities and Local Government (United Kingdom), "A Plain English Guide to the Localism Act," November 2011, https://assets.publishing.service.gov.uk/government/uploads/system/uploads/attachment_data/file/5959/1896534.pdf.

8. Department for Levelling Up, Housing and Communities and Ministry of Housing, Communities & Local Government, "Local Government Structure and Elections," UK.gov, October 19, 2021, www.gov.uk/guidance/local-government-structure-and-elections.

9. Paul Smith, "The Localism Bill Ignores the Need for Affordable Homes," *The Guardian*, December 4, 2010, www.theguardian.com/housing -network/2010/dec/14/localism-bill-ignores-need-affordable-homes.

10. Stephen M. Lepore, "Washington DC Joins New York, Philadelphia, San Francisco, and Boston in Issuing COVID-19 Vaccine Mandate for Indoor Activities, Including Gyms, Restaurants, and Bars as well as NBA and NHL Games," *Daily Mail*, December 22, 2021, www.dailymail.co.uk/news/article -10337849/Washington-DC-joins-NYC-Philly-issuing-COVID-19-vaccine -mandate-indoor-activities.html.

11. Halle Parker, "No More New Orleans Vaccine Mandate: Businesses Are Relieved amid Decision to Lift COVID Rules," *New Orleans Public Radio*, March 21, 2022, https://www.wwno.org/public-health/2022-03-21/no-more- new-orleans-vaccine-mandate-businesses-are-relieved-amid-decision-to-lift- covid-rules. Mark Ballard, "Louisiana House Passes Bill to Prohibit State, Local Government from Setting Vaccine Mandates," *The Advocate*, April 20, 2022, https://www.theadvocate.com/baton_rouge/news/politics/legislature/article _e1b7fe02-c106-11ec-a978-475f4fdce286.html.

12. Allen Kim, "Several Sheriffs in North Carolina Say They Won't En- force the State's Mask Mandate," *CNN*, June 25, 2020, https://www.cnn. com/2020/06/25/us/north-carolina-sheriffs-masks-trnd/index.html.

CHAPTER 1. LOCALISM AND WHY IT MATTERS

1. Google's Ngram Viewer indicates that the word *localism* was used more often in the year 2019 than in any other year since 1800.

2. Bill Laurance, "Vines Choking out Trees in the Tropics," in *Science Friday*, edited by John Dankosky (NPR, 2013).

3. Cf. Hans Beck, *Localism and the Ancient Greek City-State* (University of Chicago Press, 2020).

4. E. F. Schumacher, *Small Is Beautiful: Economics as If People Mattered* (London: Blond and Briggs, 1973; repr., New York: Harper Perennial, 2010).

5. Alexander Hamilton, James Madison, and John Jay, *The Federalist with Let- ters of "Brutus,"* edited by Terence Ball (Cambridge University Press, 2003), p. 104.

6. Franklin Delano Roosevelt, "Commonwealth Club Address (1932)," in *Classics of American Political and Constitutional Thought*, edited by Scott J. Ham- mond, Kevin R. Hardwick, and Howard L. Lubert, vol. 2 (Indianapolis, IN: Hackett, 2007), p. 404.

7. Since this book is about places and whether and why they matter, I should mention that most of it was written in New York City (a large city of 8 million people) and Lebanon, New Hampshire (a small city of just 13,000). Additional examples are drawn from Fremont, California, my hometown (a sub- urb of about 240,000 residents).

8. Michael Pollan, *The Omnivore's Dilemma: A Natural History of Four Meals* (New York: Penguin Press, 2006); Alisa Smith and J. B. Mackinnon, *Plenty: Eating Locally on the 100-Mile Diet* (New York: Three Rivers Press, 2007).

9. Fiona Simpson, "National Franchise Brand, Local Franchisee Marketing," *Forbes*, October 10, 2018, www.forbes.com/sites/fionasimpson1/2018/10/10/national-franchise-brand-local-franchisee-marketing/#7ebe2cc02df4.

10. Ibid.

11. Ellen Rosen, "9 Ways to Support Small Businesses," *New York Times*, November 23, 2020, www.nytimes.com/2020/11/23/business/smallbusiness/how-to-support-small-businesses.html.

12. Beck, *Localism and the Ancient Greek City-State*, p. 1.

13. Quoted in Patrick W. Watson, "The World Is Entering a 'Localism' Era," *Forbes*, January 4, 2017, www.forbes.com/sites/patrickwwatson/2017/01/04/the-world-is-entering-a-localism-era/#22d19b052d75.

14. Stephanie Muravchik and Jon A. Shields, *Trump's Democrats* (Washington, D.C.: Brookings Institute Press, 2020), p. 95.

15. Other European Intuitions meet in Frankfurt (the European Central Bank), The Hague (the European Police Office), and Luxembourg (e.g., the Court of Justice of the European Union).

16. "About the Campaign," Vote Leave, February 9, 2018, www.voteleavetakecontrol.org/campaign.html.

17. Bruce Katz and Jeremy Nowak, *The New Localism: How Cities Can Thrive in the Age of Populism* (Washington, D.C.: Brookings Institution Press, 2017).

18. The New Localism, May 15, 2021, www.thenewlocalism.com/shop/.

19. Joel Kotkin and Ryan Streeter, editors, *Localism in America: Why We Should Tackle Our Big Challenges at the Local Level* (American Enterprise Institute, 2018), pp. 1–2.

20. Lyman Stone, "We Conservatives Champion Local Power. So We Must Respect the Rights of 'Blue' Cities," Vox, August 21, 2017, www.vox.com/platform/amp/the-big-idea/2017/8/21/16176578/localism-sanctuary-cities-federalism-conservative-case.

21. Ibid.

22. During the Trump administration, liberals and progressives, normally friendly to centralized government, joined the localist bandwagon in order to protect undocumented immigrants. They argued that it should be up to cities and localities to decide what to do about immigration within their borders. Using localism to protect undocumented immigrants isn't at all straightforward, however, because borders and immigration are traditionally national issues. There are sound practical reasons to have uniform and consistent immigration rules.

23. Joseph Blocher, "A Gun Debate Compromise: Let Cities and Rural Areas Pass Different Laws," Vox, March 24, 2018, www.vox.com/the-big-idea/2018/3/21/17147398/rural-cities-gun-laws-control-culture-war-nra-second

-amendment-parkland-shootings. Also see Joseph Blocher, "Firearm Localism," *Yale Law Journal* 123 (2013).

24. Archon Fung, *Empowered Participation: Reinventing Urban Democracy* (Princeton University Press, 2004), p. 4.

25. Carole Pateman, *Participation and Democratic Theory* (Cambridge University Press, 1970), p. 20.

26. See, for example, Daniel P. Moynihan, *Maximum Feasible Misunderstanding: Community Action in the War on Poverty* (New York: Free Press, 1969).

27. Juliet F. Gainsborough, "To Devolve or Not to Devolve? Welfare Reform in the States," *Policy Studies Journal* 31, no. 4 (2003).

28. Joe Soss, Richard C. Fording, and Sanford F. Schram, "The Color of Devolution: Race, Federalism, and the Politics of Social Control," *American Journal of Political Science* 52, no. 3 (2008), p. 551.

29. Ibid. Also note the ways in which contemporary welfare localism resembles the Elizabethan Poor Laws, which were administered at the parish level.

30. As Tocqueville put it, "By *mores* I mean here what the Ancients meant by the term: I apply it not only to mores in the strict sense, what one might call habits of the heart, but also to the various notions that men possess, to the diverse opinions that are current among them, and to the whole range of ideas that shape habits of mind." Alexis de Tocqueville, *Democracy in America*, edited by Olivier Zunz, translated by Arthur Goldhammer, vol. 1 (1835–1840; New York: Library of America, 2004), p. 331.

31. Trevor Latimer, "Against Subsidiarity," *Journal of Political Philosophy* 26, no. 3 (2018); Trevor Latimer, "The Principle of Subsidiarity: A Democratic Reinterpretation," *Constellations: An International Journal of Critical and Democratic Theory* 25, no. 4 (2018).

32. Treaty on European Union (Maastricht text), July 29, 1992, 1992 O.J. C 191/1 at 6.

33. Treaty of Lisbon Amending the Treaty on European Union and the Treaty Establishing the European Community, 2007 O.J. C 306/1.

34. European Charter of Local Self-Government, October 15, 1985, 122 E.T.S. at art 3.1, www.coe.int/en/web/conventions/full-list/-/conventions /rms/090000168007a088.

35. Ibid., art 4.2.

36. Ibid., preamble.

37. Patrick J. Deneen, *Why Liberalism Failed* (Yale University Press, 2018).

38. "Enthusiasm, n.," in *Oxford English Dictionary*.

39. An inexhaustive list: Kristian Stokke and Giles Mohan, "The Convergence around Local Civil Society and the Dangers of Localism," *Social Scientist* 29, no. 11/12 (2001); Greg Sharzer, *No Local: Why Small-Scale Alternatives Won't Change the World* (Winchester, UK: Zero Books, 2012); Sheryll D. Cashin, "Localism, Self-Interest, and the Tyranny of the Favored Quarter," *Georgetown Law*

Review 88 (2000); Phil Parvin, "Localism and the Left: The Need for Strong Central Government," *Renewal: A Journal of Labour Politics* 19, no. 2 (2011); Richard C. Schragger, "The Limits of Localism," *Michigan Law Review* 100, no. 2 (2001); Giles Mohan and Kristian Stokke, "Participatory Development and Empowerment: The Dangers of Localism," *Third World Quarterly* 21, no. 2 (2000); Phil Parvin, "Against Localism: Does Decentralising Power to Communities Fail Minorities?" *Political Quarterly* 80, no. 3 (2009); Stephen Macedo, "Property Owning Plutocracy: Inequality and American Localism," in *Justice and the American Metropolis*, edited by Clarissa Rile Hayward and Todd Swanstrom (University of Minnesota Press, 2001); K. Newton, "Is Small Really So Beautiful? Is Big Really So Ugly? Size, Effectiveness, and Democracy in Local Government," *Political Studies* 30, no. 2 (1982).

40. Mark Purcell and J. Christopher Brown, "Against the Local Trap: Scale and the Study of Environment and Development," *Progress in Development Studies* 5, no. 4 (2005), p. 280.

41. Ibid. Also see Mark Purcell, "Urban Democracy and the Local Trap," *Urban Studies* 43, no. 11 (2006); Bill Cooke and Uma Kothari, editors, *Participation: The New Tyranny* (London: Zed Books, 2001).

42. See, for example, Cass R. Sunstein, *The Cost-Benefit Revolution* (MIT Press, 2018).

43. T. M. Scanlon, *What We Owe to Each Other* (Cambridge, MA: Belknap Press, 1998), p. 219.

44. Ibid.

45. John Rawls, *Political Liberalism* (Columbia University Press, 1996).

46. David Bromwich, *Moral Imagination: Essays* (Princeton University Press, 2014), p. xii.

47. Hamilton, Madison, and Jay, *The Federalist*, p. 41.

48. Tocqueville, vol. 1, *Democracy in America*, p. 15.

CHAPTER 2. WHAT IS LOCALISM?

1. Alexis de Tocqueville, *Democracy in America*, edited by Olivier Zunz, translated by Arthur Goldhammer, vol. 1 (1835–1840; New York: Library of America, 2004), p. 97. Tocqueville is referring to centralization rather than localism in this passage.

2. Paul Hildreth, "What Is Localism, and What Implications Do Different Models Have for Managing the Local Economy?" *Local Economy* 26, no. 8 (2011), p. 703.

3. Ibid.

4. Ibid.

5. Jane Wills, *Locating Localism: Statecraft, Citizenship and Democracy* (Bristol: Policy Press, 2016), p. 7.

6. Ibid., p. 9.

7. Ibid., p. 16.

8. David J. Hess, "Global Problems, Localist Solutions," in *The Localization Reader: Adapting to the Coming Downshift*, edited by Raymond De Young and Thomas Princen (MIT Press, 2012), pp. 274–75.

9. Ibid., p. 275.

10. Richard C. Schragger, "The Limits of Localism," *Michigan Law Review* 100, no. 2 (2001), p. 373.

11. Mark Evans, David Marsh, and Gerry Stoker, "Understanding Localism," *Policy Studies* 34, no. 4 (2013), p. 405.

12. Simin Davoudi and Ali Madanipour, editors, *Reconsidering Localism* (New York: Routledge, 2015), p. i.

13. Ibid., p. 1.

14. Richard Briffault, "Our Localism: Part I—the Structure of Local Government Law," *Columbia Law Review* 90, no. 1 (1990), p. 1.

15. Roderick M. Hills Jr., "Is Federalism Good for Localism? The Localist Case for Federal Regimes," *Journal of Law & Politics* 21 (2005), pp. 188–89.

16. Ibid., p. 189.

17. Mark T. Mitchell and Jason Peters, editors, *Localism in the Mass Age: A Front Porch Republic Manifesto* (Eugene, OR: Cascade Books, 2018), loc. 154 of 5648, Kindle.

18. Ibid., loc. 162 of 5648, Kindle.

19. Ibid., loc. 192 of 5648, Kindle.

20. Ibid., loc. 195 of 5648, Kindle.

21. Mike Hais, Doug Ross, and Morley Winograd, *Healing American Democracy: Going Local* (Blue Zephyr, 2018), 42, Kindle.

22. Ibid., 5, Kindle.

23. Joel Kotkin and Ryan Streeter, editors, *Localism in America: Why We Should Tackle Our Big Challenges at the Local Level* (American Enterprise Institute, 2018), pp. 1–2.

24. Bruce Katz and Jeremy Nowak, *The New Localism: How Cities Can Thrive in the Age of Populism* (Washington, D.C.: Brookings Institution Press, 2017), p. 6.

25. Neil Brenner and Nik Theodore, "Preface: From the 'New Localism' to the Spaces of Neoliberalism," *Antipode* 34, no. 3 (2002), p. 342.

26. Daniel Weinstock, "Cities and Federalism," in *NOMOS LV: Federalism and Subsidiarity*, edited by James E. Fleming and Jacob T. Levy (New York University Press, 2014), p. 283.

27. Jackson Turner Main, *Political Parties before the Constitution* (University of North Carolina Press, 1973), p. 32.

28. Forrest McDonald, *Novus Ordo Seclorum: The Intellectual Origins of the Constitution* (University Press of Kansas, 1985), p. 174.

29. Barry Alan Shain, *The Myth of American Individualism: The Protestant Origins of American Political Thought* (Princeton University Press, 1994), p. 60.

30. Saul Cornell, *The Other Founders: Anti-Federalism and the Dissenting Tradition in America, 1788–1828* (University of North Carolina Press, 1999), p. 215.

31. Kenneth A. Lockridge, *Settlement and Unsettlement in Early America: The Crisis of Political Legitimacy before the Revolution* (Cambridge University Press, 1981), p. 39.

32. Ibid.

33. David Brooks, "The Localist Revolution," *New York Times*, July 19, 2018, https://nyti.ms/2O4WsdV.

34. "-Ism, *Suffix*," in *Oxford English Dictionary*.

35. Sheryll D. Cashin, "Localism, Self-Interest, and the Tyranny of the Favored Quarter," *Georgetown Law Review* 88 (2000), p. 1988.

36. Wills, *Locating Localism: Statecraft, Citizenship and Democracy*, p. 7.

37. Davoudi and Madanipour, *Reconsidering Localism*, p. 1.

38. Hildreth, "What Is Localism, and What Implications Do Different Models Have for Managing the Local Economy?" p. 703.

39. Consolidated Version of the Treaty on European Union, 2016 O.J. C 326/13 at 16.

40. Mitchell and Peters, *Localism in the Mass Age: A Front Porch Republic Manifesto*, loc. 163 of 5648, Kindle.

41. "Extra-, *Prefix*," in *Oxford English Dictionary*.

42. Tocqueville, *Democracy in America*, vol. 1, p. 379.

43. Stephanie Muravchik and Jon A. Shields have referred to "local nationalism." Stephanie Muravchik and Jon A. Shields, *Trump's Democrats* (Washington, D.C.: Brookings Institution Press, 2020), p. 100.

44. Wayne Hemingway, "Why Do We Celebrate Localism, but Dislike Nationalism?" *Huffpost*, November 21, 2018, www.huffingtonpost.co.uk/entry/we-celebrate-localism-until-it-becomes-nationalism_uk_5bf2a531e4b0b9f7ae9c8244.

45. Douglas Adams, *The Hitchhiker's Guide to the Galaxy* (1979; New York: Balantine Books, 2005).

46. Ursula K. Heise, *Sense of Place and Sense of Planet: The Environmental Imagination of the Global* (Oxford University Press, 2008), p. 3.

47. United States Census Bureau, "Rapid City, Pennington County, South Dakota," https://data.census.gov/cedsci/profile?g=0600000US4610352980.

48. The New York City Department of Health and Mental Hygiene, "Manhattan Community District 12: Washington Heights and Inwood," www1.nyc.gov/assets/doh/downloads/pdf/data/2015chp-mn12.pdf, p. 2.

49. Quoted in Sallie A. Marston, John Paul Jones, III, and Keith Woodward, "Human Geography without Scale," *Transactions of the Institute of British Geographers* 30, no. 4 (2005), p. 416.

50. Henri Lefebvre, "Reflections on the Politics of Space," *Antipode* 8, no. 2 (1976), p. 33.

51. Harold D. Lasswell, *Politics; Who Gets What, When, How* (New York: Whittlesey House, 1936).

52. Abraham Lincoln, *The Collected Works of Abraham Lincoln*, edited by Roy P. Basler, 8 vols. (Rutgers University Press, 1953; University of Michigan Digital Library Production Services, 2001), 2:270.

53. Sallie A. Marston, "The Social Construction of Scale," *Progress in Human Geography* 24, no. 2 (2000).

54. "Localism, *n.*," in *Oxford English Dictionary*.

55. "-Ism, *Suffix*."

56. Tom Wheeler, "On Local Broadcasting, Trump Federal Communications Commission 'Can't Be Serious!,'" *Brookings*, April 12, 2018, www.brookings .edu/blog/techtank/2018/04/12/on-local-broadcasting-trump-federal -communications-commission-cant-be-serious/.

57. David Ferry, "The Dirty Secret of Violent Surf Localism: It Works," *Outside*, April 19, 2016, www.outsideonline.com/2070371/dirty-secret-violent -surf-localism-it-works.

58. Daniel Treisman, *The Architecture of Government: Rethinking Political Decentralization* (Cambridge University Press, 2007).

59. Gérard Marcou, "Postface: Essay on the Clarification of Some Key Concepts and Methodical Problems," in *Decentralization and Local Democracy in the World: First Global Report by United Cities and Local Governments* (2008), p. 311.

60. The literature on federalism is vast. Readers interested in learning about federalism should start with John Kincaid, editor, *Federalism*, 4 vols. (Los Angeles: SAGE, 2011). or with the journal *Publius*.

61. TEU, 2016 O.J. C 326/13.

62. Cf. Steve Herbert, "The Trapdoor of Community," *Annals of the Association of American Geographers* 95, no. 4 (2005).

63. For a similar argument with respect to corporations, see Lucia M. Rafanelli, "A Defense of Individualism in the Age of Corporate Rights," *Journal of Political Philosophy* 25, no. 3 (2017).

64. Gordon L. Clark, "A Theory of Local Autonomy," *Annals of the Association of American Geographers* 74, no. 2 (1984), p. 195.

65. Ibid.

CHAPTER 3. TYRANNY

1. Emma Goldman, *Anarchism and Other Essays* (New York: Mother Earth Publishing Association, 1910), p. 61.

2. Quoted in Dennis Dalton, *Mahatma Gandhi: Nonviolent Power in Action* (Columbia University Press, 2012), p. 77.

3. F. A. Hayek, *The Road to Serfdom: Text and Documents*, edited by Bruce Caldwell (University of Chicago Press, 2007), p. 234.

4. Aldous Huxley, *Brave New World Revisited* (New York: HarperPerennial, 1958), p. 18.

5. Schumacher, *Small Is Beautiful: Economics as If People Mattered* (London: Blond and Briggs, 1973; repr., New York: Harper Perennial, 2010), p. 260.

6. Robert A. Nisbet, "Rousseau and Totalitarianism," *Journal of Politics* 5, no. 2 (1943), p. 96.

7. Quoted in *Cleveland Gazette*, "Warns of Centralization," November 9, 1935.

8. Brink Lindsay, *Against the Dead Hand: The Uncertain Struggle for Global Capitalism* (New York: John Wiley & Sons, 2002), p. 2.

9. Melvin Richter, "A Family of Political Concepts: Tyranny, Despotism, Bonapartism, Caesarism, Dictatorship, 1750–1917," *European Journal of Political Theory* 4, no. 3 (2005), p. 225.

10. Localism and centralization are only roughly opposites. See the discussion of the distinction between decentralization and localism in chapter 2.

11. *Federalist* No. 47 in Alexander Hamilton, James Madison, and John Jay, *The Federalist with Letters of "Brutus,"* edited by Terence Ball (Cambridge University Press, 2003), p. 235.

12. Charles de Secondat Baron de Montesquieu, *The Spirit of the Laws*, translated and edited by Anne M. Cohler, Basia Carolyn Miller, and Harold Samuel Stone (Cambridge University Press, 1989), p. 157.

13. Ibid., p. 63. For more on uniformity, centralization, and tyranny, see Benjamin Constant, *Political Writings*, translated and edited by Biancamaria Fontana (Cambridge University Press, 1988).

14. Montesquieu, *The Spirit of the Laws*, p. 157

15. Ibid.

16. Ibid., p. 21.

17. Ibid.

18. Ibid., pp. 17–18.

19. Ibid., p. 17.

20. Ibid., p. 18.

21. Lee Ward, "Montesquieu on Federalism and Anglo-Gothic Constitutionalism," *Publius: The Journal of Federalism* 37, no. 4 (2007).

22. *Federalist* No. 47, in Hamilton, Madison, and Jay, *The Federalist*, p. 234.

23. Thomas Jefferson, *Jefferson: Political Writings*, edited by Joyce Appleby and Terence Ball (Cambridge University Press, 1999), p. 326.

24. *Federalist* No. 51, in Hamilton, Madison, and Jay, *The Federalist*, p. 253.

25. Ibid., pp. 253–54.

26. Ibid., p. 254.

27. Alexis de Tocqueville, *Democracy in America*, edited by Olivier Zunz, translated by Arthur Goldhammer, vol. 2 (1835–1840; New York: Library of America, 2012), p. 97.

28. Many scholars claim that this distinction is useful. See, for example, Christina Bambrick, "'Neither Precisely National nor Precisely Federal': Governmental and Administrative Authority in Tocqueville's Democracy in America," *Publius: Journal of Federalism* 48, no. 4 (2018). Tocqueville himself recognizes the distinction is not straightforward: "In some respects the distinction between the two kinds of centralization becomes blurred." *Democracy in America*, vol. 1, p. 98.

29. Ibid.

30. Ibid., p. 98.

31. "All the miseries of feudal society stemmed from the fact that the power not just to administer but to govern was divided among a thousand hands and fragmented a thousand ways." Ibid., p. 99.

32. Ibid., p. 108.

33. Ibid.

34. Ibid., p. 109.

35. *Democracy in America*, vol. 2, p. 317.

36. Ibid, p. 326, emphasis mine.

37. Ibid, p. 325.

38. Robinson uses the term *partial entailment* to describe "that aspect of a causal connection that is best described as one of necessity, yet which is not an instance of logical necessity." "Partial Entailment and the Causal Relation," *Mind* 70, no. 280 (1961), p. 526.

39. *Federalist* No. 47, in Hamilton, Madison, and Jay, *The Federalist*, p. 234, emphasis mine. Jefferson, *Political Writings*, p. 326, emphasis mine.

40. Montesquieu, *The Spirit of the Laws*, p. 157.

41. Jac C. Heckelman and Keith L. Dougherty, "A Spatial Analysis of Delegate Voting at the Constitutional Convention," *Journal of Economic History* 73, no. 02 (2013).

42. "Vice of the Political System of the United States (1787) in *Classics of American Political and Constitutional Thought*, 2 vols, edited by Scott J. Hammond, Kevin R. Hardwick, and Howard L. Lubert, vol. 1 (Indianapolis, IN: Hackett, 2007), pp. 370–74.

43. Madison later changed his mind about the states.

44. As Daniel Treisman notes, commenting on Tocqueville, there is a version of the argument I am contesting that says "that it is technically impossible for a central government to implement different public policies in different local units." Daniel Treisman, *Architecture of Government* (Cambridge University Press, 2007), p. 59.

45. Ibid., p. 60.

46. Ibid., p. 61.

47. Geoffrey Brennan and James M. Buchanan, *The Power to Tax: Analytical Foundations of a Fiscal Constitution* (Indianapolis, IN: Liberty Fund, 2000), p. 33.

48. Brennan and Buchanan see themselves as replacing the assumption of benevolence in public finance with that of "indifference or even possible malevolence." Ibid., p. 18.

49. Ibid., p. 20, emphasis added.

50. Adam Smith, *The Theory of Moral Sentiments*, edited by D. D. Raphael and A. L. Macfie (1759; Indianpolis, IN: Liberty Fund, 1982), p. 233–34.

51. "Adam Smith's Libertarian Paternalism" in *Oxford Handbook of Freedom*, edited by David Schmidtz and Carmen E. Pavel (Oxford University Press, 2018), p. 252.

52. "Centralization, n.," in *Oxford English Dictionary*.

53. Smith, *The Theory of Moral Sentiments*, p. 234.

54. Robert A. Caro, *The Power Broker: Robert Moses and the Fall of New York* (New York: Knopf, 1974).

55. U.S. Bureau of Economic Analysis, Federal Government Current Expenditures (AFEXPND), FRED, Federal Reserve Bank of St. Louis, July 29, 2021, https://fred.stlouisfed.org/series/AFEXPND; U.S Bureau of Economic Analysis, Gross Domestic Product (GDPA), FRED, Federal Reserve Bank of St. Louis, July 29, 2021, https://fred.stlouisfed.org/series/GDPA.

56. This is the series already cited, Federal Government Current Expenditures, minus the series for federal government current transfer payments, divided by the series for gross domestic product, also already cited. For federal government current transfer payments, see U.S. Bureau of Economic Analysis, federal government current transfer payments (W014RC1A027NBEA), FRED, Federal Reserve Bank of St. Louis, July 29, 2021, https://fred.stlouisfed.org/series/W014RC1A027NBEA.

57. For transfers to state and local government, see U.S. Bureau of Economic Analysis, federal government current transfer payments: Other current transfer payments: Grants-in-aid to state and local governments FRED, Federal Reserve Bank of St. Louis, July 29, 2021, https://fred.stlouisfed.org/series/AFGSL.

58. "Federalism (Properly Understood) Works in Welfare Policy Too," in *Localism in America: Why We Should Tackle Our Big Challenges at the Local Level*, edited by Joel Kotkin and Ryan Streeter (American Enterprise Institute, 2018), pp. 33–34.

59. Franklin Delano Roosevelt, "Commonwealth Club Address (1932)," in *Classics of American Political and Constitutional Thought*, edited by Scott J. Hammond, Kevin R. Hardwick, and Howard L. Lubert, vol. 2 (Indianapolis, IN: Hackett, 2007), p. 404.

60. FDR Presidential Library & Museum, National Archives, "A President's Evolving Approach to Fiscal Policy in Times of Crisis," February 12, 2019, https://fdrlibrary.org/budget.

61. *Federalist* No. 70 in Hamilton, Madison, and Jay, *The Federalist*, p. 342.

62. Tocqueville, *Democracy in America*, p. 583.

63. Andrew M. Colman, *A Dictionary of Psychology*, 4th ed. (Oxford University Press, 2015), p. 72.

64. Matthew White, *The Great Big Book of Horrible Things: The Definitive Chronicle of History's 100 Worst Atrocities* (New York: W. W. Norton, 2012), p. xvi. Emphasis in original.

65. Ibid., p. xvii.

66. Pinker, *The Better Angels of Our Nature*, p. xxiv.

67. Charles Spencer, *The White Ship* (London: William Collins, 2020), p. 288.

68. Tocqueville, *Democracy in America*, vol. 2., p. 342. Note that I have edited this passage deliberately. The full passage reads: The state "works willingly for their happiness but wants to be the sole agent and only arbiter of that happiness. It provides for their security, foresees and takes care of their needs, facilitates their pleasures, manages their most important affairs, directs their industry, regulates their successions, and divides their inheritances. Why not relieve them entirely of the trouble of thinking and the difficulty of living?"

CHAPTER 4. BELONGING

1. Joel Kotkin and Ryan Streeter, editors, *Localism in America: Why We Should Tackle Our Big Challenges at the Local Level* (American Enterprise Institute, 2018), p. 3.

2. "Trust in Government," *Gallup*, September 2021, https://news.gallup.com/poll/5392/trust-government.aspx.

3. Richard Florida calls this "around a fifth to a third." Kotkin and Streeter, *Localism in America*, p. 83.

4. It is perhaps worth mentioning that confidence in the federal government dipped below 50 percent only once prior to the subprime mortgage crisis in 2007 (June 1976); since then, it has hovered around 45 percent. "Trust in Government," *Gallup*.

5. "The Public, the Political System and American Democracy," Pew Research Center, April 26, 2018, www.people-press.org/2018/04/26/the-public-the-political-system-and-american-democracy/.

6. Allstate/Atlantic Media, Heartland Monitor Poll XXVI, July 2016. For a brief summary, see Ronald Brownstein, "Why Americans Argue Nationally but Act Locally," *The Atlantic*, July 2016, www.theatlantic.com/politics/archive/2016/07/looking-for-change-from-the-bottom-up/490937/.

7. Allstate/Atlantic Media, Heartland Monitor Poll XXVI.

8. Ibid.

9. Allstate/Atlantic Media, Heartland Monitor Poll XXII, February 2015. For a partial summary, see Karlyn Bowman, "Our Towns: Americans Say They

Are Alive and Working Well," *Forbes*, July 18, 2015, www.forbes.com/sites /bowmanmarsico/2015/06/19/our-towns-americans-say-they-are-alive-and -working-well/?sh=64c1e1fd170e.

10. Allstate/Atlantic Media, Heartland Monitor Poll XXII.

11. Ibid.

12. Ibid.

13. Ibid.

14. Stephanie Muravchik and Jon A. Shields have argued that local attachments are a defining feature of "Trump democrats." Stephanie Muravchik and Jon A. Shields, *Trump's Democrats* (Washington, D.C.: Brookings Institution Press, 2020).

15. Diane Jeske, "Special Obligations," *Stanford Encyclopedia of Philosophy*, August 6, 2019, https://plato.stanford.edu/entries/special-obligations/.

16. For an excellent but different account of place and special obligations, see Paulina Ochoa Espejo, *On Borders: Territories, Legitimacy, and the Rights of Place* (Oxford University Press, 2020), chapter 7.

17. For a defense of the term *ghetto*, see Richard Rothstein, *The Color of Law: A Forgotten History of How Our Government Segregated America* (New York: Liveright Publishing Corporation, 2017), p. xvi.

18. Ferdinand Tönnies, *Community and Civil Society*, edited by Jose Harris, translated by Jose Harris and Margaret Hollis (Cambridge University Press, 2001), p. 18.

19. Charles Tilly, *Durable Inequality* (University of California Press, 1998).

20. Bernard Williams and J. J. C. Smart, *Utilitarianism: For and Against* (Cambridge University Press, 1973), p. 112.

21. Ibid., p. 116.

22. Ibid., p. 143fn2.

23. Ibid., p. 110.

24. Alexis de Tocqueville, *Democracy in America*, edited by Olivier Zunz, translated by Arthur Goldhammer, vol. 1 (1835–1840; New York: Library of America, 2012), p. 75.

25. David Hume, *Enquiries Concerning the Human Understanding and Concerning the Principles of Morals*, edited by L. A. Selby-Bigge, 2nd ed. (Oxford: The Clarendon Press, 1902), 229fn1, emphasis added. Also see Rico Vitz, "Hume and the Limits of Benevolence," *Hume Studies* 28, no. 2 (2002).

26. Adam Smith, *The Theory of Moral Sentiments*, edited by D. D. Raphael and A. L. Macfie (1759; Indianapolis, IN: Liberty Fund, 1982), p. 229, emphasis added. Edmund Burke said much the same in his famous "little platoons" passage. Edmund Burke, *Reflections on the Revolution in France*, edited by J. C. D. Clark (1790; Stanford University Press, 2001), p. 202.

27. Adam Smith, *An Inquiry into the Nature and Causes of the Wealth of Nations*, edited by Edwin Cannan, vol. 1 (1776; London: Methuen, 1904), p. 16.

28. Hume, *Enquiries Concerning the Human Understanding and Concerning the Principles of Morals*, 229fn1.

29. Fonna Forman-Barzilai, *Adam Smith and the Circles of Sympathy: Cosmopolitanism and Moral Theory* (Cambridge University Press, 2010), p. 22, emphasis added.

30. Smith, *The Theory of Moral Sentiments*, p. 235. Forman-Barzilai thinks this is Smith's reconstruction of Stoicism rather than his own view. However, the passage appears in part VI on "the character of virtue" rather than part VII on "systems of moral philosophy."

31. Ibid., p. 237.

32. For a real example of the same phenomenon, see Muravchik and Shields, *Trump's Democrats*, pp. 94–96.

33. U.S. Bureau of Economic Analysis, Local government current receipts: Current transfer receipts: state government grants-in-aid (W847RC1A027-NBEA), FRED, Federal Reserve Bank of St. Louis, November 2, 2021, https://fred.stlouisfed.org/series/W847RC1A027NBEA; U.S. Bureau of Economic Analysis, Local government current receipts: Current transfer receipts: federal grants-in-aid (W846RC1A027NBEA), FRED, Federal Reserve Bank of St. Louis, November 2, 2021, https://fred.stlouisfed.org/series/W846RC1A027NBEA; U.S. Bureau of Economic Analysis, Local government current receipts (W830RC1A027NBEA), FRED, Federal Reserve Bank of St. Louis, November 2, 2021, https://fred.stlouisfed.org/series/W830RC1A027NBEA.

34. Paul E. Peterson, *City Limits* (University of Chicago Press, 1981), p. 41.

35. Ibid.

36. Ibid.

37. Paul C. Cheshire and Ian R. Gordon, "Territorial Competition and the Predictability of Collective (in)Action," *International Journal of Urban and Regional Research* 20, no. 3 (1996), p. 396.

38. Peterson, *City Limits*, p. 148.

39. Marielle Segarra, "Philadelphia Starts Small (and Cheap) with Delaware River Waterfront Revitalization," WHYY, August 14, 2015, https://whyy.org/articles/philadelphia-starts-small-and-cheap-with-delaware-river-waterfront-revitalization/.

40. Ibid.

41. Delaware River Waterfront, Spring Garden Connector, February 13, 2019, www.delawareriverwaterfront.com/places/spring-garden-connector.

42. Paul R. Krugman, "Making Sense of the Competitiveness Debate," *Oxford Review of Economic Policy* 12, no. 3 (1996).

43. Ben Casselman, "Promising Billions to Amazon: Is It a Good Deal for Cities?," *New York Times*, January 26, 2018, https://nyti.ms/2FmRm7F.

44. Alan Peters and Peter Fisher, "The Failures of Economic Development Incentives," *Journal of the American Planning Association* 70, no. 1 (2004), p. 33.

45. Daniel J. Wilson, "Competing for Jobs: Local Taxes and Incentives," *FRBSF Economic Letter*, February 23, 2015, www.frbsf.org/economic-research /files/el2015-06.pdf.

46. Peters and Fisher, "The Failures of Economic Development Incentives," p. 34.

47. Harvey Molotch, "The City as a Growth Machine: Toward a Political Economy of Place," *American Journal of Sociology* 82, no. 2 (1976), p. 320.

48. For a more comprehensive treatment, see Timothy J. Bartik, *Who Benefits from State and Local Development Policies?* (Kalamazoo, MI: W. E. Upjohn Institute for Employment Research, 1991), p. 190ff.

49. Krugman, "Making Sense of the Competitiveness Debate."

50. Bartik, *Who Benefits from State and Local Development Policies?*, p. 192, emphasis added.

51. Cheshire and Gordon, "Territorial Competition and the Predictability of Collective (in)Action," p. 397.

52. C. Clare Hinrichs and Patricia Allen, "Selective Patronage and Social Justice: Local Food Consumer Campaigns in Historical Context," *Journal of Agricultural and Environmental Ethics* 21, no. 4 (2008).

53. Nandi Robinson, *Why Buy Local? An Assessment of the Economic Advantages of Shopping at Locally Owned Businesses* (Michigan State University Center for Community and Economic Development, 2010), https://ced.msu.edu /upload/reports/why%20buy%20local.pdf.

54. Peterson, *City Limits*, p. 23.

CHAPTER 5. NATURE

1. Alexis de Tocqueville, *Democracy in America*, edited by Olivier Zunz, translated by Arthur Goldhammer, vol. 1 (1835–1840; New York: Library of America, 2012), p. 67. *Commune* is Tocqueville's word in French that Goldhammer translates as *town*. On Goldhammer's decision to use *town* instead of *township*, see pp. 508–09.

2. Aristotle, *The Complete Works of Aristotle: The Revised Oxford Translation*, edited by Jonathan Barnes, 2 vols. (Princeton University Press, 1984), p. 2105.

3. Charles de Secondat Baron de Montesquieu, *The Spirit of the Laws*, translated and edited by Anne M. Cohler, Basia Carolyn Miller, and Harold Samuel Stone (Cambridge University Press, 1989), p. 124.

4. Thomas Jefferson, *Jefferson: Political Writings*, edited by Joyce Appleby and Terence Ball (Cambridge University Press, 1999), p. 189.

5. Ibid., p. 219.

6. Wendell Berry, *Another Turn of the Crank: Essays* (Washington, D.C.: Counterpoint, 1995), p. 17.

7. Kirkpatrick Sale, *Human Scale Revisited: A New Look at the Classic Case for a Decentralist Future* (White River Junction, VT: Chelsea Green Publishing, 2017), p. 282.

8. Ibid.

9. David Popenoe, "The Roots of Declining Social Virtue: Family, Community and the Need for a 'Natural Communities Policy,'" in *Seedbeds of Virtue: Sources of Competence, Character, and Citizenship in American Society*, edited by Mary Ann Glendon and David Blakenhorn (Lanham, MD: Madison Books, 1995), p. 86.

10. Ibid., p. 85.

11. Ibid., p. 94.

12. Sale, *Human Scale Revisited*, p. 28, emphasis in original.

13. Ferdinand Tönnies, *Community and Civil Society*, edited by Jose Harris, translated by Jose Harris and Margaret Hollis (Cambridge University Press, 2001), p. 17.

14. Ibid., p. 18.

15. Alistair Sutcliffe and others, "Relationships and the Social Brain: Integrating Psychological and Evolutionary Perspectives," *British Journal of Psychology* 103 (2012).

16. Susan Pinker, *The Village Effect: How Face-to-Face Contact Can Make Us Healthier and Happier* (New York: Spiegel & Grau, 2014).

17. Bernard Chapais, "The Deep Social Structure of Humankind," *Science* 331 (2011), p. 1276.

18. Bernard Chapais, "Monogamy, Strongly Bonded Groups, and the Evolution of Human Social Structure," *Evolutionary Anthropology* 22, no. 2 (2013).

19. Joseph Henrich, *The Secret of Our Success: How Culture Is Driving Human Evolution, Domesticating Our Species, and Making Us Smarter* (Princeton University Press, 2016).

20. Peter Singer, *The Expanding Circle: Ethics and Sociobiology* (New York: Farrar, Straus & Giroux, 1981), p. 74.

21. On gigantism, see E. F. Schumacher, *Small Is Beautiful: Economics as If People Mattered* (London: Blond and Briggs, 1973; repr., New York: Harper Perennial, 2010).

22. Montesquieu, *The Spirit of the Laws*, p. 131.

23. Ibid.

24. Ibid., p. 131, emphasis added. Other translations say "contrived." See Charles de Secondat Baron de Montesquieu, *The Complete Works of M. de Montesquieu*, translated and edited by Anne M. Cohler, Basia Carolyn Miller, and Harold Samuel Stone, 4 vols. (London: T. Evans, 1777), p. 165.

25. For a technical discussion of these issues, see G. Palla and others, "Uncovering the Overlapping Community Structure of Complex Networks in Nature and Society," *Nature* 435, no. 7043 (2005).

26. Yuval Noah Harari, *Sapiens: A Brief History of Humankind* (New York: Harper, 2015), p. 45.

27. Steven Pinker, *The Blank Slate: The Modern Denial of Human Nature* (New York: Penguin, 2002), p. 435. For an updated list, see http://condor .depaul.edu/mfiddler/hyphen/humunivers.htm.

28. Smithsonian National Museum of Natural History, "What Does It Mean to Be Human?" http://humanorigins.si.edu/evidence/genetics.

29. Chapais, "The Deep Social Structure of Humankind," p. 1277.

30. Ibid., p. 1276.

31. Ibid., p. 1277.

32. Ibid.

33. Chapais, "Monogamy, Strongly Bonded Groups, and the Evolution of Human Social Structure," p. 53.

34. Chapais, "The Deep Social Structure of Humankind," p. 1276.

35. Chapais, "Monogamy, Strongly Bonded Groups, and the Evolution of Human Social Structure," p. 55.

36. The example is from Henrich, *The Secret of Our Success*, pp. 102–04.

37. U.S. Department of Health and Human Services, National Institutes of Health, U.S. National Library of Medicine, "Pellagra," *MedlinePlus*, February 14, 2019, https://medlineplus.gov/ency/article/000342.htm.

38. For the Tasmanian example, see Henrich, *The Secret of Our Success*, pp. 220–22.

39. Ibid., p. 240.

40. Quoted in Pinker, *The Blank Slate*, p. 163.

41. Quoted in Singer, *The Expanding Circle*, p. 62.

42. Pinker, *The Blank Slate*, p. 150.

43. Ibid., p. 162.

44. "Pro-Attitude," in *The Oxford Dictionary of Philosophy*, edited by Simon Blackburn (Oxford University Press, 2016).

45. Mikaël Molet and others, "Guilt by Association and Honor by Association: The Role of Acquired Equivalence," *Psychonomic Bulletin & Review* 20, no. 2 (2013).

46. Immanuel Kant, *Critique of the Power of Judgment*, edited by Paul Guyer, translated by Paul Guyer and Eric Matthews (1790; Cambridge University Press, 2000).

47. Harari, *Sapiens*, p. 236.

48. In doing so, I draw on Peter Singer's work on the implications of evolutionary biology for ethics. See Singer, *The Expanding Circle*.

49. Ibid., p. 152.

50. Jean-Paul Sartre, *Being and Nothingness: An Essay on Phenomenological Ontology* (New York: Philosophical Library, 1956).

51. Pius XI, *Quadragesimo Anno* (1931).

52. See David Golemboski, "Federalism and the Catholic Principle of Subsidiarity," *Publius* 45, no. 4 (2015); Russell Hittinger, "Social Roles and Ruling Virtues in Catholic Social Doctrine," *Annales Theologici* 16 (2002); Russell Hittinger, "The Coherence of the Four Basic Principles of Catholic Social Doctrine: An Interpretation," in *The Proceedings of the 14th Plenary Session of the Pontifical Academy of Social Sciences, Pursuing the Common Good: How Solidarity and Subsidiarity Can Work Together*, edited by Margaret S. Archer and Pierpaolo Donati (Vatican City: Pontifical Academy of the Social Sciences, 2008).

53. Lynn Hunt, *Inventing Human Rights: A History* (New York: W. W. Norton, 2007).

54. TEU, 2016 O.J. C 326/13 at 16.

55. Golemboski, "Federalism and the Catholic Principle of Subsidiarity."

CHAPTER 6. DEMOCRACY

1. Amartya Sen, "Democracy as a Universal Value," *Journal of Democracy* 10, no. 3 (1999).

2. Dana Ott, *Small Is Democratic: An Examination of State Size and Democratic Development* (New York: Garland Publishing, Inc., 2000).

3. Gilbert Livingston, Convention Debates, 24 June 1788 in *The Documentary History of the Ratification of the Constitution*, Digital Edition, edited by John P. Kaminski and others, vol. 22 (University of Virginia Press, 2009), p. 1837.

4. Thomas Paine, *Common Sense; Addressed to the Inhabitants of America, on the Following Interesting Subjects* (Philadelphia: R. Bell, 1776), p. 4.

5. Jean-Jacques Rousseau, *Rousseau: The Social Contract and Other Later Political Writings*, translated and edited by Victor Gourevitch, 2nd ed. (Cambridge University Press, 2018).

6. Thomas Jefferson, *Jefferson: Political Writings*, edited by Joyce Appleby and Terence Ball (Cambridge University Press, 1999), p. 326.

7. John Stuart Mill, "Considerations on Representative Government," in *Essays on Politics and Society*, edited by J. M. Robson, Collected Works of John Stuart Mill (University of Toronto Press, 1977), p. 412.

8. Trevor Latimer, "Plural Voting and Political Equality: A Thought Experiment in Democratic Theory," *European Journal of Political Theory* 17, no. 1 (2018).

9. Alexis de Tocqueville, *Democracy in America*, edited by Olivier Zunz, translated by Arthur Goldhammer, vol. 1 (1835–1840; New York: Library of America, 2012).

10. Bernard Manin, *The Principles of Representative Government* (Cambridge University Press, 1997).

11. Civil Disobedience (1859) in *Classics of American Political and Constitutional Thought*, edited by Scott J. Hammond, Kevin R. Hardwick, and Howard L. Lubert, vol. 1 (Indianapolis, IN: Hackett, 2007), pp. 932–39.

12. Robert A. Dahl and Edward R. Tufte, *Size and Democracy* (Stanford University Press, 1973), p. 13.

13. Ibid., p. 20, emphasis in original.

14. Ibid., p. 21.

15. Ibid.

16. E. E. Schattschneider, *The Semisovereign People: A Realist's View of Democracy in America* (New York: Holt, Rinehart and Winston, 1960).

17. On this point, see Bas Denters and others, *Size and Local Democracy* (Cheltenham, UK: Edward Elgar, 2014), p. 333.

18. Philip Pettit, "Three Conceptions of Democratic Control," *Constellations* 15, no. 1 (2008), p. 46.

19. Carole Pateman, *Participation and Democratic Theory* (Cambridge University Press, 1970).

20. James Bohman and William Rehg, *Deliberative Democracy: Essays on Reason and Politics* (MIT Press, 1997).

21. Jack L. Walker, "A Critique of the Elitist Theory of Democracy," *American Political Science Review* 60, no. 2 (1966).

22. Josiah Ober, "Natural Capacities and Democracy as a Good-in-Itself," *Philosophical Studies* 132, no. 1 (2007).

23. Carole Pateman, "Participatory Democracy Revisited," *Perspectives on Politics* 10, no. 1 (2012).

24. C. B. Macpherson, *The Life and Times of Liberal Democracy* (Oxford University Press, 1977).

25. Steven E. Finkel, "Reciprocal Effects of Participation and Political Efficacy: A Panel Analysis," *American Journal of Political Science* 29, no. 4 (1985).

26. Alan S. Gerber, Donald P. Green, and Ron Shachar, "Voting May Be Habit-Forming: Evidence from a Randomized Field Experiment," *American Journal of Political Science* 47, no. 3 (2003).

27. James Miller, *"Democracy Is in the Streets": From Port Huron to the Siege of Chicago* (New York: Simon and Schuster, 1987).

28. External efficacy, by contrast, is the belief that the political system is responsive to its citizens. External efficacy is cognitive; internal efficacy is affective.

29. Finkel, "Reciprocal Effects of Participation and Political Efficacy."

30. Ibid.

31. Also see Steven E. Finkel, "The Effects of Participation on Political Efficacy and Political Support: Evidence from a West German Panel," *Journal of Politics* 49, no. 2 (1987).

32. Nicholas A. Valentino, Krysha Gregorowicz, and Eric W Groenendyk, "Efficacy, Emotions and the Habit of Participation," *Political Behavior* 31, no. 3 (2009).

33. Anne Phillips, "Why Does Local Democracy Matter?" in *Local Democracy and Local Government*, edited by Lawrence Pratchett and David Wilson (Houndmills, UK: Macmillan Press, 1996), p. 22.

34. Sidney Verba, Kay Lehman Schlozman, and Henry E. Brady, *Voice and Equality: Civic Voluntarism in American Politics* (Harvard University Press, 1995).

35. Denters and others, *Size and Local Democracy*, p. 315.

36. Denters and others, *Size and Local Democracy*, p. 16, emphasis in original.

37. Ibid., p. 315.

38. K. Newton, "Is Small Really So Beautiful? Is Big Really So Ugly? Size, Effectiveness, and Democracy in Local Government," *Political Studies* 30, no. 2 (1982), p. 203. Quoted in Denters and others, *Size and Local Democracy*.

39. Bonnie M. Meguid, "Bringing Government Back to the People? The Impact of Political Decentralization on Voter Engagement in Western Europe," Working Paper, Department of Political Science, University of Rochester, 2011, p. 8, www.bonniemeguid.com/uploads/1/1/7/8/117833082/meguid _bringing_govt_back_to_the_people.pdf.

40. Meguid, "Bringing Government Back to the People," p. 9.

41. Ghazala Mansuri and Vijayendra Rao, *Localizing Development: Does Participation Work?* (Washington, D.C.: The World Bank, 2013), p. 3.

42. Ibid., p. 8.

43. Ibid., p. 5.

44. Ibid.

45. Joseph A. Schumpeter, *Capitalism, Socialism, and Democracy*, 5th ed. (London: George Allen & Unwin, 1976), p. 261.

46. Ibid., p. 260.

47. J. Eric Oliver, Shang E. Ha, and Zachary Callen, *Local Elections and the Politics of Small-Scale Democracy* (Princeton University Press, 2012), p. 64.

48. Ibid., p. 65. Also see Zoltan L. Hajnal and Paul G. Lewis, "Municipal Institutions and Voter Turnout in Local Elections," *Urban Affairs Review* 38, no. 5 (2003).

49. Oliver, Ha, and Callen, *Local Elections and the Politics of Small-Scale Democracy*, p. 84.

50. Jessica Trounstine, "Turnout and Incumbency in Local Elections," *Urban Affairs Review* 49, no. 2 (2012), p. 168.

51. On this point, see Scott L. Althaus, "Information Effects in Collective Preferences," *American Political Science Review* 92, no. 3 (2014).

52. Paul E. Peterson, *City Limits* (University of Chicago Press, 1981).

53. Harry Brighouse and Adam Swift, "Equality, Priority, and Positional Goods," *Ethics* 116, no. 3 (2006), p. 472.

54. U.S. Department of Commerce, United States Census Bureau, CPS Historical Time Series Tables, Table A-1. Years of School Completed by People 25 Years and Over, by Age and Sex: Selected Years 1940 to 2017, April 20, 2021, www2.census.gov/programs-surveys/demo/tables/educational-attainment /time-series/cps-historical-time-series/taba-1.xlsx.

55. The reference is to Henry St. John Viscount Bolingbroke, "The Idea of a Patriot King," in *Political Writings* (Cambridge University Press, 1997).

56. Monica Langley, "As Economic Crisis Peaked, Tide Turned against McCain," *Wall Street Journal*, November 5, 2008, www.wsj.com/articles /SB122586043326400685.

57. For a discussion, see Richard F. Fenno, *Home Style: House Members in Their Districts* (Boston: Little, Brown, 1978).

58. Dahl and Tufte, *Size and Democracy*, p. 13.

59. Alameda County Library, "Who We Are," January 23, 2022, https:// aclibrary.org/who-we-are/.

60. Alameda County Library, "Alameda County Library Advisory Commission," January 23, 2022, https://aclibrary.org/library-commissions/.

61. This was true as of May 2021. Emma G. Fitzsimmons, "Who Really Runs New York City's Subway?" *New York Times*, July 25, 2017, www.nytimes .com/2017/07/25/nyregion/who-runs-new-yorks-subway.html.

62. Christopher H. Achen and Larry M. Bartels, *Democracy for Realists: Why Elections Do Not Produce Responsive Government* (Princeton University Press, 2016).

63. Danny Hayes and Jennifer L. Lawless, "The Decline of Local News and Its Effects: New Evidence from Longitudinal Data," *Journal of Politics* 80, no. 1 (2017), p. 333.

64. Danny Hayes and Jennifer L. Lawless, "As Local News Goes, So Goes Citizen Engagement: Media, Knowledge, and Participation in US House Elections," *Journal of Politics* 77, no. 2 (2015), p. 448.

65. James M. Snyder and David Strömberg, "Press Coverage and Political Accountability," *Journal of Political Economy* 118, no. 2 (2010), p. 359.

66. Ibid., p. 360.

67. Pew Research Center, Newspapers Fact Sheet, June 23, 2018, www .journalism.org/fact-sheet/newspapers/; U.S. Bureau of Economic Analysis, Population (B230RC0A052NBEA), FRED, Federal Reserve Bank of St. Louis, February 15, 2019, https://fred.stlouisfed.org/series/B230RC0A052NBEA.

68. Daniel J. Hopkins, *The Increasingly United States: How and Why American Political Behavior Nationalized* (University of Chicago Press, 2018), p. 207.

69. Ibid., p. 215.

70. Ibid., p. 213.

71. Christopher R. Berry and William G. Howell, "Accountability and Local Elections: Rethinking Retrospective Voting," *Journal of Politics* 69, no. 3 (2007).

72. Daniel Walker Howe, *What Hath God Wrought: The Transformation of America, 1815–1848* (Oxford University Press, 2007).

73. Mathew D. McCubbins and Thomas Schwartz, "Congressional Oversight Overlooked: Police Patrols versus Fire Alarms," *American Journal of Political Science* 28, no. 1 (1984).

74. Ben Terris, "He's Got a 'Downton Abbey'-Inspired Office, but Rep. Aaron Schock Won't Talk About It," *Washington Post*, February 2, 2015, www .washingtonpost.com/lifestyle/style/hes-got-a-downton-abbey-inspired -office-but-rep-aaron-schock-wont-talk-about-it/2015/02/02/1d3f1466-ab1f -11e4-abe8-e1ef60ca26de_story.html?utm_term=.0131911587ee.

75. Schattschneider, *The Semisovereign People*.

76. Cass R. Sunstein, *The Cost-Benefit Revolution* (MIT Press, 2018), p. 33.

CHAPTER 7. KNOWLEDGE

1. Joel Kotkin and Ryan Streeter, editors, *Localism in America: Why We Should Tackle Our Big Challenges at the Local Level* (American Enterprise Institute, 2018), p. 36.

2. F. A. Hayek, "The Use of Knowledge in Society," *American Economic Review* 35, no. 4 (1945), pp. 521–22.

3. Patsy Healy, "Civic Capacity, Place Governance and Progressive Localism," in Simin Davoudi and Ali Madanipour, editors, *Reconsidering Localism* (New York: Routledge, 2015), p. 112.

4. Hayek, "The Use of Knowledge in Society," p. 524.

5. Ibid., p. 527.

6. Ibid., p. 524.

7. Ibid.

8. Cf. Daniel J. Hopkins, *The Increasingly United States: How and Why American Political Behavior Nationalized* (University of Chicago Press, 2018).

9. James C. Scott, *Seeing Like a State: How Certain Schemes to Improve the Human Condition Have Failed* (Yale University Press, 1998).

10. Ibid., p. 4.

11. Ibid., p. 90.

12. Ibid., p. 248.

13. Ibid., p. 249.

14. Ibid., p. 250.

15. Alex de Waal, *Evil Days: 30 Years of War and Famine in Ethiopia* (Africa Watch, 1991), p. 223.

16. Scott, *Seeing Like a State*, p. 6.

17. Ibid.

18. Richard A. Epstein, "The Uses and Limits of Local Knowledge: A Cautionary Note on Hayek," *NYU Journal of Law & Liberty* 1, no. 0 (2005), pp. 206–07.

19. Cass R. Sunstein, *The Cost-Benefit Revolution* (MIT Press, 2018), p. 82.

20. New State Ice Co. v. Liebmann, 285 U.S. 252 (1932).

21. For some suggestions, see Sunstein, *The Cost-Benefit Revolution*.

CHAPTER 8. EFFICIENCY

1. Andrés Rodríguez-Pose and Adala Bwire, "The Economic (in)Efficiency of Devolution," *Environment and Planning A: Economy and Space* 36, no. 11 (2004), p. 1907.

2. TEU, 2016 O.J. C 326/18.

3. For a lucid account of the distinction, see David Golemboski, "Federalism and the Catholic Principle of Subsidiarity," *Publius* 45, no. 4 (2015). On this point, also see John Douglas Wilson, "Theories of Tax Competition," *National Tax Journal* 52, no. 2 (1999), p. 270.

4. Kaldor Nicholas, "Welfare Propositions of Economics and Interpersonal Comparisons of Utility," *The Economic Journal* 49, no. 195 (1939); J. R. Hicks, "The Foundations of Welfare Economics," *The Economic Journal* 49, no. 196 (1939).

5. Wallace E. Oates, "An Essay on Fiscal Federalism," *Journal of Economic Literature* 37, no. 3 (1999), p. 1112. Quoting Wallace E. Oates, *Fiscal Federalism* (New York: Harcourt Brace Jovanovich, 1972), p. 54.

6. Property tax in the United States is typically a percentage of the assessed value of property, where the assessed value is some percentage (up to 100 percent) of its market value. Property tax regimes vary by state, but in New York, the property tax rate is determined by dividing the jurisdiction's tax levy (the amount it needs to raise from the property tax) by the total value of assessed property in the jurisdiction. Rates can go up when the jurisdiction needs more money, holding assessed values fixed, and down when assessed values increase, holding the tax levy fixed. For a primer, see New York State Department of Taxation and Finance, "How Real Property Taxation Works," www.tax.ny.gov/pdf/publications/orpts/taxworks.pdf.

7. Note, however, that in a recent study of Danish local government reform, Jens Blom-Hansen, Kurt Houlberg Kora, Søren Serritzlew, and Daniel Treisman found that "jurisdiction size has no unequivocal effect on costs for

multipurpose units." This does not mean "that no economies of scale exist," of course, just "that the relevant kind of fixed costs are difficult to reduce by municipal amalgamation" of the kind implemented in Denmark. Jens Blom-Hansen and others, "Jurisdiction Size and Local Government Policy Expenditure: Assessing the Effect of Municipal Amalgamation," *American Political Science Review* 110, no. 4 (2016), p. 828.

8. With a few minor exceptions.

9. David R. Mayhew, *Congress: The Electoral Connection*, 2nd ed. (Yale University Press, 2004).

10. Stephen J. Bailey, *Local Government Economics: Principles and Practice* (Basingstoke, UK: Macmillan, 1999), p. 22.

11. Christopher R. Berry, *Imperfect Union: Representation and Taxation in Multilevel Governments* (Cambridge University Press, 2009), p. 88.

12. Bailey, *Local Government Economics: Principles and Practice*, p. 23.

13. On this point, see William H. Riker, *Federalism: Origin, Operation, Significance* (Boston: Little, Brown and Company, 1964).

14. Alexis de Tocqueville, *Democracy in America*, edited by Olivier Zunz, translated by Arthur Goldhammer, vol. 1 (1835–1840; New York: Library of America, 2012), p. 134.

15. Cf. Paulina Ochoa Espejo, *On Borders: Territories, Legitimacy, and the Rights of Place* (Oxford University Press, 2020).

16. Bailey, *Local Government Economics: Principles and Practice*, p. 23.

17. Ibid., p. 38.

18. Albert O. Hirschman, *Exit, Voice, and Loyalty: Responses to Decline in Firms, Organizations, and States* (Harvard University Press, 1970).

19. Charles M. Tiebout, "A Pure Theory of Local Expenditures," *Journal of Political Economy* 64, no. 5 (1956), p. 417–18.

20. Bill Bishop, *The Big Sort: Why the Clustering of Like-Minded America Is Tearing Us Apart* (Boston: Houghton Mifflin, 2008).

21. Gregory Weiher, *The Fractured Metropolis: Political Fragmentation and Metropolitan Segregation* (State University of New York Press, 1991), p. 11.

22. Tiebout, "A Pure Theory of Local Expenditures," p. 424.

23. Daniel Treisman, *The Architecture of Government: Rethinking Political Decentralization* (Cambridge University Press, 2007), p. 76.

24. Ibid., pp. 77–78.

25. Tiebout made seven assumptions in his original paper. Taking the subsequent literature into account and rearranging Tiebout's exposition somewhat, Treisman identified a total of eleven assumptions.

26. On this point, see Treisman, *Architecture of Government*, p. 79.

27. For a discussion, see The Clash, "Should I Stay or Should I Go?" in *Combat Rock* (CBS, 1982).

28. Also see Bryan Caplan, "Standing Tiebout on His Head: Tax Capitalization and the Monopoly Power of Local Governments," *Public Choice* 108, no. 1 (2001).

29. Wallace E. Oates, "The Effects of Property Taxes and Local Public Spending on Property Values: An Empirical Study of Tax Capitalization and the Tiebout Hypothesis," *Journal of Political Economy* 77, no. 6 (1969), p. 968. Also see Oded Palmon and Barton A. Smith, "New Evidence on Property Tax Capitalization," *Journal of Political Economy* 106, no. 5 (1998); Vincent La, "Capitalization of School Quality into Housing Prices: Evidence from Boston Public School District Walk Zones," *Economics Letters* 134 (2015).

30. In the United States, as of 2002, there were 3,405 water supply districts in forty-eight states. See Berry, *Imperfect Union*, tables 2.1 and 2.2.

31. Wilson, "Theories of Tax Competition," p. 270.

32. Ibid., p. 298.

33. Christopher Berry, "Piling On: Multilevel Government and the Fiscal Common-Pool," *American Journal of Political Science* 52, no. 4 (2008).

34. Ibid., p. 17.

35. Ibid., p. 7.

36. Ibid., p. 100.

37. U.S. Department of Commerce, United States Census Bureau, Quarterly Residential Vacancies and Homeownership, First Quarter 2021, April 7, 2021, www.census.gov/housing/hvs/files/currenthvspress.pdf, table 4.

38. Ibid., table 7.

39. Ibid., table 8.

40. Ibid., table 6.

41. William A. Fischel, *The Homevoter Hypothesis: How Home Values Influence Local Government Taxation, School Finance, and Land-Use Policies* (Harvard University Press, 2001), p. 12.

42. Paul E. Peterson, *City Limits* (University of Chicago Press, 1981).

43. Richard W. England, "Tax Incidence and Rental Housing: A Survey and Critique of Research," *National Tax Journal* 69, no. 2 (2016), p. 447.

44. Joshua Green, "What Is the Average Moving Cost?," *My Moving Reviews*, January 7, 2021, www.mymovingreviews.com/move/average-moving-cost/.

45. Neil Bhutta and others, "Changes in U.S. Family Finances from 2016 to 2019: Evidence from the Survey of Consumer Finances," *Federal Reserve Bulletin* 106, no. 5 (2020), p. 16.

46. Survey of Consumer Finances, 1989–2019, "Transaction Accounts by Percentile of Income," May 22, 2021, www.federalreserve.gov/econres/scf/dataviz/scf/chart/#series:Transaction_Accounts;demographic:inccat;population:all;units:median;range:1989,2019.

47. Ibid.

48. Also see Douglas S. Massey and Nancy A. Denton, *American Apartheid: Segregation and the Making of the Underclass* (Harvard University Press, 1993); William J. Wilson, *The Truly Disadvantaged: The Inner City, the Underclass, and Public Policy* (University of Chicago Press, 1987).

49. Steven N. Durlauf, "A Theory of Persistent Income Inequality," *Journal of Economic Growth* 1, no. 1 (1996).

50. Richard Fry and Paul Taylor, *The Rise of Residential Segregation by Income* (Washington, D.C.: Pew Research Center, 2012), p. 3.

51. CPS Historical Geographic Mobility/Migration Graphs, United States Census Bureau, May 22, 2021, www.census.gov/library/visualizations /time-series/demo/historic.html.

52. Timothy Noah, "Staying Put: Why Income Inequality Is Up and Geographic Mobility Is Down," in *Tell Me More*, edited by Michel Martin (NPR, 2013).

53. Quoted in "Declining Mover Rate Driven by Renters, Census Bureau Reports," *United States Census Bureau*, November 15, 2017, https://census .gov/newsroom/press-releases/2017/mover-rates.html.

54. United States Census Bureau, Geographical Mobility: 2017 to 2018, November 2018, www2.census.gov/programs-surveys/demo/tables/geographic -mobility/2018/cps-2018/tab15.xls, table 15.

55. Jack Ewing, "Volkswagen, Hit by Emissions Scandal, Posts Its First Loss in Years," *New York Times*, October 28, 2015, https://nyti.ms/1WhgtiQ.

56. Ibid.

57. John Phillips, "Honda Cr-V Ex," *Car and Driver*, November 1, 2001, www .caranddriver.com/reviews/a15137918/honda-cr-v-ex-road-test/; Daniel Pund, "Best Forgotten: The Story of the Pontiac Aztek," *Car and Driver*, December 8, 2017, www.caranddriver.com/features/a14989657/pontiac-aztek-the-story-of-a -vehicle-best-forgotten-feature/.

58. Weiher, *The Fractured Metropolis*, p. 58.

59. Ibid.

60. Ibid., p. 59.

61. Julie L. Rose, *Free Time* (Princeton University Press, 2016).

62. Elizabeth Anderson, *The Imperative of Integration* (Princeton University Press, 2010).

63. For a defense of the term *ghetto*, see Richard Rothstein, *The Color of Law: A Forgotten History of How Our Government Segregated America* (New York: Liveright Publishing Corporation, 2017), p. xvi.

64. Jonathan Kozol, February 15, 2019, www.ucpress.edu/book/9780520 274747/educational-delusions.

65. Gary Orfield and Erica Frankenberg, *Educational Delusions? Why Choice Can Deepen Inequality and How to Make Schools Fair* (University of California Press, 2013), p. 257.

66. Ibid.

67. Ibid.

68. Ibid., p. 262.

69. Michael Henry Adams, "The End of Black Harlem," *New York Times*, May 27, 2016, https://nyti.ms/1U0bvjX.

70. Alexis de Tocqueville, *Democracy in America*, vol. 1, pp. 97–98.

71. Ibid., p. 74.

72. Gordon L. Clark, "A Theory of Local Autonomy," *Annals of the Association of American Geographers* 74, no. 2 (1984), p. 198.

73. For a discussion of these issues, see J. Mitchell Pickerill and Paul Chen, "Medical Marijuana Policy and the Virtues of Federalism," *Publius: The Journal of Federalism* 38, no. 1 (2008); David S. Schwartz, "High Federalism: Marijuana Legalization and the Limits of Federal Power to Regulate States," *Cordozo Law Review* 35, no. 2 (2013).

74. National Conference of State Legislatures, Marijuana Overview, December 14, 2018, www.ncsl.org/research/civil-and-criminal-justice/marijuana-over view.aspx.

75. Kastalia Medrano, "The Best Countries around the World to Smoke Weed," *Thrillist*, March 11, 2019, www.thrillist.com/vice/30-places-where -weed-is-legal-cities-and-countries-with-decriminalized-marijuana.

76. C. Vann Woodward, *The Strange Career of Jim Crow* (Oxford University Press, 1955).

77. *Parents Involved in Community Schools v. Seattle School Dist. No. 1*, 551 U.S. 701 (2007).

78. Clint Bolick, *Grassroots Tyranny: The Limits of Federalism* (Washington, D.C.: CATO Institute, 1993).

79. Centers for Medicare & Medicaid Services, "Eligibility," January 25, 2022, www.medicaid.gov/medicaid/eligibility/index.html.

80. Rodríguez-Pose and Bwire, "The Economic (in)Efficiency of Devolution," p. 1912, internal citations omitted.

81. Ibid., p. 1912.

82. Andrés Rodríguez-Pose and Roberto Ezcurra, "Is Fiscal Decentralization Harmful for Economic Growth? Evidence from the OECD Countries," *Journal of Economic Geography* 11, no. 4 (2011), p. 637.

83. Ibid.

84. Yolanda Ubago Martínez, Pedro Pascual Arzoz, and Belén Iráizoz Apezteguía, "Does Decentralization Contribute to Efficiency? Evidence from OECD Countries," *Applied Economics* 50, no. 7 (2018), p. 736.

85. Wen Wang, Xinye Zheng, and Zhirong Zhao, "Fiscal Reform and Public Education Spending: A Quasi-Natural Experiment of Fiscal Decentralization in China," *Publius: The Journal of Federalism* 42, no. 2 (2012), p. 352.

86. Susan Rose-Ackerman, "Risk Taking and Reelection: Does Federalism Promote Innovation?," *Journal of Legal Studies* 9, no. 3 (1980), p. 594.

87. Ibid.

88. Hongbin Cai and Daniel Treisman, "Political Decentralization and Policy Experimentation," *Quarterly Journal of Political Science* 4, no. 1 (2009), p. 37.

89. Ibid.

90. Ibid.

91. Ibid., p. 38.

CHAPTER 9. AGAINST LOCALISM

1. Maria Alvarez, "Reasons for Action: Justification, Motivation, Explanation," *Stanford Encyclopedia of Philosophy*, April 24, 2016, https://plato.stanford.edu/entries/reasons-just-vs-expl/.

2. *Milliken v. Bradley*, 418 U.S. 717, p. 742.

3. It is interesting in this regard that Justice Powell, from whom Chief Justice Burger borrowed the discourse of local control, is regarded as a proponent of judicial balance. According to Paul Kahn, for Justice Powell, "the goal of constitutional adjudication was to find the center, to strike the balance between competing interests." Paul W. Kahn, "The Court, the Community and the Judicial Balance: The Jurisprudence of Justice Powell," *Yale Law Journal* 97, no. 1 (1987), p. 2.

4. Shelly Kagan, *The Limits of Morality* (Oxford University Press, 1989), p. 17, emphasis in original.

5. Franklin Delano Roosevelt, "Commonwealth Club Address (1932)," in *Classics of American Political and Constitutional Thought*, edited by Scott J. Hammond, Kevin R. Hardwick, and Howard L. Lubert, vol. 2 (Indianapolis: Hackett, 2007), p. 404.

6. In this passage, I'm assuming that race exists; it doesn't. See, for example, Anthony Appiah and Amy Gutmann, *Color Conscious: The Political Morality of Race* (Princeton University Press, 1996).

7. For a discussion of normative reasons, see T. M. Scanlon, *What We Owe to Each Other* (Belknap Press of Harvard University Press, 1998).

8. Blackburn Simon, editor, *The Oxford Dictionary of Philosophy* (Oxford University Press, 2016).

CHAPTER 10. BEYOND LOCALISM

1. David Hume, *A Treatise of Human Nature*, edited by L. A. Selby-Bigge (1739; Oxford: Clarendon Press, 1896), p. 535.

2. David A. O'Connor and others, "Behavioral Sensitivity to Reward Is Reduced for Far Objects," *Psychological Science* 25, no. 1 (2013), p. 276.

3. Ibid., p. 275.

4. Marlone D. Henderson and others, "Transcending the 'Here': The Effect of Spatial Distance on Social Judgment," *Journal of Personality and Social Psychology* 91, no. 5 (2006), p. 845.

5. Marlone D. Henderson and Cheryl J. Wakslak, "Over the Hills and Far Away: The Link between Physical Distance and Abstraction," *Current Directions in Psychological Science* 19, no. 6 (2010), p. 392.

6. Lawrence E. Williams and John A. Bargh, "Keeping One's Distance: The Influence of Spatial Distance Cues on Affect and Evaluation," *Psychological Science* 19, no. 3 (2008), p. 304.

7. Ibid., p. 305.

8. Ibid., p. 306.

9. Adam L. Alter and Emily Balcetis, "Fondness Makes the Distance Grow Shorter: Desired Locations Seem Closer because They Seem More Vivid," *Journal of Experimental Social Psychology* 47, no. 1 (2011), p. 16.

10. Ibid., p. 18.

11. Ibid., p. 17.

12. Jerry J. Han and Andrew D. Gershoff, "When Good Things Feel Closer and Bad Things Feel Farther: The Role of Perceived Control on Psychological Distance Perception," *Journal of Consumer Psychology* 28, no. 4 (2018), p. 633.

13. Daniel Kahneman, *Thinking, Fast and Slow* (New York: Farrar, Straus and Giroux, 2011), p. 130.

14. Joshua DeLung and others, "Proximity and Framing in News Media: Effects on Credibility, Bias, Recall, and Reader Intentions," *Journalism and Mass Communication* 2, no. 7 (2012), p. 749.

15. Kirby Goidel and others, "Sources of Economic News and Economic Expectations," *American Politics Research* 38, no. 4 (2010), p. 761.

16. Phyllis Kaniss, *Making Local News* (University of Chicago Press, 1991), p. 155.

17. Andrew M. Colman, *A Dictionary of Psychology*, 4th ed. (Oxford University Press, 2015), p. 299.

18. Alexis de Tocqueville, *Democracy in America*, edited by Olivier Zunz, translated by Arthur Goldhammer, vol. 1 (1835–1840; New York: Library of America, 2004), p. 75.

19. Ibid., p. 271.

20. Peter Singer, *The Expanding Circle: Ethics and Sociobiology* (New York: Farrar, Straus & Giroux, 1981), p. 153.

21. Nira Liberman and Yaacov Trope, "Traversing Psychological Distance," *Trends in Cognitive Sciences* 18, no. 7 (2014).

22. Ibid., p. 365.

23. Ibid., p. 366.

24. Adam Smith, *The Theory of Moral Sentiments*, ed. D. D. Raphael and A. L. Macfie (1759; Indianapolis: Liberty Fund, 1982), p. 9.

25. Ibid.

26. Ibid., p. 21.

27. Stephen Darwall, "Empathy, Sympathy, Care," *Philosophical Studies: An International Journal for Philosophy in the Analytic Tradition* 89, no. 2/3 (1998).

28. Fonna Forman-Barzilai, *Adam Smith and the Circles of Sympathy: Cosmopolitanism and Moral Theory* (Cambridge University Press, 2010), p. 144.

29. Peter Flindell Klarén, *Peru: Society and Nationhood in the Andes* (Oxford University Press, 2000), p. 37.

30. Ibid.

31. Smith, *The Theory of Moral Sentiments*, p. 140.

32. Fonna Forman-Barzilai, "Sympathy in Space(s): Adam Smith on Proximity," *Political Theory* 33, no. 2 (2005); Forman-Barzilai, *Adam Smith and the Circles of Sympathy: Cosmopolitanism and Moral Theory.*

33. At most, he says we would "gain nothing" by changing human nature so as to lead us to care equally about what's distant and what's near.

34. David Bromwich, *Moral Imagination: Essays* (Princeton University Press, 2014), p. xii.

35. Ibid.

36. Percy Shelley, *A Defense of Poetry*, quoted in Ibid., p. 12.

37. Ibid.

38. Ibid.

39. Ibid.

40. Matthew 5:46, quoted in Ibid.

41. Mark Purcell and J. Christopher Brown, "Against the Local Trap: Scale and the Study of Environment and Development," *Progress in Development Studies* 5, no. 4 (2005).

42. Trevor Latimer, "The Principle of Subsidiarity: A Democratic Reinterpretation," *Constellations: An International Journal of Critical and Democratic Theory* 25, no. 4 (2018).

43. Cf. Paulina Ochoa Espejo, *On Borders: Territories, Legitimacy, and the Rights of Place* (Oxford University Press, 2010), especially chapter 7.

44. Steven Pinker, *Enlightenment Now: The Case for Reason, Science, Humanism, and Progress* (New York: Viking, 2018), p. 367.

45. E. F. Schumacher, *Small Is Beautiful: Economics as If People Mattered* (London: Blond and Briggs, 1973; repr., New York: Harper Perennial, 2010), p. 70.

46. Ibid.

47. Ibid.

Index